Marketing Sovereign Promises

How did England, once a minor regional power, become a global hegemon between 1689 and 1815? Why, over the same period, did it become the world's first industrial nation? Gary W. Cox addresses these questions in *Marketing Sovereign Promises*. This book examines two central issues: the origins of the great taxing power of the modern state, and how that power is made compatible with economic growth.

Part I considers England's rise after the revolution of 1689, highlighting the establishment of annual budgets with shutdown reversions. This core reform effected a great increase in per capita tax extraction.

Part II investigates the regional and global spread of British budgeting ideas. Cox argues that states grew only if they addressed a central credibility problem afflicting the *ancien régime* – that rulers were legally entitled to spend public revenue however they deemed fit.

Gary W. Cox is the William Bennett Munro Professor of Political Science at Stanford University. Cox has written numerous articles and is the author of *The Efficient Secret* (winner of the 1983 Samuel H. Beer Dissertation Prize and the 2003 George H. Hallett Award), coauthor of *Legislative Leviathan* (winner of the 1993 Richard F. Fenno Prize), author of *Making Votes Count* (winner of the 1998 Woodrow Wilson Foundation Award, the 1998 Luebbert Prize, and the 2007 George H. Hallett Award), and coauthor of *Setting the Agenda* (winner of the 2006 Leon D. Epstein Book Award). Cox was elected to the American Academy of Arts and Sciences in 1996 and the National Academy of Sciences in 2005.

POLITICAL ECONOMY OF INSTITUTIONS
AND DECISIONS

Series Editors

Stephen Ansolabehere, Harvard University
Jeffry Frieden, Harvard University

Founding Editors

James E. Alt, Harvard University
Douglass C. North, Washington University of St. Louis

Other books in the series

Alberto Alesina and Howard Rosenthal, *Partisan Politics, Divided Government and the Economy*

Lee J. Alston, Thrainn Eggertsson and Douglass C. North, eds., *Empirical Studies in Institutional Change*

Lee J. Alston and Joseph P. Ferrie, *Southern Paternalism and the Rise of the American Welfare State: Economics, Politics, and Institutions, 1865–1965*

James E. Alt and Kenneth Shepsle, eds., *Perspectives on Positive Political Economy*

Josephine T. Andrews, *When Majorities Fail: The Russian Parliament, 1990–1993*

Jeffrey S. Banks and Eric A. Hanushek, eds., *Modern Political Economy: Old Topics, New Directions*

Yoram Barzel, *Economic Analysis of Property Rights, 2nd edition*

Yoram Barzel, *A Theory of the State: Economic Rights, Legal Rights, and the Scope of the State*

Robert Bates, *Beyond the Miracle of the Market: The Political Economy of Agrarian Development in Kenya*

Jenna Bednar, *The Robust Federation: Principles of Design*

Charles M. Cameron, *Veto Bargaining: Presidents and the Politics of Negative Power*

Kelly H. Chang, *Appointing Central Bankers: The Politics of Monetary Policy in the United States and the European Monetary Union*

Peter Cowhey and Mathew McCubbins, eds., *Structure and Policy in Japan and the United States: An Institutionalist Approach*

Gary W. Cox, *The Efficient Secret: The Cabinet and the Development of Political Parties in Victorian England*

Gary W. Cox, *Making Votes Count: Strategic Coordination in the World's Electoral Systems*

(*continued after Index*)

Marketing Sovereign Promises

Monopoly Brokerage and the Growth of the English State

GARY W. COX

Stanford University

CAMBRIDGE
UNIVERSITY PRESS

CAMBRIDGE
UNIVERSITY PRESS

32 Avenue of the Americas, New York NY 10013-2473, USA

Cambridge University Press is part of the University of Cambridge.

It furthers the University's mission by disseminating knowledge in the pursuit of
education, learning, and research at the highest international levels of excellence.

www.cambridge.org
Information on this title: www.cambridge.org/9781316506097

© Gary W. Cox 2016

First published 2016

Printed in the United States of America by Sheridan Books, Inc.

A catalogue record for this publication is available from the British Library.

Library of Congress Cataloging in Publication Data
Names: Cox, Gary W., author.
Title: Marketing sovereign promises: monopoly brokerage and the growth
of the English state / Gary W. Cox.
Description: New York, NY: Cambridge University Press, 2016. |
Series: Political economy of institutions and decisions |
Includes bibliographical references and index.
Identifiers: LCCN 2015043647| ISBN 9781316506097 (paperback) |
ISBN 9781107140622 (hardback)
Subjects: LCSH: Taxing power – Great Britain – History. | Sovereignty – History. |
Debts, Public – Great Britain – History. | Economic development – Great Britain –
History. | Great Britain – Politics and government. | Great Britain – Foreign relations.
Classification: LCC HJ2613.C69 2016 | DDC 336.3/409420903–dc23
LC record available at http://lccn.loc.gov/2015043647

ISBN 978-1-107-14062-2 Hardback
ISBN 978-1-316-50609-7 Paperback

Contents

Tables and Figures

Tables

Figures

Preface

How did England transform from a minor regional power into a global hegemon over the long eighteenth century (1689–1815)? Why, over roughly the same period, did it become the world's first industrial nation?

A powerful line of argument holds that the reform of England's political institutions after 1689 laid the ground for its later military and economic success. Yet, many prominent economic and political historians have argued that the facts just do not support the institutionalist theory. The stakes in this debate are high because institutionalist ideas have been deployed to explain not only England's rise but also the great military and economic divergence between Europe and the rest of the world.

The first part of this book reconsiders England's rise. My account of what changed constitutionally differs from both previous institutionalists and their critics. I stress, for example, a reengineering of the budgetary reversion – to establish what I call rule-of-law budgets – as the root reform. Relatedly, my account of the consequences of constitutional reform differs. For example, I view the enormous increase in per capita tax extraction as the most important single consequence of the Revolution's reforms, with the revolution in debt being a side effect. Understanding the historical origins of the British state's great taxing power, and why and how it could be made compatible with political liberty and economic growth, are central issues that this book addresses.

The second part of this book investigates the spread of British constitutional ideas about budgeting to the rest of the world. Theoretically, I argue that states could attain "modern" levels of revenue extraction only if they addressed a central credibility problem afflicting all *ancien régime* states: because rulers were legally entitled to spend any revenues they might receive however they saw fit, they could not credibly commit to spend those revenues in particular ways. Empirically, I provide various kinds of evidence that tax receipts per capita reached modern levels only after reforms bolstering the credibility of the executive's expenditure promises. At the same time, I show that many rulers have reengineered the budgetary reversion in their own favor, with fundamental political and economic consequences.

This work has benefited from the generosity of many colleagues. For sharing their respective data sets, I thank Dan Bogart, Mark Dincecco, and David Stasavage. For sharing their comments and insights, I thank Lucy Barnes, Emily Beaulieu, Lisa Blaydes, Dan Bogart, Michael Braddick, Lawrence Broz, Torun Dewan, Mark Dincecco, Tiberiu Dragu, Jeffry Frieden, Peter Gourevitch, Phil Hoffman, David Lake, Alison McQueen, Doug North, Jean-Laurent Rosenthal, Ken Scheve, Ken Shepsle, Barry R. Weingast, and participants in seminars at Harvard, LSE, Stanford, UCSD, and Warwick.

Finally, I thank my wife, Karen, for her love and support.

Sovereign Credibility and Public Revenue

Rulers throughout history have sought monetary and labor contributions from their subjects in exchange for promises to provide future benefits. Military officers have been asked to serve now, in exchange for a promise of salary and pension later. Contractors have been asked to supply goods now, in exchange for a promise of remittance later. Investors have been asked to loan money now, in exchange for a promise of repayment later.

In all these promissory markets, rulers have been beset by credibility problems. In seventeenth-century Europe, for example, elites would have known Niccolò Machiavelli's notorious advice that a "wise ruler ... should not keep his word when such an observance of faith would be to his disadvantage" (1979[1532], ch. 18). Many would also have known Hugo Grotius's related observation that "almost all jurists believe that the contracts, which a king enters into with his subjects, [cannot be enforced] by [state] law" (1949[1625], bk. 2, ch. 14).

Scholars such as North and Weingast (1989), Root (1989), and Myerson (2008) have highlighted the fiscal consequences that ensue when agreements with sovereigns cannot be legally enforced. Simply put, subjects will not willingly buy the king's promises if they are not credible, whereupon the flow of revenues from voluntary sales will dry up. Thus, we arrive at a fundamental question in political economy: How can sovereigns make their promises credible enough to sell if they cannot be legally enforced?

In this book, I analyze the English solution to this problem, which entailed three main steps: (1) giving Parliament a monopoly right to make, revise, and transfer sovereign promises; (2) granting certain actors a monopoly right to broker the resulting sales (and earn commissions);

and (3) removing the legal discretion of executive officials, at both the policy-making and administrative levels, over performance. The earliest version of this tripartite system, which I dub "monopoly brokerage," emerged in the late thirteenth century to protect real property rights. The same design principles were, after the Glorious Revolution of 1688, used to enhance the credibility of sovereign promises to spend money for stipulated purposes. Later still, English ideas were imperfectly transcribed into post-Enlightenment European constitutions. Part I of this book describes the English experience with monopoly brokerage, while Part II considers the checkered dispersion of monopoly brokerage to the rest of Europe and the world.

In this introduction, I first review previous ideas about sovereign credibility – both in general and in the case of England. I then explain the logic of monopoly brokerage in more detail. Finally, I provide a road map to the rest of the chapters.

Theories of Sovereign Credibility

Extant theories of sovereign credibility hinge on different visions of how sovereign promises are crafted, sold, and redeemed. To take the simplest example first, suppose promises can be made and unmade by royal decrees, which the monarch can emit at will. In this case, royal promises can be credible only if the monarch's cost of performance falls short of the costs that promise-holders can impose in retaliation to default. This is the bleak Machiavellian conclusion of the *punishment school* of sovereign credibility (e.g., Eaton and Gersovitz 1981 on debt; Haber, Maurer, and Razo 2003 on property).

Now suppose that sovereign promises can be made and unmade only by statutes, which Parliament can emit at will. In this case, promise-holders may again seek to deter default by threatening retaliatory punishment. In addition, however, they can seek to block the statutes needed to repudiate or revise the promises they hold.

The *constitutional school* assumes that new statutes require approval by various constitutional veto players. In the English case, for example, acts of Parliament required formal approval by the House of Commons, House of Lords, and Crown. From this perspective, England's promises – to provide a pension, pay an invoice, and so forth – were credible to the extent that promise-holders could expect at least one veto player to block statutes revising their promises (North and Weingast 1989; Stasavage 2003).

The *majoritarian school* takes a different view of the statutory process, one that emphasizes the freedom of governing majorities to act on their preferences. Indeed, pure majoritarian theories assume that a sovereign commitment will be honored if and only if a majority of voters wish to do so when performance comes due (e.g., Dixit and Londregan 2000 on debt; Lamoreaux 2011 on property).

In both the punishment and majoritarian schools, promise-holders are at the mercy of a Machiavellian state. A monarch or ruling majority can solemnly promise *now* to perform *later*. Yet, when later arrives, the then-monarch or then-majority can decide afresh what to do. If new circumstances render it disadvantageous to perform as originally promised, then no veto players exist to prevent default. In contrast, in the constitutional school, promise-holders need not continuously maintain the support of the ruler or ruling majority. They can rely on past promises, if they or their political allies can block statutes.

The Case of England

By far the best-known single case in which punishment, majoritarian, and constitutional arguments have been debated is that of England. Interpretations of England's (and, after 1707, Great Britain's) rise to power have long divided into a Whig school, emphasizing the importance of the constitutional settlement after the Glorious Revolution, and an anti-Whig school, emphasizing the freedom that parliamentary majorities have had to act on their political preferences.

North and Weingast (1989) provided such an analytically sharp statement of the Whig position that it has framed much of the subsequent scholarly debate. They argued that the emergence of parliamentary supremacy after the Revolution enabled the Crown to commit much more credibly to sovereign promises because revising such commitments now required approval by the Commons and Lords. The Crown's enhanced ability to commit, in turn, had enormous consequences. Investors were willing to lend vastly larger amounts of money over longer time horizons – financing global conquest and colonization. Entrepreneurs were willing to invest much larger amounts of money over longer time horizons – sparking the Industrial Revolution.[1]

---

[1] North and Weingast were circumspect in connecting the Glorious to the Industrial Revolution but, as we shall see in Chapter 8, others have asserted such a connection forcefully.

No one doubts that explaining why Great Britain became the world's hegemonic power in the nineteenth century and why it led the world into the Industrial Revolution are explananda of the first order. Yet, scholarly opinions on the North-Weingast thesis divide sharply. I shall review supportive work later but for now focus on their critics.

Several scholars assert that England's constitution simply did not change much after the Revolution. Epstein (2000), O'Brien (2002, 2005), Murrell (2009), and others argue that England's reforms were more technical than political and accrued slowly during the Civil War, Commonwealth, and Restoration. The Revolution was just one step in a gradual process. Relatedly, Pincus and Robinson (2011a) point out that not one of the specific constitutional reforms that North and Weingast highlighted constituted a sharp or unprecedented break with the past.

Other critics argue that the credibility of England's sovereign promises simply did not improve at the Revolution. As Murphy puts it, "by 1696 … faith in parliament's ability to honour its financial commitments was not substantially increased, as North and Weingast argue, but significantly eroded" (2012, p. 58). Moreover, when interest rates on English debt did eventually improve, critics claim they were driven by factors other than constitutional reform – such as lobbying by creditors (Carruthers 1996; Murphy 2013), the emergence of a stable pro-creditor majority party (Stasavage 2003, 2007; Pincus and Robinson 2011), victory at war (Sussman and Yafeh 2013), and the maturation of secondary markets (Carlos et al. 2014). At least when one looks at the interest rates on England's national debt, it seems hard to escape Sussman and Yafeh's blunt conclusion: "the notion that financial markets swiftly reward countries for the establishment of investor-friendly institutions is not grounded in historical facts" (2006, p. 907).

North and Weingast's thesis about property rights has fared no better. If such promises became more credible after the Revolution, their critics say, then rates of return on property should have declined. Yet, studies by Clark (1996), Epstein (2000), and Quinn (2001) find no reduction in such rates at the Revolution, not even a delayed one. Hoppit, based on a detailed study of property confiscation by the state, concludes that "property rights became *less* secure after 1688" (2011, p. 94, italics added).

All told, then, North and Weingast's critics have said there was neither a large constitutional change at the Revolution nor an improvement in the English state's credibility afterward. Whatever drove England's global conquest and Industrial Revolution, it wasn't the Revolution settlement.

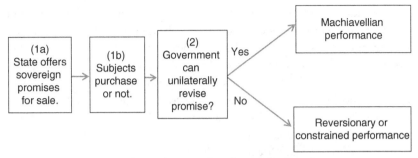

FIGURE 1.1. Sovereign promises from sale to performance.

Promise and Performance

In this book, I reconsider the debate between punishment, majoritarian, and constitutional theories. To introduce my approach, Figure 1.1 displays the sequence of events in an abstract promissory market, from sale to performance.

In stage 1a, the state offers to sell some sovereign promises. In England, for example, the Treasury sold interest-bearing Treasury Orders, while the Exchequer sold common-law writs. Each of these scraps of parchment or paper promised that the bearer would receive something of value – whether as simple as "payment" or as complex as "legal recourse" – in the future.

After subjects purchase them (stage 1b), the government in office when performance comes due (stage 2) might be able unilaterally to revise the initial promises (e.g., via a decree). If so, then the state's performance is *Machiavellian*.

Otherwise, if the government is not able unilaterally to revise the legal terms of performance, then it has two legal options. One is to revise the promise by negotiation with the other veto players. I call this *negotiated* performance and ignore it here. One can imagine, for example, that one of the veto players rejects all revisions. The only other legal option is to abide by the terms of the original promise, in which case I say that the government's performance is *reversionary* or *constrained*.

Most analyses of sovereign promises assume Machiavellian performance is the only possibility. In economic models of sovereign debt, for example, the state *always* reconsiders how to perform, in light of conditions prevailing at maturity. The ruler-at-issuance cannot constrain the ruler-at-maturity. Similarly, in majoritarian models of debt, the median-voter-at-issuance cannot bind the median-voter-at-maturity.

I consider a more general model, in which both Machiavellian and constrained governments can exist. Let P be the probability, as gauged by purchasers in stage 1, that the government in stage 2 will *not* be able unilaterally to revise a promise sold in stage 1. Let $E(V_r)$ be what investors expect to get if the government is constrained (reversionary performance); and $E(V_M)$ be what they expect to get when the government is not constrained (Machiavellian performance). The overall expected value of the sovereign promise – the maximum price that risk-neutral investors would be willing to pay for it – can be written as

$$E(V) = PE(V_r) + (1 - P)E(V_M) \qquad (1)$$

The expected value of constrained performance, $E(V_r)$, depends on both the *face value* and the *transfer value* of the original promise. The face value is what the bearer of a promise expects to get at maturity, if performance is strictly as promised (discounted to the date of purchase). The transfer value reflects investors' option of selling their promises before maturity. Throughout this book, I consider how improvements in the credibility of constraint, face value, and transfer value affected the English (and later the British) state's ability to raise revenues from the sale of sovereign promises.

Credibility of Constraint (P)

I begin with two conceptual points about the nature of commitment. First, commitment is not a feature of a state or constitutional order; rather, it is a feature of an individual sovereign promise. A given state can simultaneously issue some promises that its government-of-the-day will be legally free to revise (royal or Machiavellian promises) and other promises that its government-of-the-day will not be legally free to revise (parliamentary or rule-of-law promises). Second, a government can legally evade complying with a given promise in three main ways: (1) revising (in the extreme, voiding) the promise; (2) eroding the value of the promise by issuing more promises of the same or similar type (e.g., inflation); and (3) coercively transferring the promise to another party (e.g., eminent domain).

In any state, the government-of-the-day will seek to evade an inconvenient commitment by pursuing the most convenient legal tactic – whether revision, erosion, or transfer – via the most convenient legal device – whether statute, decree, or court decision. Thus, *legal commitment to a particular sovereign promise is only as strong as the weakest link in a chain of legal constraints placed upon the executive.*

Because the prerevolutionary English Crown could potentially evade promises in multiple ways, achieving "limited government" was no easy task. Although Parliament had fettered the prerogative before 1688, the overall constraint it succeeded in imposing was quite limited. Some Crown prerogatives, such as the right to borrow money, remained legally unchallenged. Other prerogatives, such as the right to levy taxes, were trammeled by chains that still had weak links (which the Crown assiduously identified and exploited).

What made the Revolution a watershed, rather than merely another signpost, in England's constitutional development was its comprehensiveness. *All* sovereign promises were brought under Parliament's monopoly control, through the introduction of ministerial responsibility; and *all* legal devices by which the executive might escape a particular commitment were put under Parliament's regulation. Thus, the English body politic, which had received many small and ineffective doses of limited government throughout the short seventeenth century, received its first large and effective dose after the Revolution.

How did parliamentarians convert sovereign promises from merely royal to fully parliamentary commitments? North and Weingast summarize the crucial element as *parliamentary supremacy*, whereas I shall argue – as a matter of both abstract logic and English history – for a stronger condition: a *parliamentary monopoly* on making sovereign promises combined with *monopoly brokerage* of the resulting sales.[2] In the next two subsections, I explain the logic of these twin monopolies.

Why Credibility of Constraint Requires a Parliamentary Monopoly

In standard usage, "parliamentary supremacy" means that Parliament can make or unmake any law; no court can revise or reject its decisions; and no executive decree can in any way alter statute law. So defined, parliamentary supremacy ensures that the formal statutory process – requiring approval by the Commons, Lords, and Crown – cannot be circumnavigated by royal decrees or executive-dictated judicial decisions. To put it in the lingo of contemporary political science, parliamentary supremacy ensures that revising statutes really does require the approval of the formal veto players.[3]

---

[2] I sometimes use the term "monopoly brokerage" to refer to the full tripartite system ensuring the credibility of sovereign promises and sometimes to the specific role played by the brokers.

[3] On veto player theory in general, see Cox and McCubbins (2001) and Tsebelis (2002).

A "parliamentary monopoly" means both parliamentary supremacy as just defined, plus a further stipulation: that only an act of Parliament (or a decree approved by Parliament) can authorize the sale of sovereign promises. When this additional stipulation does not hold, sovereign promises can be sold on both royal initiative (by decree) and parliamentary initiative (by statute). The market, in other words, becomes a sort of duopoly.

When promises are embedded in statutes, parliamentary supremacy protects promise-holders against unilateral *revision* of their promises by the executive. However, supremacy does not protect promise-holders against unilateral executive actions that *erode* the value of their promises.

Consider, for example, an entrepreneur who has purchased a royal patent conferring the right to build a turnpike road. Even if the legal terms of the original grant remain in force, the value of those rights can be eroded if the Crown later authorizes a competing turnpike road or canal in the near vicinity (cf. Lamoreaux 2011). Another example concerns inflation. When James I put baronetcies up for sale, he initially charged £1,095 and promised that only a fixed number would be created. Later, however, he reneged on his pledge, selling more baronetcies and driving the market price down to £220 (North and Weingast 1989, p. 811). The general point is that the value of many sovereign promises can be eroded by the sale of further promises of the same type.

Parliamentary monopoly defends promise-holders against erosion of their promises' value, by removing the Crown's ability to sell future promises. Indeed, because it is easier to issue new royal promises (just the Crown has to think this is a good idea) than to issue new parliamentary promises (which requires assent by the Commons, Lords, and Crown), a parliamentary monopoly on issuance removes the larger of the two erosion risks.

All told, then, only a parliamentary monopoly can protect promise-holders against both *direct revision* and *indirect erosion*. English promise-holders of various kinds – for example, public creditors holding debts, landowners holding titles to real property, and entrepreneurs holding corporate charters – cared deeply about both kinds of risk. Thus, they pushed for a parliamentary monopoly, aka the rule of law.

Constructing Parliamentary Monopolies
To secure a parliamentary monopoly required ensuring that only a statute, or a decree with equivalent support, could authorize the sale of a particular kind of sovereign promise. Decrees issued unilaterally by the monarch had to be rendered either illegal or unconstitutional.

The oldest tactic was to render decrees explicitly illegal. For example, by 1285 only an act of Parliament could authorize the sale of new common-law writs; decrees for this purpose were illegal. Explicit prohibition, however, left the Crown free to invent close substitutes for the promises it was forbidden to sell, which could then indirectly erode the value of parliamentary promises. In the case of common-law writs, for example, the Crown created entirely new prerogative courts and transferred politically sensitive cases to those courts.

Thus, a safer approach was to control how the royal prerogative was used. Once established, ministerial responsibility enabled Parliament to exert such control and thereby take over markets in which the royal prerogative remained legally intact. For example, the prerogative right to borrow has never been questioned at law. Yet, *unilateral* borrowing by the Crown became unconstitutional. The Crown could only borrow on advice of ministers who could be removed by a vote of no confidence.

The Brokers' Monopolies

When Parliament solidified its monopoly over a particular kind of sovereign promise, specialists quickly emerged to broker the resulting sales to the public. For example, lawyers purchased writs for litigants, parliamentary solicitors steered private bills for entrepreneurs seeking development rights, and bankers handled the flotation of sovereign debts.

In most cases, brokers earned commissions and thus sought to *monopolize* the conduct of sales. In this book, I explore several different species of monopoly broker in distinct markets – such as the Inns of Court (property rights), the Bank of England (sovereign debt), and the somewhat different case of the ministry (which acquired a monopoly right to propose public expenditures in 1706). In each case, I describe when and how the brokers secured their monopolies; how they were compensated; and why they were consistently more opposed to default than the Crown.

Limiting Executive Discretion (to Increase $E(V_r)$)

Even if a sovereign promise remained legally binding, it might not be worth much. In particular, the wording of some promises left executive officials complete discretion over how and when to perform. Officials constrained to comply with such vacuous promises could be just as Machiavellian as those able to unilaterally revise the legal terms of performance. Thus, the expected value of a state's reversionary performance depended on crafting the original promise in order to limit executive discretion.

As more of England's sovereign promises were embedded in statutes, a sea change occurred in the elaboration and precision of those promises. The content of these more elaborate promises varied but investors sought two key limits on executive discretion.

First, investors wanted *senior claims*. Debt-holders, for example, wanted specific revenue streams earmarked to repay them and they wanted their claims on these revenues to have priority over all other claims. Landowners (who held sovereign promises known as titles) wanted their usage rights to be exclusive and absolute. MPs wanted the expenditures they were promised to have first claim on specific revenue streams; unfunded mandates were no more popular with MPs than junior debt claims were with investors.

Second, investors wanted the state to line up *sufficient resources to perform*. Debt-holders, for example, wanted the revenues dedicated to repaying them to be obviously enough to retire the entire debt. Landowners wanted the resources dedicated to enforcing their rights to be clearly adequate to the task. MPs wanted the revenues dedicated to their pet expenditure items to cover all costs.

By enhancing the seniority and sufficiency of their claims, promise-holders could deprive administrative staff in the executive branch of any legal discretion. I describe some of the battles for seniority and sufficiency in later chapters.

Not all sovereign promises could be spelled out completely, however. Some promises to expend public revenues in particular ways were inherently "incomplete contracts." In such cases, the highest executive officials – ministers – had to be left with some residual discretion. The English method of policing the exercise of this residual discretion was, again, ministerial responsibility.

Part I: Reconsidering the Revolution

In contrast to those who argue that the Revolution brought gradual or only de facto political changes, I argue that a series of important de jure constitutional reforms occurred. While the specific reforms differed from market to market, in each case they promoted a parliamentary monopoly, thereby preventing the Crown from unilaterally revising, eroding, or transferring sovereign promises. In other words, they established the rule of law in a particular market.

In Part I of this book, I describe how Parliament's monopoly was established in several distinct markets. I begin with public expenditure

(Chapters 2–3), an area that North and Weingast and their critics have relatively neglected, and then proceed to debt (Chapters 4–6) and property rights (Chapters 7–8), before providing a summary overview in Chapter 9.

Did Reforms Matter for Taxation and Public Expenditure?

Many scholars have modeled taxation as an exchange in which a ruler promises public goods in return for the citizenry's payment of taxes (Bates and Lien 1985; Levi 1988; Tilly 1990; Congleton 2011). A central issue in such models is whether citizens can hide their taxable assets from the Crown. The more they can do so, the more their payment of taxes must be voluntary rather than coerced.

Here, I focus on a different exchange, not between Crown and subjects but rather between Crown and representatives. The Crown offers what I call a *platform* – a sovereign promise to expend specific state revenues on specific purposes. Those purposes might include providing public goods or redressing various "grievances." The House of Commons can "buy" the platform by voting for the associated supply bill.[4]

The exchange of tax grants for platforms just described is only a slight stylization of deals actually struck in England over many centuries. However, many negotiations between Crown and Commons foundered because the Crown's platforms lacked credibility. Indeed, the Crown was legally free to spend any money it got in whatever fashion seemed appropriate in light of changing circumstances. This unfettered ability to control expenditure meant that royal platforms – typically articulated in the Summons to Parliament, the Speech from the Throne, or other royal communications – could be revised at royal will.

After the Revolution, three interlocking reforms substantially improved the credibility of platforms. First, and most fundamentally, expenditure promises were embedded in the appropriations clauses of statutes. Second, the Commons acquired much more information – via reporting requirements and audits – about how public revenues were actually being spent. It is no accident that standardized statistics on English public revenues and expenditures begin in 1689. Third, to punish ministers for violating the letter or spirit of the Crown's expenditure promises,

---

[4] Throughout this book, I focus on the Crown–Commons relationship, in light of the superior constitutional position the House of Commons had established vis-à-vis money bills. In particular, the Commons exclusively proposed such bills and the Lords could not amend them (it could only accept or reject).

the Commons shifted from impeachment (cumbersome, legalistic, and extreme) to removal via votes of censure.[5]

But why would the Crown dismiss ministers, simply because the House of Commons censured them? The answer is that, after the Revolution, the government's legal authority to collect certain taxes, as well as its legal authority to disburse funds from certain state coffers, automatically lapsed at the end of each fiscal year. In other words, *the budgetary reversion was a government shutdown*. That carefully engineered constitutional fact ensured royal respect for votes of censure, which constituted the Commons' threat to cut supply at the next opportunity, were the offending ministers not removed.

Annual budgets with shutdown reversions removed the Crown's unilateral ability to decide how to spend public monies. The executive had been constrained. However, no single MP internalized the tax cost of public expenditure. Thus, the initial reforms mitigated executive moral hazard at the expense of exacerbating the fiscal common pool problem.

Moreover, the reforms did not by themselves ensure the credibility of platforms. If the Commons could propose revisions of the budget at any time (which it could), and the budget simply allocated a fixed sum across competing uses, then standard results on "divide the dollar" politics imply no budget could be stable. Regardless of the status quo budget, another could always be found that would command a statutory majority (i.e., a majority in both chambers and the royal assent).

The English thus faced twin problems inherent in fiscally strong assemblies – insufficiently internalized tax costs and unstable budgets. They dealt with these troublesome twins by giving ministers a monopoly right to propose expenditure of public revenues. With such a right, permanent since 1706, ministers became the monopoly brokers of deals between the tax-granting Commons and the platform-peddling Crown.

Collectively the reforms just sketched – annual budgets, shutdown reversions, a ministerial monopoly on proposing expenditures – amounted to what I call a budgeting revolution (see Chapters 2 and 3). The main effect was that platforms became much more credible, so that MPs were willing to grant much greater tax revenues in exchange for them. Indeed, tax receipts tripled the Restoration average within a decade of the Revolution (Brewer 1988; O'Brien 1988).

---

[5] The credibility of the Crown's platforms depended on all three reforms working together. If promises were not statutory, then Crown officials could revise them at will. If either information or punishment were lacking, then Crown officials could skirt appropriations with impunity.

It is important to stress, however, that growth in public expenditures was concentrated in those areas governed by annual appropriations proposed by ministers. As will be seen, the state grew rapidly where, and only where, platforms were rule-of-law promises.

Did Reforms Matter for Loans and Debts?

The fiscal cost of England's sovereign debt after the Revolution varied substantially but this was not because investors feared their promises would be revised by a Machiavellian government-at-maturity. English debt faced high interest rates and stiff price discounts because much of it was either junior or underfunded. The senior and better-funded debts were paid off reliably, but the junior and underfunded debts accumulated until they reached crisis proportions. In the first quarter century after the Revolution, England suffered two such cycles, driving the fiscal cost of debt sharply upward in both cases. The problem was not solved until the seniority and funding of the debt were addressed, and this could not happen until a parliamentary monopoly on debt issuance had emerged, which required ministerial responsibility.

In other words, I argue (in Chapters 4–6) that English sovereign debts became very credible almost immediately after the Revolution, through the simple device of making them parliamentary. However, in the first generation after the Revolution, England issued a lot of debt promises with low face values (because they were junior and/or underfunded). The reason England sold debt with low face value was entirely political: Parliament refused to grant the long-term taxes that were essential to fund long-term debts, until it had wrested control over the expenditure of public revenues from the Crown. The capstone achievement in controlling expenditure was, as noted earlier, ministerial responsibility. Once all Crown acts had to be on the advice of ministers removable by vote of censure, Parliament promptly adjusted the term structure of taxation and almost all debt became long-term and funded.

Did Reforms Matter for Property Rights?

The credibility of domestic real property rights did not change at the Revolution because monopoly brokerage in that market had emerged long before, as I describe in Chapter 7. Thus, one does not expect to see, nor does one find, a decline in rates of return on domestic property after 1688.

That said, the right to transfer one's usage rights to others was underdeveloped in England before 1688. The key change in property rights

after 1688 was not an improvement in credibility but rather an improvement in transferability. I explore this point in connection with the tre-
mendous boom in turnpikes, canals, and estate acts that ensued after the
Revolution (Bogart 2005, 2011a; Bogart and Richardson 2011).

Britain's private bill procedure was unique among its European competitors, and it enabled substantially more efficient bargaining between
local stakeholders in development contests. The result was that Britain
experienced exponential growth (literally) in its turnpike road mileage,
along with sharp improvements in canal density and coastal waterway
transport. By the mid-eighteenth century Britain had by far the best transportation system in the world, which created the largest national market
in Europe. In combination with high labor and low energy costs, the size
of England's market sparked the series of innovations and workplace
reorganizations known as the Industrial Revolution (see Chapter 8).

Part II: Exporting the Revolution

England's Glorious Revolution had admirers aplenty – not just the Whig
grandees who publicized a particular account of its events (Pincus 2009);
and not just Montesquieu, whose *Spirit of the Laws* echoed revolutionary ideas. Indeed, generations of continental observers sought to "reverse
engineer" the Revolution. In Part II of this book (Chapters 10–12), I consider one aspect of the constitutional diaspora from the Revolution: how
the world's constitutions have regulated the power of the purse.

When a given polity established annual budgets, thereby converting
its platforms into statutory rather than decretal promises, the executive's commitment to following the budgetary plan became substantially
more credible (Dincecco 2011). However, two important caveats must be
registered.

First, annual budgets could improve executive commitment to a
one-year plan but longer-term commitments hinged on the budgetary
reversion. The major west European states all established annual budgets in the period 1790–1861. In several of these countries, however, the
budgetary reversion was the executive's proposal (or a variant thereof).
As I show in Chapter 10, public revenues grew substantially faster in
countries adopting shutdown reversions than in those failing to do so.

Second, sound fiscal management required more than establishing
annual budgets and shutdown reversions. Such reforms reduced executive moral hazard but did nothing to address the fiscal common pool
problem. Indeed, this latter problem was *worsened* by conferring fiscal

control on assemblies. The English had prevented MPs from draining the fiscal common pool by endowing ministers with a monopoly on proposing expenditures. Polities that did not adopt this crucial feature of monopoly brokerage, such as the Third Republic in France, experienced chaotic budgets and unstable ministries.

All told, then, the main lesson I draw from examining the first imitators of British fiscal practices is as follows. Only countries that fully adopted monopoly brokerage of platforms – which entailed annual budgets, shutdown reversions, and a ministerial monopoly on proposing expenditures – were able both to increase their revenues rapidly and to expend them responsibly.

I draw similar lessons from examining how Western budgetary procedures spread to the rest of the world (Chapter 11). While the British Parliament's right to deny supply was unquestioned after the Revolution, the analogous right has been engineered away in many of the world's constitutions. Where the budgetary reversion favors the executive, tax revenues are lower. Moreover, executives with favorable budgetary reversions are more likely to end democracy via auto-coups than those facing a shutdown reversion.

Part II focuses on the power of the purse in order to bring down to earth a range of questions perennially asked of institutionalist accounts. For example, was monopoly brokerage of platforms necessary or sufficient for either the proximal effects (taxes, loans, development) or the distal effects (conquest, industrialization) that seem to have followed in Great Britain? I take up some of these issues in the final chapter.

PART I

THE GLORIOUS REVOLUTION AND THE ENGLISH STATE

2

The Market for Taxes and Platforms

By the 1340s and 1350s, Parliament had asserted and largely established an exclusive right to grant new taxes (Waugh 1991, p. 203; Sacks 1994, p. 19; Payling 2009, p. 76). Thereafter, until the Revolution, taxation was supposed to proceed as follows. The monarch would ask for new taxes and, in exchange, offer some general remarks about the purposes to which the new revenues would be put. Those purposes were typically war-related and invoked the doctrine of necessity (Sacks 1994, pp. 17–18). In my lingo, the monarch offered to "sell" Parliament some platforms – sovereign promises about expenditure – in exchange for taxes. If MPs liked what they heard, they could "buy" the platform by granting taxes.

Virtually all platforms before the Revolution were royal; very few were embedded in statutes. Thus, the monarch could change his or her mind about the proper use of the revenues at will. Even if the monarch did not abandon his/her original promise, however, Parliament typically had little idea whether it was being honored, as MPs lacked even the most basic accounts of the public revenues and expenditures.

The low credibility of royal platforms led, especially during the Stuart years, to the Commons denying supply. Why buy a platform whose performance one cannot verify and can be changed at royal whim? The Crown, anticipating that its dodgy pledges would elicit no new taxes, did not summon Parliament – and sought to find revenues without it.

There were only two logical ways out of the fiscal impasse facing Stuart England. One, the Stuarts' preferred solution, was royal absolutism (Pincus 2009). The other required making sovereign promises about expenditure more credible, so that bargains between the tax-granting Commons and the platform-peddling Crown would no longer fail so often.

After the Revolution, Parliament simultaneously defended against absolutism and reengineered the credibility of platforms. To make platforms harder to change legally, Parliament embedded them in statutes, in what were called appropriations. To bolster its ability to verify that promises were kept, Parliament required executive officials to provide vastly more information about the public finances. To enhance its ability to punish ministers for violating its instructions, Parliament forced ministerial responsibility on a reluctant monarch.

Inextricably connected to the rapidly evolving appropriations-audit-punishment system was the emergence of ministers as the monopoly brokers of the taxes-for-platforms market. Ministers assembled a set of rights, entrenched in both written and unwritten rules, enabling them to control the crafting of both platforms and supply bills.

As platforms became parliamentary and the ministers' position as monopoly brokers solidified, the taxes-for-platforms trade between Crown and Commons boomed. The main consequence of England's budgeting revolution, documented in the next chapter, was a huge and permanent run-up in tax revenues. Taxes, in turn, crucially underpinned the "financial revolution" in sovereign debt (on which more in Chapters 4–6).

The Age of Royal Platforms and Parliamentary Taxes: 1350–1688

Prior to the Revolution, an English king was supposed to "live of his own." Some revenues were collected by hereditary right and needed no parliamentary authorization. At the beginning of each new reign, Parliament would routinely grant additional revenues for the life of the monarch. After that, with one exception, the king was on his own (Reitan 1970; Chandaman 1975, pp. 276–277; Roberts 1977).

The exception was that the monarch could ask Parliament for temporary levies to meet extraordinary needs. In the Summons to Parliament, Speech from the Throne, or other public documents the monarch would explain why s/he sought new funds. For example, Edward I promised in 1295 to fend off an impending invasion by the king of France, who "proposes to destroy the English language altogether from the earth, if his power should correspond to the detestable proposition of the contemplated injustice" (Cheyney 1897, pp. 33–35). At other times, the monarch might take notice of specific "grievances" mentioned by the Commons, promising redress.

The Summons or the Speech contained royal platforms (i.e., promises about how the monarch would spend the new tax money s/he sought). Parliament was then free to grant the supply requested – "buying" the platform – or reduce or deny it.

Once they had the money in their hands, monarchs were predictably tempted to alter their platforms by diverting funds to other purposes. In other words, they were prone to reneging. Rulers throughout medieval Christendom mitigated their credibility problems by creating councils or parliaments with monopoly rights to grant new taxes (cf. Marongiu 1968; Barzel and Kiser 2002). The Council's or Parliament's monopoly, if respected, meant that the sovereign could not easily find new sources of taxation after reneging on whatever commitments had been made to procure the original taxes. Tax-granting monopolies thus enhanced the credibility of Parliament's threat to withhold funds in the future, should current funds be misspent. In the English case, Waugh reckons that "parliament's monopoly [over the granting of taxes] was not firmly established until the 1340s" (1991, p. 203), while Payling casts the 1350s as the crucial decade (2009, p. 76).

Although only Parliament could grant taxes, the Crown fully controlled the crafting, sale, and performance of platforms. The monarch and royal officials wrote the Summons and the Speech. They decided when to call Parliament and present MPs with a sales pitch. And, once the money was in the royal coffers, Crown officials had complete legal discretion over how to spend it.

The Crown's unchallenged legal control of expenditure, along with the merely royal nature of its promises, meant that its platforms were Machiavellian. In the case of defensive wars against dire threats, the Machiavellian nature of royal promises might not matter much. Taxpayers could trust the monarch to spend as promised, since their interests were transparently aligned.

The Stuarts, however, sought to expand their domestic authority and international stature (cf. Pincus 2009). The old system choked on their ambitions. MPs were obviously reluctant to grant supplies that might be used against them – for example, in the run-up to the English Civil War. But even when the Crown had identified a tempting offensive opportunity in the burgeoning Atlantic economy, or offered redress of burning grievances, MPs mistrusted royal promises.

Their mistrust was partly due to simple logic – why put faith in a monarch able to repudiate platforms with impunity? – and partly due to bitter experience. Charles II, for example, had secured a subsidy from Parliament by "pointing to the probable cost of outfitting the fleet for … employment against Louis XIV" (De Krey 2007, pp. 96–97). Yet, Charles II had previously concluded the secret treaty of Dover with Louis XIV, and he used the subsidy to wage war against the Dutch. On another occasion, Charles II informed Parliament that "money provided … for the disbandment of the newly raised land forces had in fact been applied to their maintenance" and asked for yet another subsidy to disband them (Chandaman 1975, p. 155).

The proximal effect of the Stuarts' lack of credibility was that the Commons often refused supply.[1] In my lingo, bargaining between Commons and Crown failed because the latter could not credibly commit to its platforms.

Distal effects followed. Knowing no new taxes would be granted, the Crown refused to call Parliament for long periods and sought to raise revenues in ways that undermined the Commons' authority.

One means of raising revenue without Parliament was to skirt the (none too clear) legal definition of a tax and ensure that sympathetic judges heard the resulting litigation. The two most obvious examples of this gambit were Charles I's collection of ship money, which led to John Hampden's imprisonment for refusing to pay; and Charles' imposition of a forced loan, which led to the jailing of five knights who refused to lend. By the Restoration, however, Parliament had overturned Hampden's conviction and the prerogative courts, which kept the five knights in jail, had been abolished. Thus, after 1660, raising taxes or forced loans by royal prerogative no longer looked like a viable tactic (cf. Roseveare 1973, p. 22).

Another tactic, dating back to the fourteenth century, was the sale of lucrative monopolies to business syndicates (Power 1942; North and Weingast 1989; Harris 2000, pp. 46–47). The monopolies themselves were royal promises (conferred by letters patent). Their sale generated substantial revenues while burdening English consumers with higher prices.

---

[1] The Commons' refusal of supply is one example of a broader pattern identified in the literature – viz., that European monarchs' lack of credibility as regards the division of spoils from offensive wars caused elites (whether or not acting through parliaments) to withhold their contributions to the war effort. See Levi (1988), Rosenthal (1998), Kiser and Linton (2002, pp. 891–892).

An important step toward closing down the royal market occurred with the Statute of Monopolies, enacted on 25 May 1624. Henceforth, patents were supposed to be temporary monopolies given only to those with truly novel inventions. Charles I managed to continue selling dubious patents by exploiting exceptions in the statute and ensuring that legal challenges were referred to pliant conciliar courts (Gregg 1984, pp. 215–220). Thus, a further important step occurred at the Restoration, when jurisdiction over patent litigation transferred to the common-law courts.

As the Crown found it more and more difficult to raise revenues without parliamentary approval, it increasingly turned to yet another tactic – creating a subservient House of Commons. The main tactics here were (1) re-chartering and packing the parliamentary corporations; (2) buying seats and votes in elections; and (3) buying votes in the House of Commons (George 1940; Foord 1947; Kemp 1957).

The root cause of the various royal gambits described in the previous four paragraphs, along with the constitutional crises they sparked, was the nature of the taxes-for-platforms market. Any polity that gives its legislature a monopoly right to grant taxes and its executive a monopoly right to craft and perform platforms will risk the sort of inefficient constitutional strife that Stuart England suffered. For the executive's inability to credibly commit to how it will spend revenues granted by the assembly will cause bargains over raising taxes to fail.[2]

Theoretically, the Commons' threat of withholding future taxes could render the Crown's expenditure promises more credible. However, this punishment theory of taxation, like punishment theories of sovereign debt, implies a "credit limit." The Commons' threat to withhold future supplies would only carry so much weight and could be outweighed if fiscal shocks made the Crown desperate for immediate funds. Thus, if the threat of punishment (withholding future supplies) were to deter the Crown from reneging on its platforms, then the Commons would have to grant small amounts of revenue for short periods.

As described later, the Commons vigorously pursued just such a short-leash strategy in the immediate aftermath of the Revolution. However, a short leash left the underlying structural problem – created by combining a legislature that grants taxes with an executive that spends them – unresolved.

---

[2] That inability to commit leads to a higher risk of bargaining failure is a central result in rationalist models of bargaining. See, e.g., Fearon 1995a; Jackson and Morelli 2011.

To remedy this structural dilemma, England might have taken two constitutional paths. One path was to transfer the legislature's power to grant taxes to the executive. The other was to make the executive's expenditure promises more credible. In the next two sections, I describe how England's parliamentarians blocked the first option and took the second.

Preventing Absolutism

Throughout the short seventeenth century (1603–1688), Parliament frequently asserted its power over the purse and the Crown repeatedly sought to evade that power and establish financial independence. While the battle at any particular historical moment was not always between the extremes of "parliamentary monopoly" and "royal absolutism," those were the polar outcomes the two sides craved and feared. Most of the time, the war over the constitution was cold, with revenue-hungry monarchs respecting the letter of parliamentary rights while violating their spirit. Occasionally, as in the Civil War, the conflict over the sinews of power turned hot.

The Crown employed a three-pronged strategy to promote absolutism. The first and least radical prong of royal strategy was to control Parliament by re-chartering parliamentary corporations, buying seats, and buying votes in Parliament. The second prong was to rule legally without Parliament; the Stuarts could and did refuse to call Parliament for long periods, seeking to find sufficient revenues via various technically legal gambits. The third and most radical prong was to crush Parliament and establish a more absolutist regime by force.

Parliament's strategy to bolster its constitutional position was not simply to proclaim its rights in the broadest possible terms. It had tried that before – for example, in the 1628 Petition of Right – without success. Thus, radical parliamentarians began to devise constitutional shields that would blunt each prong of absolutist strategy. After the Revolution, new shields were enshrined in the settlement documents *sensu lato*, as I note in the next few subsections.

Crushing Parliament Militarily

To prevent the monarch from crushing Parliament militarily, the Bill of Rights (1689) and the Mutiny Act (1689) forbade raising or maintaining a standing army during peacetime without parliamentary assent. Neither prohibition had ever been embodied in statutory form before. Together they ensured that the Crown, were it determined to coerce Parliament, would need to undertake illegal acts early in the process of implementing its coercive strategy, thereby giving parliamentary forces more time to coordinate their countermeasures. As Redlich put it, "the first constitutional change made after 1688, and a momentous one it was, consisted in the institution of the annual Mutiny Act, whereby an army was in fact founded and received a legal status by means of a yearly approval in parliament, together with a grant of sufficient means to supply a year's needs" (1908, vol. III, p. 168).

End-Running Parliament

Although Parliament had placed time limits on revenue grants before the Revolution, the Bill of Rights for the first time stipulated that "levying money ... *for longer time* ... than the same is or shall be granted [by statute], is illegal" (italics added). Such a prohibition had been proposed in 1674. As Jones notes, its purpose was to make "it illegal to extend taxes arbitrarily beyond the time limits set by parliament" (1994, p. 70), thereby removing the "operationally easiest method" of evading parliamentary control. The necessity for such a prohibition was illustrated again in 1685, when a newly crowned James II continued to collect the taxes granted to his predecessor, prior to obtaining parliamentary approval.

After the Revolution, parliamentarians exploited the "for longer time" clause to put the Crown on a far shorter financial leash than ever before (see, e.g., Roberts 1966, 1977; Reitan 1970; Hill 1976; Hoppit 2000). For example, when William III came to the throne, Parliament granted him the customs tax revenues for six months, then another six months, then one year, then four years, and then five (Hill 1976, pp. 38, 40, 42, 49, 62; Hoppit 2000, pp. 25–26). A deadline always loomed at which the king would lose more than a fifth of his total revenues, unless he could cut another deal with Parliament. This put William III in a very different bargaining position than either Charles II or James II, both of whom had received the customs for life. I provide new evidence on just how much weaker William III's bargaining position was later in this chapter.

Controlling Parliament

To prevent the Crown from controlling Parliament, the settlement erected new defenses against each of the main tactics of royal influence – viz., re-chartering, seat buying, and vote buying. Let's consider each in turn.

To deter re-chartering, a 1690 Act reversed a King's Bench judgment rendered in 1683 against the City of London. The original judgment had entailed forfeiture of the City of London's charter and franchises to the Crown and constituted a landmark in the Stuarts' long campaign to control Parliament by destroying old and issuing new charters of parliamentary corporations (George 1940). Parliament's explicit reversal of the decision was designed to make it more difficult for future monarchs to void parliamentary charters.

To deter royal seat buying, the Bill of Rights called for freedom to elect Members of Parliament without royal interference. Admittedly, however, there was nothing new in this demand.

The Act of Settlement (1701), however, contained a new legal defense against royal vote buying in Parliament. Reacting to William III's vigorous attempts to influence the House of Commons, clause 5 declared that anyone who held an office under or received a pension from the Crown was ineligible to sit in Parliament. Statutes passed in 1705–1707 weakened this prohibition, allowing members to accept various executive offices, so long as they resigned their seat in the Commons and stood for reelection. Even in this weakened form, however, the attack on placemen was a significant new attempt to reduce the Crown's vote buying.[3] As Brewer notes, the effort succeeded: "The number of placemen in the lower house grew remarkably little between 1688 and 1714 when viewed in the context of the overall growth in the number of state servants" (1988, p. 159).

Making Platforms More Credible

In addition to defending against absolutism, the Commons played offense: it sought to make sovereign promises about expenditure more binding. The first step was to entrench such promises in statutes, thereby making it more likely they would still be legally in force when performance was due. The next step was to remove all executive discretion in interpreting statutory provisions.

Appropriations

To show how dramatically platforms shifted from being merely royal to being parliamentary promises, I examined all appropriations made by

---

[3] See Foord 1947; Kemp 1957. Once ministerial responsibility was in place, the need to prevent MPs from holding positions of profit under the Crown diminished. Since such posts were now all filled on advice from ministers, the battle over placemen henceforth was as much between the back and front benches as between Parliament and Crown.

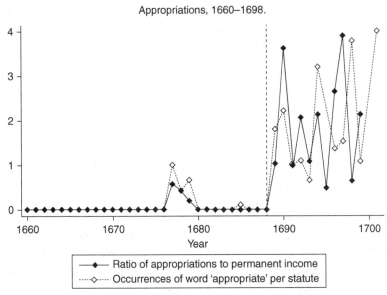

FIGURE 2.1. Appropriations, 1660–1698.

Parliament from 1660 to 1699. Prior to the Revolution, the Commons experimented only briefly with embedding platforms in statutes. Figure 2.1 displays the ratio of money appropriated – that is, earmarked by act of Parliament for expenditure on a particular purpose – to the king's permanent annual income.[4] As can be seen, this ratio was zero in all but three years before 1689, reaching a maximum of 0.57 in 1677. After the Revolution, the ratio immediately jumps over 1 and, for the most part, stays over 1 thereafter. In essence, after 1688 the Commons embarked on a spree of appropriation unprecedented in size, scope, and duration.

Another way to see how dramatically platforms shifted from royal to parliamentary in nature is to count the number of times the verb "appropriate" (or its derivatives) appears in the statutes of the realm. In most years before the Revolution, the word is not used in any statute. After

---

[4] I do not count money appropriated to repay loans here, only money appropriated to some specific item of current expenditure. It is harder to attach specific amounts to appropriations for loan repayment but, were one able to do so, the contrast between pre- and post-1688 would be just as stark. I also do not count money as appropriated unless the word "appropriate" is used explicitly. Instances in which Parliament in fact appropriates without using the word explicitly are rare but examples do exist (e.g., 17 Charles II, c. 1, section 5).

the Revolution, as Figure 2.1 shows, "appropriate" seems to be one of Parliament's favorite verbs. Maitland was largely correct when he opined that the practice of appropriation after the Revolution "never varied; in granting money to the crown, parliament ... appropriated the supply to particular purposes" (1908, p. 433).[5]

The trend toward ever-greater appropriation was so powerful that one can say that a rudimentary system of annual budgeting is in place by the mid-1690s (Redlich 1908, vol. III, pp. 161–170; Kemp 1957, pp. 72–73; Roseveare 1973, p. 44; Horwitz 1977, pp. 87–88; Harling 2001, p. 18). Initially, however, annual appropriation applied only to the armed forces, which consumed about 75 percent of public expenditures at the time (Brewer 1988, pp. 40, 137).

Civil expenditures – paying the salaries and pensions of civil servants, ministers, judges, ambassadors, and other state officials, as well as providing for the expenses of the royal household – remained the domain of the monarch. The Crown was given a permanent annual income with which to defray the expenses of the so-called Civil List. Because the Crown "had full power of disposition over all sums granted in the Civil List" (Redlich 1908, vol. III, p. 162) and did not need annual reauthorization of its income, any promises it chose to make about how Civil List monies would be spent remained merely royal promises.

Over the course of the eighteenth century, some civil expenses – the so-called supply services – came to be annually appropriated. In 1830, the Civil List was substantially reduced, so that it covered only the monarch's personal and family expenses. After this point, all the main expenditures of the state, except those Parliament made permanent charges on the Consolidated Fund, were subject to annual appropriation – and a full public budget in modern form emerges.[6]

MPs stipulated a strict chain of custody for revenues they appropriated, along with stiff penalties for administrators who deviated from parliamentary intent.[7] In this way, the abrupt shift from royal to parliamentary platforms (for military expenditures) facilitated control of lower-level executive branch officials.

---

[5] In a few early cases, such as 1 William & Mary, c. 13, Parliament does not say clearly how surplus revenues should be spent, thereby implicitly leaving them to Crown discretion. By 1695, however, the practice of appropriating "overplus" or "residue" funds seems to be well established.

[6] See Redlich 1908, vol. III, pp. 161–170; Kemp 1957, pp. 72–73; Binney 1958.

[7] The standard provisions can be found in 1 William and Mary, session 2, c. 1, sections xlv–lv.

Chains of custody and penalties did not greatly constrain the highest executive officials' discretion, however, since appropriations clauses still described the purposes to which funds were to be put in very broad terms. For example, the army estimate was not divided (into seven headings) until 1711, and "the expenses of the navy ... were appropriated in one total sum until 1798" (Redlich 1908, vol. III, p. 169). Thus, the Commons had somehow to reduce ministers' ability to violate the spirit of their grants, and this involved better controlling pretty much everything they did.

Ministerial Responsibility

According to the dominant political analysis of the time, the key to controlling the monarch's actions was holding those through whom s/he took those actions accountable: "the king ... is not punishable or blameable by our Constitution, but the ministry is" (quoted in Roberts 1959, p. 580). The great constitutional puzzle, with which parliamentarians had struggled throughout the seventeenth century, concerned how to hold the Crown's advisors accountable for their advice. The solution involved developing Parliament's capacities in three distinct but related areas. First, MPs had to know who the advisors were. Second, MPs had to know when advisors had given advice of which they would disapprove. Third, MPs had to be able to punish bad advice.

As regards *who* the king's advisors were, there was a substantial and intellectually organized push to make the Privy Council the responsible body. Proponents of conciliar responsibility dominated throughout the settlement period (1689–1701) and their views were clearly embodied in clause 4 of the Act of Settlement (1701). Yet, as Roberts (1959, 1966) explains, public discourse shifted rapidly in the next few years, with repeated calls for the ministry – a term just then gaining wide currency – to bear responsibility.

As regards *when* the king's advisors had given bad advice, a key issue was whether Parliament needed explicit evidence that advisor X had promoted policy Y, or whether implicit evidence sufficed. The standard of evidence in turn connected to the mode of punishment. The dominant viewpoint earlier in the seventeenth century was that Parliament's main weapon against evil councilors was impeachment. Impeachment, however, required legal proof of individual responsibility for bad advice. The new view, which developed rapidly in conjunction with the shift in focus from the Council to the Cabinet, was that Parliament's main weapons would not be legal but political: Parliament would force bad ministers from office by denying supply. This weapon was far more flexible and did not require explicit proof of wrongdoing; Parliament could mount attacks on individual ministers or on the ministry as a whole simply because it disagreed with their policies.[8]

The vote of censure soon became a formal warning that supply would be cut, were the offending minister(s) not removed from office. The Commons' threat was credible because MPs could reduce whatever appropriations they wished out of the package proposed by ministers, and add whatever additional restrictions they wished regarding how monies should be spent. The Commons could then send its amended budget to the Lords and the Crown, each of whom would be constrained either to wholly accept it or wholly reject it. Rejection triggered a very unpalatable reversionary budget with no spending on items covered by annual appropriations. The Commons' ability to present the Crown with a take-it-or-leave-it offer, in which leaving the offer led to a drastic reduction in military spending, ensured that it could reliably punish the Crown for retaining ministers whom the Commons no longer trusted.

By 1706 (on which date more later in this chapter) Parliament's control of revenue and appropriation had become so extensive and regular that threats to cut supply typically did not need to be carried out; the Crown preferred simply to remove the censured minister(s). Thus, the key elements of ministerial responsibility were in place: the monarch had always to act on advice of ministers; and Parliament could force ministers out by votes of censure, backed by the threat of denying supply (Roberts 1966).

Denying Supply

The argument laid out in the previous section hinges on the notion that the Commons became sharply more able to deny supply after the Revolution. Yet, scholars debate whether Parliament's rights over taxation underwent any significant de jure change at the Revolution. As Murrell (2009) and Pincus and Robinson (2011a) point out, the Bill of Rights (1689) mostly repeats Parliament's ancient rights. As Epstein (2000) and O'Brien (2002, 2005) point out, fundamental changes in the tax system had occurred

---

[8] Roberts notes that the standard of evidence became "common fame" (1956, p. 222). The older tactic of impeachment – which had been resuscitated in the 1620s (after a long lapse) precisely in an attempt to control the Crown's actions (see Anderson 1962; Greif 2007, pp. 40–41) – continued for a short while after the emergence of ministerial responsibility, mostly helping to punish violations of the new norms of ministerial responsibility. After 1715, however, impeachments became rare (the last occurring in 1806). Once a cheaper and more flexible way to exert control had been invented, the older and more cumbersome procedure fell into disuse.

during the Civil War and Restoration. For example, "prerogative revenues ... were all abolished or replaced by tax revenues in 1660" and henceforth all forms of taxation were legally under parliamentary control (Braddick 1996, pp. 10, 14). From this perspective, it is hard to see why the Glorious Revolution should be given the leading role in the history of Parliament's control over taxation.

Yet, although England's transition from what Schumpeter (1918[1954]) called a demesne state to a tax state was complete by 1660, that transition by itself was compatible with either an absolutist or a parliamentary future. Plenty of countries exist today in which the legislature legally controls taxation and yet a dictator rules as absolutely as any monarch. Thus, further constitutional reforms were necessary to secure Parliament's monopoly.

The key reform, embodied in the Bill of Rights' "for longer time" clause, enabled Parliament to impose strict time limits on revenue grants. Having asserted its right in principle, Parliament proceeded to impose time limits in practice. Whigs and Tories immediately agreed that the customs and other revenues should be granted only for short periods and neither side wavered thereafter (cf. Roberts 1966, 1977, pp. 66–69; Reitan 1970; Hill 1976, pp. 38–62). Quantifying how much Parliament's use of time-limited grants increased after the Revolution is an important exercise that, so far as I know, no one has previously undertaken.[9]

My approach is to calculate the discounted present value of the funds that Parliament could potentially terminate, as a percentage of each monarch's total annual revenues. For example, if a monarch had a revenue stream of size T that could be terminated in n years; had a permanent revenue stream of P; and used a discount rate r; then the discounted present value of a threat to end the time-limited funds, expressed as a share of total annual revenue, would be $T(1 + r)^{-n}/(P + T)$. Table 2.1 shows how important terminable grants were to the last prerevolutionary and first post-revolutionary monarchs.

Soon after his accession, James II was granted most of his revenues for life but also received time-limited customs duties on wines and vinegar (for eight years), tobacco and sugar (for eight years), and linens and silks (for five years). The discounted present value of his potentially disappearing revenues, over the first two years of his reign, represented about 7 percent of James' total revenues. In contrast, William III had essentially no settled revenues over the first two years of his reign. Even if one credits him as having a permanent income equal to that he eventually acquired,

---

[9] Roberts (1977) comes closest. The figures here are from Cox (2012).

TABLE 2.1. *Parliamentary Use of Time Limits on Tax Grants*

Monarch	Discounted Present Value of Terminable Tax Grants, as Percentage of Crown's Annual Income[a]
James II	7%[b]
William and Mary	69%[c]

Source: Cox (2012).

[a] My calculations use the formula in the text, focusing on each monarch six months after accession. I assume the Crown was risk neutral, was an unbiased estimator of future revenues, and discounted future revenues at a rate of 10 percent. Moderate alterations of these assumptions affect the results only slightly. The raw data for my calculations come from "Revenue Accounts," *Calendar of Treasury Books, Volume 9: 1689–1692* (1931), pp. CCIV–CCXVII. URL: http://www.british-history.ac.uk/report.aspx?compid=104740&strquery=income and expenditure (Date accessed: 23 December 2010).

[b] Reitan estimates James' total annual revenue as £1,900,000 (1970, p. 572).

[c] William and Mary's total income (not counting loans) over the period November 1688 to September 29, 1691 was £8,693,331. Their yearly income was thus on average £2,897,777. I estimate their permanent income at £691,836, following Roberts (1977, p. 62). Finally, I assume that their unsettled revenues could be terminated in a year. This is too generous for customs revenues, which initially had a six-month time limit, and too generous also for those revenues that Parliament had not yet addressed at all (as these could in principle have been withdrawn at any time).

the discounted present value of the revenues that Parliament could potentially terminate was roughly 69 percent. This tenfold increase in Crown revenues under effective parliamentary control qualitatively altered their bargaining relationship.

It is quite clear, moreover, that MPs knew what they were doing (Roberts 1959, 1966, 1977; Reitan 1970). Brewer's discussion of the intensity of direct taxation imposed by Parliament is particularly revealing:

In the long-term history of English taxation, the period between 1688 and 1714 stands out as an anomaly. Before the Glorious Revolution indirect taxes provided most of the government's revenue. After the Hanoverian Succession a similar pattern obtained. Only under William and Mary and Anne did direct imposts in the form of the land tax dominate revenue collection. The land tax, despite its heavy incidence on the landed classes, was preferred by the House of Commons over other taxes because it was the most limited ... limited because both its imposition and rate were approved annually by parliament; limited also because its collection was controlled by gentry in the localities ... and not through the deployment of a large body of centrally appointed officials. (1988, pp. 99–100)

In other words, MPs of the "country persuasion" were so determined to put a short leash on the Crown that they were willing to place the burden of taxation on their own estates. They allowed the imposition of more efficient (and long-term) indirect taxes only after their grip on the purse had become sufficiently clear and stable.

Ministers as Monopoly Brokers of the Taxes-for-Platforms Market

Their responsibility made ministers the monopoly facilitators of trade between Crown and Parliament. The Crown could offer platforms to the Commons only via ministers and on their advice, and the Commons could offer supplies to the Crown only via bills that ministers had the exclusive right to draft.

In this section, I first describe the ministers' monopoly on the taxes-for-platforms trade, from both the Crown's and the Commons' perspective. I then briefly comment on ministers' compensation and why they improved the efficiency of the market they brokered. This particular kind of monopoly brokerage is unlike any other I describe in this book. Yet it too ensured that the brokers (in this case, ministers) were reliably more hostile to default (in this case, unauthorized virement or impoundment) than the Crown.

Ministerial Responsibility from the Crown's Perspective

If the king doubted that his current ministers were the monopoly suppliers of new expenditures and taxes, then he might pursue other means to secure supply. In particular, he might assemble an ad hoc parliamentary majority for each major new grant, buying as many votes in Parliament as needed. Two elements of the settlement clearly aimed to prevent such royal influence in Parliament: the ban on sovereign interference with parliamentary elections (in the Bill of Rights of 1689), and the ban on MPs accepting places of profit from the Crown (in the Act of Settlement of 1701).

Another important institutional innovation came shortly after, in 1706, when the House of Commons resolved that it would "receive no petition for any sum of money relating to public service, but what is recommended from the crown." Historical accounts view this rule as solidifying the ministry's position vis-à-vis backbench MPs. Todd argues that the rule was brought in – first as a resolution (which had to be annually renewed) in 1706 and then as a standing order in 1713 – to prevent private members from raiding unallocated funds (1867 vol. I, pp. 428–429). Brewer suggests that the new rule simply codified the ministry's success in securing control over financial legislation: in the 1690s, private members had often significantly altered the Treasury's course with counterproposals; by the early 1700s, the ministry had secured a de facto monopoly on fiscal proposals; the new rule created a de jure monopoly (1988, pp. 149–50).

The implementation of the "rule of 1706" left no loophole by which unofficial members might breach the ministerial monopoly. First, the ministry had the exclusive right to submit the estimates (i.e., to propose expenditures). Second, after 1706 no legislative committee was ever again empowered, as the Committee on Public Accounts had been, to amend the ministry's estimates before forwarding them to the Committee of Supply. Third, MPs could amend the estimates in the Committee of Supply only by *reducing* proposed items of expenditure (and a similar rule applied in the House itself). In sum, the entire legislative process was reengineered to deny unofficial members any means to propose expending public revenues.

It is important to note that the new rule also bolstered the ministry's position vis-à-vis the Crown. It helped ensure – and make clear to all – that *ministers* would have the exclusive right to propose charges upon the public revenue.[10] It thus reflected and reinforced the new consensus that ministers were the king's primary advisors.

More importantly, the new rule prevented the king from seeking to split or end run his own ministers in Parliament. No sovereign could ask a friendly MP to propose a new expenditure and then buy enough votes to pass it. The "friendly MP" could never find an opportunity to propose. Moreover, royal purchase of votes was made more difficult in 1707 by transferring the initial consideration of supply to the Committee of the Whole, a tactic which had been invented under James I precisely to insulate MPs from Crown influence. All told, the "rule of 1706" had the following consequence: *henceforth, the Crown's only constitutional route to new expenditures authorized by Parliament lay through the ministry.*

Ministerial Responsibility from Parliament's Perspective
The ministry's monopoly on access to the Crown was ensured by Parliament's determination to force the Crown to dispense with secret and irresponsible advisors. Holding ministers responsible for all public acts necessarily meant that new coalitions within Parliament could

---

[10] Only ministers could convey recommendations from the Crown to Parliament. Later precedents extended the scope of the standing order, making clear that only ministers could recommend new taxes.

approach the king only through the existing ministry, or by replacing the current ministry.

Although the desire to get rid of hidden advisors helped ensure ministers' monopoly on brokering Crown–Parliament deals, important institutional changes facilitated their job. In particular, ministers formally controlled the committees in charge of writing supply bills after 1693 and, as noted earlier, had a monopoly on proposals for new charges upon the public revenue after 1706.[11] Thus, Parliament could offer supplies to the Crown only via supply bills that ministers drafted and proposed. *Henceforth, the only constitutional route for parliamentarians to deal with the Crown lay through the ministry.*

Ministers' Compensation and Incentives to Perform

Unlike the other markets I explore in this book, ministers shared both the costs of performance and the benefits of repudiation. If they chose to abide by an appropriations clause that constrained their actions in ways they disliked, then they bore the consequences. If they chose to skirt such a clause, then they got something closer to their preferred expenditure.

To limit their mischief, ministers were given an even more straightforward reason to perform than the other brokers considered later in this book. In particular, ministers who defaulted on platforms risked losing office via vote of censure.[12] Responsible ministers thus had much better incentives than hereditary monarchs to honor their expenditure promises to the Commons (or to revise them only by agreement).

Conclusion

It is hard to exaggerate how much more structurally sound sovereign promises to spend money in particular ways became after the Revolution. Before 1688, almost all such promises were royal and Parliament had great difficulty in discovering, much less punishing, nonperformance. Afterward, virtually all platforms were parliamentary (embedded in the appropriations clauses of statutes); the Commons received annual reports on the public finances; and its vigorous use of time limits meant it could quickly punish misappropriation by allowing old taxes to lapse or denying new ones.

---

[11] See Hayton (2002, pp. 393, 425–426) for a description of the 1693 change.

[12] As discussed earlier, the vote of censure was merely a warning that supply would be cut, if offending ministers remained in office; but such threats were credible because the Commons could present the Crown with a take-it-or-leave-it budget embodying its chosen cuts.

Fairly quickly, the Commons established annual budgets. The legal authority to disburse funds for certain purposes automatically lapsed at the end of every financial year. In other words, the budgetary reversion entailed what the American colonists eventually called a "government shutdown."

Adam Smith, in his *Lectures on Jurisprudence* (1762–1766, pp. 267–268), identified the budgetary reversion as key to England's liberty. Echoing earlier English commentaries (on which see Roberts 1966), Smith explained that the annual character of English budgets meant that "the whole of the government must be at an end if the Parliament was not regularly called." Moreover, he viewed Parliament's ability to stop supply as crucial to establishing "a system of liberty … in England."

By 1706, the key elements of ministerial responsibility had emerged. Ministers' primary responsibility was to steer supply bills through to enactment. That is, they were responsible for brokering deals between the Crown and Commons, with the former offering platforms embodied in statutes, the latter granting statutory authority to collect taxes and expend revenues. In the next chapter, I investigate the consequences of post-revolutionary England's new rule-of-law system of budgeting.

3

More Credible Platforms, More Taxes

In the previous chapter, I documented four important changes in how the taxes-for-platforms trade between Crown and Commons operated after the Glorious Revolution. First, before the Revolution, virtually all platforms had been royal (embedded in royal documents); afterward, they were almost exclusively parliamentary (embedded in the appropriations clauses of statutes). Second, before the Revolution, MPs' threats to deny supplies typically affected small amounts relative to the Crown's permanent income; afterward, thanks to vigorous exploitation of the "for longer time" clause of the Bill of Rights, the amounts involved were much larger. Third, before the Revolution, the Commons had no effective means to hold the Crown's advisors accountable for their advice; afterward, ministerial responsibility developed into a credible system. Fourth, before the Revolution, the Crown might have chosen any number of avenues through which to approach the Commons; afterward, there was only one constitutional route – through the ministers – who emerged as the monopoly brokers of the taxes-for-platforms market.

In this chapter, I consider the consequences of the reforms just noted. The most important consequence was that a lot more taxes were granted, once MPs had more credible assurances about how the resulting revenues would be spent. More broadly, the entire market – in which platform-selling Crown met tax-granting Commons – worked much more smoothly.

However, in those parts of the British budget that remained purely royal, there was no revenue growth. In other words, state revenues grew where, and only where, platforms became more credible.

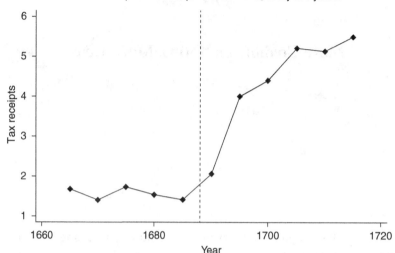

Tax receipts at Exchequer, 1665–1715, every five years.

FIGURE 3.1. Tax receipts at Exchequer, 1665–1715, every five years.
O'Brien (1988). Table 2. Cox (2012).
The vertical axis gives tax receipts in millions of constant pounds sterling.

Another vital consequence of Britain's budgeting revolution was the regulation of the fiscal common pool. I elaborate this accomplishment by comparing Great Britain's experience after the Revolution with that of France's Third Republic (a case to which I return in Chapter 10).

Proximal Consequences

The most direct consequences of England's budgetary revolution were that the volume, variety, and efficiency of trade surged. Let's consider each point in turn.

The Volume of Trade

One can estimate the volume of the taxes-for-platforms trade by the aggregate taxes granted. During the Restoration, notwithstanding the many improvements in tax *collection* (Roseveare 1973; Brewer 1988), tax *receipts* showed a shallow decline from 1665 to 1685, averaging £1.53 million. After the Glorious Revolution, tax receipts more than doubled the Restoration average by 1695 and tripled it by 1700 (see Figure 3.1). By 1815, taxes had risen sixteen-fold.

This surge in receipts was due primarily to the House of Commons' increased willingness to grant new taxes after the Revolution, rather than to any increased yield of old taxes. Hoppit shows that Parliament enacted public finance bills about 2.7 times per year during the Restoration, versus 7.1 times per year during the first post-Revolution generation (1689–1712) (2002, p. 270).

The Variety of Trade

The variety of platform promises also increased. Prior to the Revolution, royal platforms consisted mostly of promises to spend on particular wars. Afterward, parliamentary platforms became more diverse, including promises to pay creditors, to allocate revenues to the heir, and so on. Pincus and Robinson (2014) show that Britain's expenditures during the eighteenth century were considerably less concentrated on purely fiscal-military matters than were the expenditures of its major competitors.

The reason that platforms became more varied is that, once they were entrenched in statutes, it became worthwhile to elaborate them. Previously, as merely royal promises, they were more like suggestive guidelines. It made little sense to specify details, because the Crown remained free to revise expenditures in response to events.

The Efficiency of Trade

A key index of the efficiency of the taxes-for-platforms market is simply the frequency with which Parliament met.[1] By that index, the Revolution's effect is clear. Parliament did not sit in six of the ten years 1680–1689. In contrast, Parliament met in every year of the decade 1690–1699 and typically stayed in session for longer periods than it had under the Stuarts. Nothing in the settlement documents directly required the Crown to hold frequent parliaments, as Pincus and Robinson point out (2011, pp. 8–9). Thus, I take the greater frequency of meetings as reflecting the Crown's greater belief that it could get funds by selling platforms to the Commons.

Relatedly, the success rate of money bills improved substantially. "In the Restoration period only 45 per cent of attempts at public-finance legislation succeeded; under William III it was 55 per cent; between 1702 and 1748 it was about 80 per cent; and in the second half of the eighteenth century it was about 90 per cent" (Hoppit 2002, p. 269).

---

[1] Early European parliaments that refused to grant taxes – indicating that the sovereign's credibility problems were too great to overcome in that particular forum and time – were generally not called. The most famous exemplar of this logic – why convene a taxes-for-platforms assembly if no trade could foreseeably be arranged? – was the Estates General in France. But the logic, as Major (1960) noted, was more general.

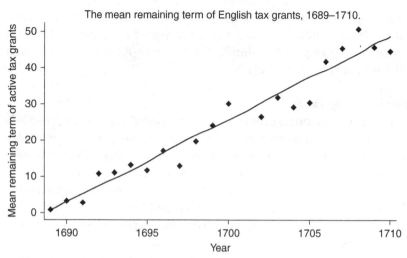

Source: Author's calculations from Statutes of the Realm.
The curve displayed is a locally weighted regression line.

FIGURE 3.2. The mean remaining term of English tax grants, 1689–1710.

Another indicator of market efficiency is the steadily increasing term of
Parliament's tax grants. Figure 3.2 displays, for each year 1689–1710, the
mean remaining term of all active tax grants. In 1689, Parliament granted
a lot of revenue but the average term of its grants was less than a year. By
1710, the average remaining term of the then-active grants was more than
forty years. Between 1689 and 1710, the average remaining term increased
almost linearly.[2]

The steadily lengthening term of the House of Commons' tax grants
shows that MPs became increasingly confident they could control expenditures. I count this as an efficiency gain because longer-term tax grants
meant a less frequent need to renegotiate them. Thus, the transaction costs
of taxation – in the form of negotiations between Crown and Commons –
steadily declined.

A related measure of market efficiency is the cumulative number of
long-term tax grants, displayed in Figure 3.3. For present purposes, I define
a tax grant as "long-term" if its initial term exceeded twenty years.[3] As can
be seen, the Commons granted no long-term taxes between 1670 and 1692.

---

[2] The line in the figure is the best-fitting locally weighted regression line.
[3] If a grant was for the life of the monarch, I count it as equivalent to a grant whose term
stretched to the year in which the monarch in fact died. For example, I count the life
grants made to James II in 1685 as sixteen-year grants, given that James died in 1701.

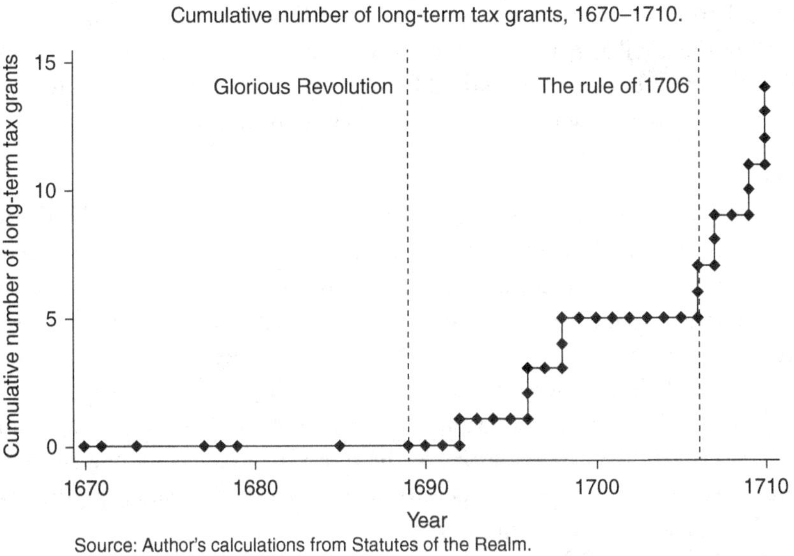

Cumulative number of long-term tax grants, 1670–1710.

FIGURE 3.3. Cumulative number of long-term tax grants, 1670–1710.

Thereafter, long-term grants accrued slowly. When ministers acquired an exclusive right to propose platforms in 1706, however, long-term grants increased substantially in frequency.

My interpretation is that platforms were protected against unilateral revision by the Crown when they were embedded in statutes (after 1689). This reform sufficed to loosen the purse strings considerably, as shown in Figure 3.1. When ministers secured a monopoly on proposing expenditures (after 1706), platforms were protected against vacillating floor majorities in the Commons and unilateral erosion by the Crown. This second reform further enhanced the credibility of platforms, enabling the term structure of taxation to be rationalized, as shown in Figure 3.3.

Not Much Taxation without Appropriation

I have argued that MPs were unwilling to grant much in the way of taxes, unless the revenues were appropriated by statute and MPs could detect and punish misappropriation. The big run-up in taxes granted after the Revolution, documented in Figure 3.1, gibes with this argument.

However, the wave of parliamentary appropriation after 1688 did not reach all parts of Great Britain's budget. In the immediate aftermath of the Revolution, neither Scottish nor Civil List revenues were subject to annual appropriation. Thus, one expects neither Scottish taxes nor taxes feeding the Civil List to have grown, until such time as promises about how the resulting revenues would be spent became more credible. In this section, I provide evidence supporting these expectations.

Scotland

In 1689, when William and Mary accepted the co-regency of the then-independent kingdom of Scotland, they quickly led their new subjects into war against France, as they had done upon assuming the crown of England. While the Scottish parliament sat more often after the Revolution (Hayton 1995, p. 281), there was no burst of appropriation. Of the supply bills enacted between 1689 and 1695, only one specifically appropriated the revenue it granted.[4] The co-regents thus exercised much greater control over expenditure of their Scottish than their English revenues. At the same time, Scottish tax rates remained considerably below English rates before the Union (1707).

After the Union, the apparatus of appropriation applied as much to Scotland as to the rest of the United Kingdom and "taxation did rise sharply, by all accounts" (Devine 2005, p. 23), in order to match Scottish with English rates. Scottish MPs knew full well that taxes would rise but found the package of promises made in the Act of Union sufficient compensation.

The Civil List

As noted in Chapter 2, the Crown retained full control over how it spent the Civil List grant. MPs should thus have been less willing to increase that grant than they were to increase grants whose expenditure they controlled via appropriations.

Plainly this expectation is borne out. As a percentage of total government expenditure, the Civil List shrank from 12.8 percent in 1697 to 9.2 percent in 1739 to 4.9 percent in 1775.[5]

The relatively slow growth of the Civil List was directly connected to the curious parochialism of domestic policy during the eighteenth century. In Maitland's famous characterization:

[A]ny alteration of the general rules of law, was much rarer [in the eighteenth century] than it is in our own day ... I take up a list of the statutes of 1786. There

---

[4] The supply acts are listed at http://www.rps.ac.uk/.

[5] The Civil List grew from £700,000 in 1697 to £811,000 circa 1739 to £965,000 circa 1775, falling in the next century (Redlich 1908, vol. III, pp. 161–162). Meanwhile total government expenditure grew from £5,456,555 (1697) to £8,778,900 (1739) to £19,831,333 (1775), continuing to rise in the next century (Brewer 1988, p. 40).

are 160 so-called public acts, and 60 so-called private acts. But listen to the titles of a few of the public acts: an act for establishing a workhouse at Havering, an act to enable the king to license a playhouse at Margate, ... an act for widening the roads in the borough of Bodmin. Fully half of the public acts are of this petty local character. ... One is inclined to call the last century the century of *privilegia*. It seems afraid to rise to the dignity of a general proposition. (1908, pp. 382–383)

Maitland's explanation for this legislative parochialism was "jealousy of the crown":

To have erected boards of commissioners empowered to sanction the enclosure of commons or the widening of roads, to have enabled a Secretary of State to naturalize aliens, would have been to increase the influence and patronage of the crown. (p. 383)

To this I would simply add that any such boards and officials would, at least earlier in the century, naturally have formed part of the Civil List. Thus, the growth of the civilian bureaucracy was stunted by Parliament's desire to avoid increasing the Civil List grant, over the expenditure of which it exercised relatively poor control.[6]

Later in the eighteenth century, civil expenses were increasingly placed onto the annual appropriations. In 1830, Parliament took "a decisive step" (Redlich 1908, vol. III, p. 163), driving royal platforms almost entirely from the field of public expenditure. Soon thereafter, the bureaucracies that Parliament had feared to create in the previous century sprang into existence. After the Naturalization Act of 1844, for example, one no longer needed a private act of Parliament to secure British citizenship. Instead, one applied to the Secretary of State for the Home Department.

Regulating the Fiscal Common Pool

The more MPs control how public revenues will be spent, the more their appetites for expenditure should worry taxpayers. A clear risk of over-spending arises because individual MPs fully appreciate the value of public projects located in their own constituencies but only partly internalize the tax cost of those projects. Similarly, MPs fully appreciate the value of public policies (e.g., tariffs) benefiting allied special interests but only partly internalize the fiscal costs of those policies. If we metaphorically equate spending public revenues to fishing in a common pool, then letting MPs set the budget invites overfishing.

---

[6] In terms of Chapter 1's terminology, the Commons had only Machiavellian control: it could threaten to cut the Civil List in the future, if it disliked expenditures today.

As noted in Chapter 2, in 1706 the British mitigated the risk of over-fishing in the fiscal common pool by denying unofficial MPs the right to propose expenditures. The "rule of 1706" meant that backbench MPs had to lobby ministers for local or special-interest expenditures. Ministers, after hearing all requests, decided which to satisfy in light of an overall revenue constraint. Thus, they better internalized the tax costs of expenditures than did the individual MPs pushing for them.

To illustrate how important the "rule of 1706" was, I contrast Great Britain's budgetary experience with France's during the Third Republic. The British ministry's monopoly on making budgetary proposals both stabilized it in office and induced it to internalize the tax costs of special-interest expenditures. Meanwhile, the dispersal of budgetary proposal power in France III both destabilized ministries and left no one with as good an incentive to internalize tax costs. Let's elaborate each point in turn.

Monopoly Proposal Power and the Stability of Ministries

One way to explore the difference between France III and Britain is by reference to the well-known Baron-Ferejohn (1989) model of legislative bargaining. In the simplest version of this model, someone gains the right to make a proposal about how state revenues should be spent, and the other legislators then vote the proposal up or down. No amendments are allowed, no side payments are possible, and everyone knows everyone else's preferences.

Britain vested monopoly proposal rights in a single actor, the ministry. Non-ministerial MPs – the "irresponsible" members – could neither directly propose a charge upon the public revenues nor sneak one in during committee or under guise of amendment.

The theoretically predicted outcome in the Baron-Ferejohn model, when the ministry has monopoly proposal power, is that its budget will be adopted and it will remain in office.[7] Intuitively, the ministry holds all the cards. It can pick the budget it most prefers, from among all those it reckons could secure enactment.

If, through some imperfection in its knowledge of MPs' preferences, a British ministry's first budget were rejected, then the budget ball would simply be returned to its court. That is, it would have another opportunity to make a proposal; no one else could compete with it, except by first ousting it from office.

---

[7] In Diermeier and Feddersen's (1998) version of the model, one also expects that the ministry will allocate expenditures in a stable pattern to the same coalition.

In France III, the ministry's bargaining position was vastly inferior. Although the government introduced the first version of the budget, the legislative Commission on the Budget then prepared its own version, which became the basis for discussion in the National Assembly (Stourm 1917, pp. 280–291). Moreover, any member could seek amendments to the Commission's draft or propose wholly new expenditure items when the budget reached the floor (p. 305).

The Commission on the Budget was effectively chosen by lottery.[8] The theoretically expected outcome in this case is that each chosen Budget Commission will propose a somewhat different budget. A particular Commission's budget may well exclude one or more sitting ministerial factions from participation in the budgetary feast, as there is no special reason to include them. Because the majority coalition supporting the budget will want ministers sympathetic to its budget to oversee the resulting expenditures, the losing ministerial factions will fall from office.

In France III, then, the theoretical expectation is twofold. First, because they lack a de jure monopoly on making budgetary proposals, ministers will sometimes lose control of the budget. Second, when they do lose control of the budget, ministers will fall from office. These predictions fit the stylized facts of the Third Republic well.

Another way to explain the stabilizing effect of monopoly proposal power is by analyzing the value of blocking power. In France, a factional chief with the power to block the budget could withhold assent and immediately make a counterproposal. In Britain, a factional chief with blocking power could also withhold assent. However, since only ministers had the right to make proposals, the best that a dilatory factional chief could expect would be a new budget just enough better than the old one to secure his/her assent. Balancing this prospect would be the risk that the ministry might cut a deal with some other holdout(s), while reducing the dilatory faction's slice. Thus, blocking power was much more valuable in France III than in Britain, as a direct consequence of the rules governing budgetary proposals.[9]

---

[8] As Stourm explains, "the Chamber of Deputies … divides its members periodically into eleven bureaus … the composition of which is determined each month by lot" (1917, p. 280). Each bureau then elects four members to the Budget Commission.

[9] Might not the factional chief in Britain form a majority coalition, repeal the "rule of 1706," and then enact the budget? Sure. But if the faction can form a majority, then it should prefer to oust the ministry, install itself in power, and exploit the monopoly proposal power for its own benefit.

A third way to express the importance of the British ministry's monopoly on budgetary proposals is to say that the House of Commons' "rule of 1706" effectively required a constructive vote of no confidence.[10] To see this, consider a majority coalition united in its dislike of the current ministry but unable to agree on who should replace it. Will such a coalition go ahead and expel the incumbents?

In the United Kingdom, the budgetary consequences of throwing the incumbents out would depend on what new ministry happened to form thereafter. Thus, if MPs cared only about getting a better budget, then they would want to know who the new ministers would be – and what budget they would propose – before ousting the sitting government. Thus, the only votes of no confidence worth tabling would effectively be constructive.

Incentives to topple governments were quite different in France III. Any majority coalition in France III that reached agreement on a budget could proceed directly to enacting that budget. If that budget excluded one or more sitting ministers, they would resign. Who exactly would replace them did not have to be worked out in advance, since ministers' cooperation was not essential in passing the budget.

Monopoly Proposal Power and the Internalization of Tax Costs

The British government's monopoly proposal powers affected the internalization of tax costs in two profound ways, via the ministry's time horizon and the party system. Let's consider each in turn.

British ministries had longer time horizons than their French counterparts, because (as just explained) they had structural advantages in budgetary bargaining. Their longer expected duration in office gave them a better incentive to consider the tax costs of their expenditures (and how those tax costs would be perceived by the electorate). The ministry's collective incentive to police tax costs in turn helped sustain the Chancellor of the Exchequer's strong institutional position vis-à-vis the spending ministers – an early instance of a budgetary control mechanism that political scientists have repeatedly identified as important in controlling expenditure (see, e.g., Hallerberg, Strauch, and von Hagen 2010).

British ministries also headed majority parties, whereas their French counterparts represented coalitions of factions. Several works in political

---

[10] A vote of no confidence is constructive if those moving no confidence must nominate a specific candidate to replace the incumbent premier.

economy (e.g., Perotti and Kontopoulos 2002; Bawn and Rosenbluth 2006; Wehner 2010) have shown, theoretically and empirically, that more fragmented ministries lead to fiscal indiscipline.

I would simply add that Britain's budgetary institutions underpinned her two-partyism. The ministerial monopoly on proposing budgets meant that mere blocking coalitions were less valuable and majority coalitions more valuable. The purely legislative incentive to forge a majority was thus considerably higher in Britain than in France.

The United Kingdom's legislative impetus toward bipartism, moreover, was considerably stronger than any electoral incentives. Until the first Reform Act, electoral competition was quite rare, partly due to the Septennial Act and partly due to the highly restricted suffrage. Until 1867, moreover, Britain had mostly multimember electoral districts. Thus, the purely electoral incentives to build a majority party were mild at best until the later nineteenth century.

The Back Benches and the "Rule of 1706"
Backbench MPs did seek to evade the restrictions placed on them. As regards committees, for example, Todd notes that

attempts have occasionally been made to induce the House of Commons to appoint select committees to revise the estimates before they should be submitted to the Committee of Supply; but these attempts have been uniformly unsuccessful. In one or two instances, during the reign of William III, we read of the estimates ... being referred to a select committee; but since the doctrine of ministerial responsibility has been properly understood, no such proceedings have been permitted. (1867, vol. II, p. 475)

The select committee to which Todd refers was the Committee on Public Accounts, which had sometimes directly involved itself in decisions about expenditure. Such micromanaging ceased after 1704 (Desan 1998, p. 277), just as ministerial responsibility was emerging. The committee then went into abeyance after 1714 (Roseveare 1973, p. 59).

Some interpret the somnolence of the Committee on Public Accounts after 1714 as exposing the debility of the Commons' fiscal control (e.g., Desan 1998, pp. 265–278; Harris 2004, p. 226). My interpretation is that ministerial responsibility provided a superior method of budgetary control. Thus, once it had been invented, the experiment with the Committee on Public Accounts – which might otherwise have turned into something like France III's Budget Commission – was ended.

An Aside on the Navy-Industrial Complex

Firms supplying Britain's armed forces, especially those at the technological or logistical cutting edge, must frequently have contemplated investments that would be profitable only if the armed forces' budget remained stable over some number of years. Thus, they were in much the same position as other promise-holders considered in this book: the value of their investments depended on the credibility of particular sovereign promises.

The improved credibility of parliamentary as opposed to royal platforms should have sparked growth in economic sectors devoted to supplying the armed forces. This hypothesis deserves a more careful consideration than I can provide here, but it seems to fit the facts of England after the Glorious Revolution. The part of the budget that became thoroughly parliamentary fed the armed forces; and soon after we see a fiscal-military state (Brewer 1988) or a naval-industrial complex (Findlay and O'Rourke 2007, p. 347, citing Patrick O'Brien). As I note in Chapter 10, similar military-industrial responses followed when Prussia and Piedmont imitated British budgetary institutions in the nineteenth century.

Conclusion

Recent scholarship, whether embracing or rejecting the Whig view of the Glorious Revolution's importance, has focused on debt and property. I shall turn to these matters in the next five chapters but have begun with the relatively neglected topic of taxes and expenditures.

The central problem was that the House of Commons granted taxes but the Crown spent the resulting revenues. The Crown's inability to commit itself to particular patterns of expenditure was the root cause of a syndrome of debilitating, albeit intermittent, constitutional conflicts throughout the long seventeenth century.

The Revolution took one logically possible route to ending the fiscal stalemate of the prerevolutionary era. It converted platforms from merely royal into parliamentary promises by embodying them in the appropriations clauses of statutes. When combined with better information on how public revenues were actually spent and better means to punish misappropriation, MPs asked to grant taxes had a much more precise idea of what they were buying in the way of public expenditures.

Because this effort to improve the credibility of platforms was comprehensive and systematic, a rudimentary national budget emerged after 1688 for the first time in English history. This budgeting revolution crucially underpinned the debt revolution on which the literature since Dickson (1967) has tended to focus, as the next several chapters will show. Yet, the conversion of platforms from dodgy royal pledges into sturdy parliamentary appropriations was initially confined to the armed forces. The rule of law came to govern civilian expenditures much later.

The variable credibility of British platforms explains two macro-features of eighteenth-century British governance. Why was there a huge run-up in tax revenues? Because fiscal-military platforms became more credible. Why was the century an age of *privilegia*, bereft of parliamentary intervention in domestic politics? Because the Civil List was not annually appropriated.

The crowning accomplishment of the Revolution – the relatively abrupt establishment of ministerial responsibility in the period 1701–1706 – explains several other puzzles. Why was there a temporary reliance on land taxes in 1689–1715? Because MPs seeking to secure control over expenditures insisted on granting taxes over which the Crown exerted the least control. Why did MPs relent in their insistence on land taxes by the Hanoverian succession? Because the combination of annual budgets, shutdown reversions, and ministerial responsibility had by then proven a workable means of control, allowing MPs to trust the Crown with more efficient taxes collected by centralized bureaucracies. Why was there a shock to the term structure of taxation in 1689, rationalized only after 1706? Because a ministerial monopoly on proposing expenditures enabled MPs to trust the Crown (and each other) with long-term grants. Why did MPs reverse the Act of Settlement's strict prohibition on placemen holding seats in the Commons via the Regency Act (1706)? Because the appointment of placemen was now on advice of responsible ministers. Why was no parliamentary committee ever appointed after 1706 with power to amend the estimates? Because that would have violated the "rule of 1706."

Looking beyond the British case, constitutional commitment – the embedding of platforms in statutes – sparked a more general European budgeting revolution in the nineteenth century (see Chapter 10), which was then imitated worldwide (see Chapter 11). As will be seen, however, those imitating Britain's budgeting practices often failed to follow the Revolution's recipe, with predictable consequences.

4

Pricing Sovereign Debts

Sovereign debts are a subspecies of the sovereign platforms studied in Chapters 2 and 3. They are promises to use future revenues to repay immediate loans.

What price will investors pay for a sovereign debt? At issuance, investors will consider two distinct reasons that the government-at-maturity might repay them. First, the government may *prefer* to repay the debt, all things considered. Second, the original promise of repayment may remain legally in force and *constrain* the government's actions.

Whether the original promise of repayment remains in force depends on the number and diversity of veto players who must approve its revision. Royal debts, for example, can be revised at will by the monarch. Holders of such debts should thus expect only a Machiavellian repayment – one hinging on their influence at court and their ability to make trouble should they not be repaid.

Even if the original terms of a debt remain legally binding, however, the government-at-maturity may not be significantly constrained. Some debts confer senior claims on ample revenue streams; these leave the government no discretion. Other debts confer junior or underfunded claims; these leave the government substantial discretion over whether and how to repay them.

Debt seniority and funding jointly determine creditors' attitudes toward "constitutional commitment." While holders of senior and well-funded debt crave better commitment, holders of junior or underfunded debt can only be hurt by increasing the number of veto players in the legislative process. Thus, the idea – widespread since North and

Weingast (1989) – that improving constitutional commitment can only improve the credibility of debt repayment is mistaken.

I shall argue that England, in the first generation after the Revolution, issued many debt promises of high credibility but low face value. The high interest rates these early debts had to offer, and the discounts they suffered at sale, were not evidence that investors doubted the state would perform as promised. Rather, they were evidence of junior or poorly funded – and hence low-value – promises.

Those readers who find the argument sketched earlier straightforward may wish to skip to the next chapter. For those who seek a more careful exposition, this chapter provides a general model of the value of sovereign debts, shows that previous analyses have focused on special cases, and begins to discuss when and why English debt became more valuable. Chapter 5 then describes when institutions of monopoly brokerage emerged in the debt market, while Chapter 6 explores the consequences.

The Value of Sovereign Debts

Suppose a state issues one-period sovereign bonds offering interest at rate i. The maximum price that risk-neutral investors would be willing to pay for such bonds can be written as $(1 + i)\delta V$. Here, $\delta \in [0,1]$ represents the value of a pound paid one period in the future, and V is a random variable representing investors' beliefs about the fraction of the promised amount the state will repay.

I shall unpack V as follows. When the government-at-maturity decides how much of a debt to repay, it may face constraints on its ability to adjust performance. I represent the degree of constraint by a parameter $P \in [0,1]$. If $P = 0$, then the government-at-maturity is legally unconstrained by the original promise. On the other hand, if $P = 1$, then the government-at-maturity is fully constrained: it must comply with all terms of performance laid out in the original loan prospectus.

I represent investors' beliefs about how much the government would pay them, if unconstrained, by a random variable V_M; call this their Machiavellian repayment. I represent investors' beliefs about how much the government would pay them, if fully constrained by the original promise, by a random variable V_r; call this their reversionary repayment. All told, then, the fraction of their claims that investors believe will be repaid can be written as follows:

$$V = (1 - P)V_M + PV_r \qquad (1)$$

One interpretation of Equation (1) is that the government pays an amount that is a compromise between what was promised, V_r, and what the government would now like to do, V_M, with weights P on the promise and 1-P on current preferences. Another interpretation is that the government-at-maturity will either be entirely free to pursue its preferences or fully constrained by the original promise; and P represents investors' estimates of the probability of constraint. Now consider the Machiavellian and reversionary repayments at greater length.

The Machiavellian repayment depends on who turns out to be in government-at-maturity (friends or foes of repayment?), competing demands on the government's discretionary revenues, and bondholders' ability to punish relative to other stakeholders' ability to punish. In other words, V_M reflects the considerations on which punishment and majoritarian theories typically focus.

Now consider the reversionary repayment, V_r. Prospective lenders can read the law authorizing a sovereign loan before they decide whether to purchase the associated debt. They can see what taxes, if any, are dedicated to repayment and form a judgment about their adequacy. If the earmark is not repealed, then a certain, estimable amount of tax revenues will help pay off debt-holders.

One can express V_r as the product of two terms. Let $S = 1$ if the promise of repayment confers a senior claim, and $S = 0$ if it confers a junior claim. That is, $S = 1$ if specific revenues are earmarked to repay the loan *and* debt-holders have top priority to these funds, $= 0$ otherwise. Let A denote the conditional adequacy of the taxes earmarked for repayment. That is, A is the fraction of the face amount that will be repaid out of the earmarked funds, if the earmark remains in force. With this notation, one can write $V_r = SA$.

All told, the bond's expected fractional repayment, E(V), can be expressed as follows:

$$E(V) = (1 - P)E(V_M) + PSE(A) \qquad (2a)$$
$$= E(V_M) + P[SE(A) - E(V_M)] \qquad (2b)$$

If P is interpreted as a probability, then Equation (2a) says that the expected fractional repayment equals the probability of an unconstrained government times the expected Machiavellian repayment, plus the probability of a constrained government times the expected reversionary repayment.

Some Special Cases

The model of sovereign debt just presented yields, as special cases, the main previous arguments in the literature.

Senior and Well-Funded Debt

North and Weingast focused on the case in which ample funds have been earmarked, so that bondholders' reversionary repayment is better than what they could expect to get when the government-at-maturity is free to pursue its preferences. In this case, adding veto players helps – or at least never hurts (Stasavage 2003) – because such players can only entrench a valuable promise.

In terms of Equation (2b), North and Weingast can be viewed as focusing on the special case in which $SE(A) > E(V_M)$. In this case, the credibility of debt increases linearly in the state's ability to constitutionally commit itself, as represented by the parameter P.

More generally, increasing constitutional commitment (P) may either hurt or help bondholders. As Equation (2b) shows, increasing P worsens their repayment if $SE(A) < E(V_M)$, leaves it unchanged if $SE(A) = E(V_M)$, and improves it if $SE(A) > E(V_M)$. The first case, in which increasing constitutional commitment worsens bondholders' expected repayment, can be explained intuitively as follows: The holders of poorly funded debt need the government to find the ways and means to pay them, which becomes more difficult when P is larger.

Unentrenched Promises

Punishment models, as well as majoritarian models such as Stasavage's (2003, ch. 2), explicitly assume the weight on the original promise is nil (P = 0). Conceptually, this assumption ensures that the model embodies the commitment problem in its starkest form. The original promise of repayment is "cheap talk" and bondholders' expected repayment depends entirely on their ability to influence the government-at-maturity.

More generally, how much debt-holders benefit when they gain influence over the government-at-maturity depends on the weight placed on the original promise (P). Political influence is crucial if P = 0 but is less and less important as legislative stasis becomes more and more likely ($P \rightarrow 1$). If legislative stasis is assured (P = 1), then the expected repayment reduces to $E(V) = SE(A)$. Thus, the creditors' influence over the government-at-maturity no longer matters.

To restate the last point, suppose that the legislative process makes it foreseeably hard to change the status quo, as would be the case if new laws required the approval of many (and predictably diverse) veto players, or defenders of the status quo enjoyed built-in advantages à la Groseclose and Snyder (1996).[1] In such circumstances, bondholders can just look at the loan prospectus to see if it is fully funded. They do not have to worry much about who will control the government in the future, because only a large anti-creditor coalition can do them harm and such coalitions are unlikely to emerge. Nor do they need to worry about how much the government would be willing to pay out of its discretionary funds, because discretionary funds will not be called on to retire the debt.

How Much Will Investors Pay for Sovereign Debts?

Another point to draw from Equation (2) is that governments seeking higher prices for their debts can choose from two strategies – increasing their expected Machiavellian repayment, $E(V_M)$; or increasing their expected reversionary repayment, $PSE(A)$.[2] Let's consider each of these broad strategies in turn.

The expected Machiavellian repayment, $E(V_M)$, can be increased by ensuring that a friendly government will be in office at maturity, that the government will face substantial punishments for default, or that other claimants will be less able to compete for the government's discretionary funds. Stasavage (2003, 2007), for example, argues that the onset of the Whig Supremacy enhanced the credibility of English debt by creating a one-party state run by a pro-creditor party. Root (1989) argues that the French king made his debt promises more credible by allowing all his creditors to incorporate, thereby increasing their ability to punish default. An example of the third tactic is the House of Commons' "rule of 1706," which gave debt-holders a great victory over the champions of current expenditures.[3]

To improve the expected reversionary repayment, $PSE(A)$, the main tactics are to increase its three components: P, S, and E(A). It is on these

---

[1] On the "built-in advantages," see Chapter 5.

[2] More precisely, $E(V_M)$ is the *conditional* expected Machiavellian repayment because it is the repayment expected conditional on the government being free to pursue its own preferences.

[3] As noted in Chapter 2, prior to 1706, unofficial MPs could and did make claims on the public revenues via amendments on the floor. These claims ate up discretionary revenues that might otherwise have gone to service unfunded debts. After 1706, only ministers had the right to propose new charges upon the public revenues.

tactics that I shall focus in the next two chapters. To set the stage, I begin with briefer descriptions here.

Increasing P

My view of how states can better commit to their promises (i.e., increase P) differs from the veto-player approach advanced by North and Weingast (1989) and elaborated by Stasavage (2003). In that approach, debts can be made more credible by requiring that the legislature must approve any revision of their terms. Such "parliamentary supremacy" cannot harm debt-holders' interests and helps them whenever the legislature vetoes an executive request for default.

In my approach, assuring that a particular promise of repayment cannot be unilaterally revised by the executive is not enough. If the executive remains legally free to issue debt, then outstanding debt claims can be undermined. For example, new debt issued by the executive can compete for repayment with already-issued parliamentary debts, especially if the latter have only junior claims on repayment. Thus, the credibility of sovereign debt requires a parliamentary monopoly on both revising old and issuing new debts.

My view of the kind of legislative support creditors needed also differs from prominent strands in the literature. In particular, Stasavage emphasizes that creditors should form stable majority alliances with other minority interests, in order to protect their claims. This makes good sense if creditors seek to optimize their Machiavellian repayment.

In my view, many post-revolutionary creditors – those holding senior claims – sought to optimize their reversionary repayments. For this, a majority alliance was overkill. They just needed to block legislation revising their promises, and block the issuance of new debt, if it would harm their interests.

In the task of blocking, creditors had several advantages. The House of Lords had a preponderance of Whigs. Defenders of the status quo in either chamber had strategic advantages in "vote-buying" (per Groseclose and Snyder 1996). And creditors could rely on a deep-pocketed ally in the Bank of England.

Increasing S and E(A)

Those who purchased England's sovereign debt after the Revolution, I shall argue, sought not just a well-entrenched (high-P) promise. They also sought a *senior* claim (S = 1) to repayment from an *ample* fund

$(E(A) = I)$. Indeed, per Equation (2), their expected reversionary repayment was the product of all three: $PSE(A)$.

This meant that knocking off any one of the three legs of the stool would cause investors' repayments to collapse. Merely royal promises were unreliable (low-P), even if they conferred senior claims on ample funds. Parliamentary promises of junior claims were reliable but not valuable. Parliamentary promises of senior claims from insufficient funds were not much better.

Once sovereign debts became parliamentary (higher P), public creditors devoted more lobbying effort to improving the seniority and funding of their debts. MPs resisted their entreaties for several years. Their reluctance was a necessary consequence of Parliament's strategy to wrest fiscal control from the Crown. While Parliament was putting short time limits on its tax grants, long-term funded debt was not possible. As Parliament gained confidence, and especially after it had imposed ministerial responsibility, the funding of debt could be rationalized. The state sharply improved funding 1710–1715 and the fiscal cost of English debt declined accordingly, as will be seen in Chapter 6.

5

Establishing Monopoly Brokerage
of Sovereign Debts

In this chapter, I describe the emergence of Parliament's monopoly over the issuance of sovereign debt, the Bank of England's monopoly over the sale of such debt, and effective limits on executive discretion over repayment. In other words, I describe the emergence of monopoly brokerage in the loans-for-debts market.

Establishing a parliamentary monopoly over debt issuance meant that, whereas the vast bulk of sovereign promises to repay loans prior to the Revolution had been merely royal, afterward they quickly became almost wholly parliamentary.[1] The process was completed by the development of ministerial responsibility, after which the prerogative right to borrow could no longer be exercised by the Crown unilaterally.

Establishing the Bank of England's monopoly took some time, but the first important steps were taken over the period 1694–1708. As its monopoly strengthened, I argue that the Bank should have become reliably more hostile to sovereign default than the Crown.

Limiting executive discretion over repayment involved securing seniority and proper funding for all debts. As seniority and funding improved, a sea change occurred in how English debts were repaid. A very substantial fraction of debts before the Revolution were paid out of discretionary funds; debt-holders had only junior claims or senior claims on inadequate funds. By 1715, the vast bulk of payments flowed out of earmarked accounts; debt-holders held senior claims on more ample funds.

---

[1] What the literature typically calls "national" debt, I call "parliamentary." By this I mean that the promise of repayment is embedded in a statute.

Parliament's Monopoly over Debt

In this section, I consider how Parliament came to control the issuance of all debt. To begin, it is important to note that English monarchs had long borrowed on their own initiative, and had long been free to revise the terms of such loans. In other words, sovereign promises to repay loans were, for most of English history, merely royal.

The Commons' Dislike of Royal Borrowing

The Commons disliked unilateral royal borrowing for two main reasons. First, as Jones observed, "Loans from bankers, secured on taxes already voted or on the permanent revenue, could enable the crown to evade the restrictions imposed by appropriation" (1994, p. 71). In other words, if the Commons wished to control expenditure, it had to control borrowing.

Second, unilateral royal borrowing undermined the Commons' bargaining position. The monarch could present Parliament with a series of take-it-or-leave-it propositions: raise taxes to repay this loan or repudiate it. That such strong agenda control confers a formidable bargaining advantage is well known theoretically (Romer and Rosenthal 1978) and was presumably appreciated as a practical matter by contemporaries. As Maitland put it: Borrowing "is one of the king's expedients of practically forcing parliament to grant him money; his debts must be paid, or his credit among foreigners will be ruined" (1908, p. 438).

For the same reasons that Parliament disliked it, kings valued their prerogative right to borrow. Thus, imposing parliamentary control over the issuance of debt would not be easy.

The Commons' Efforts to Curb Royal Borrowing

Parliament's first – prerevolutionary – strategy to discourage royal borrowing was to leave the royal prerogative unchallenged and go after the lenders. On 7 January 1680, the House of Commons resolved that "whosoever shall hereafter lend ... any money upon the branches of the King's revenue arising by customs, excise, or hearth money shall be judged to hinder the sittings of parliament and shall be responsible for the same tax" (Einzig 1959, p. 98). In 1682, the House resolved more broadly that "anyone who lent to the crown without parliamentary authority would be judged an enemy of parliament" (O'Brien 2005, 25). It is not clear how many lenders were cowed by such pronouncements but, in any event, sovereign debts continued to be contracted by the Crown throughout the 1680s.

After the Revolution, Parliament continued to avoid directly challenging the prerogative right to borrow. However, the Commons appropriated virtually all the revenue it granted, meaning among other things that the Crown could not secure royal loans on parliamentary revenues.

The next step was to secure *parliamentary* loans on the *hereditary* revenues. The Commons had tried this in 1690. But, although it offered to back a loan of £250,000 when the king was hungry for revenues, William III vetoed the bill. He was unable to stomach parliamentary intrusion into his hereditary revenues (Reitan 1970, p. 582). By 1695, however, the still revenue-hungry king conceded the principle: he assented to 7 & 8 Wm. III, c. 30, which authorized a loan of up to £445,000 secured on the hereditary revenues. By this time, the revenues on which the Crown might have secured royal loans were very minor.

In parallel with starving the Crown of funds on which to secure royal loans, the Commons also specified the maximum amount the Crown could borrow on the security of specific tax grants, thereby establishing a series of soft debt ceilings.[2] Moreover, when created, the Bank of England was forbidden to lend to the monarch without parliamentary sanction (Kemp 1957, p. 75).

Early Successes: Measuring Parliamentary Debts

To gauge the success of Parliament's effort to starve the Crown of funds on which royal debts could be secured, one can examine how fast England's sovereign debts became parliamentary after the Revolution. To do this, I examined every supply bill in the periods 1672–1690 and 1699–1700. As can be seen in Table 5.1, the (estimated) loans authorized by Parliament per year, as a percentage of the Crown's annual income, averaged 5.1 percent in the last years of Charles II's reign (1672–1684), 5.3 percent during James II's reign (1685–1688), and 74.8 percent during the first two years of William and Mary's reign.

Warfare does not fully explain the fourteen-fold increase. Parliament was no more involved in Charles' loans during the Third Anglo-Dutch War (1672–1674) than afterward (1675–1684). And Parliament authorized loans amounting to 46.4 percent of Crown income in 1699–1700, two years after the Nine Years' War had ended.

---

[2] I say soft because there were no prohibitions on the Crown securing purely royal loans on any revenues left over after the parliamentary debt had been paid off. Had Parliament provided ample funds to pay off the parliamentary debts it authorized, this could have been a problem. In practice, however, most loans were underfunded, leaving no surplus revenues on which to secure royal loans.

TABLE 5.1. *Parliamentary Debt, 1672–1700*

Monarch	Years	Average Loans Authorized by Parliament per Year, as Percentage of Crown's Annual Income	Comments Regarding War
Charles II	1672–1684	5.1%	Third Anglo-Dutch War, 1672–74
James II	1685–1688	5.3%	-
William and Mary	1689–1690	74.8%	Nine Years War, 1688–1697
William III	1699–1700	46.4%	-

Source: Detailed calculations are provided in the appendix.

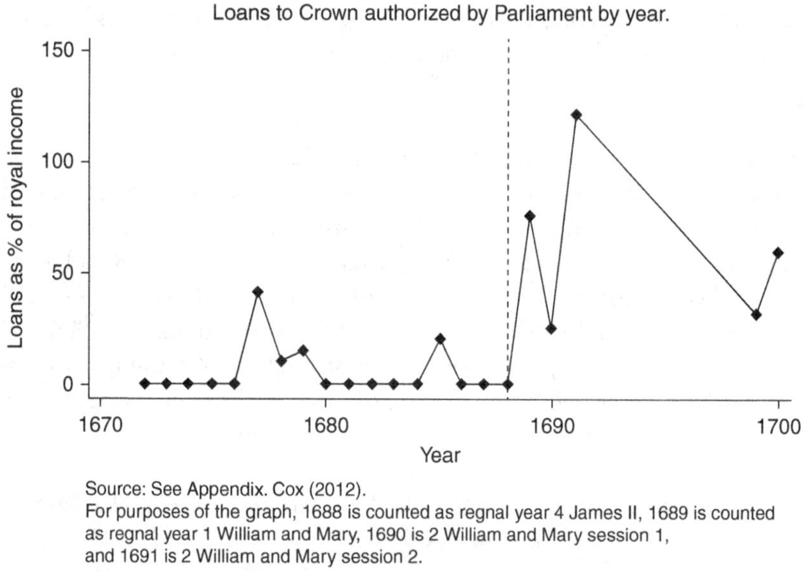

Loans to Crown authorized by Parliament by year.

Source: See Appendix. Cox (2012).
For purposes of the graph, 1688 is counted as regnal year 4 James II, 1689 is counted as regnal year 1 William and Mary, 1690 is 2 William and Mary session 1, and 1691 is 2 William and Mary session 2.

FIGURE 5.1. Loans to Crown authorized by Parliament by year.

To further illustrate the Revolution's impact, Figure 5.1 plots the estimated amount of new loans authorized by Parliament per year, 1672–1700. Parliamentary loan authorizations clearly increase sharply after the Revolution.

A Parliamentary Monopoly

Although the evidence just provided shows a marked upsurge in parliamentary, as opposed to royal, debt after the Revolution, recall that this alone would not suffice to ensure the credibility of debt. If the Crown remained legally free to issue new debt, then it might erode the value of outstanding parliamentary debt, even if it could not overtly revise it.

By 1695, when it secured a loan on the hereditary revenues, Parliament had removed royal borrowing as a practical worry. Even so, the king's prerogative right to borrow remained legally intact. Thus, the Commons (and prospective purchasers of debt) might still have worried that the king would discover clever new forms of royal borrowing.

The ultimate solution to the risk posed by an unchallenged prerogative right to borrow was the establishment of ministerial responsibility. Over the period 1701–1707, parliamentarians rather quickly turned the vote of censure from a mere expression of parliamentary disapproval into a demand to remove the censured ministers, backed by the threat of denying supply. This ensured that, if government borrowing occurred of which the House of Commons disapproved, ministers would suffer the consequences. In effect, Parliament had secured a constitutional right to veto the issuance of new debt, similar to its ancient right to veto the levying of new taxes.

The Bank of England's Monopoly over Sales

The creation of the Bank of England in 1694, the expansion of its rights in 1697, and its re-chartering in 1708 have been cited as important contributors to the credibility of English debt (cf. North and Weingast 1989; Broz 1998; Broz and Grossman 2004). The Bank obtained a de jure monopoly in its core business of banking in 1697, and it increasingly attained a de facto monopoly on floating new sovereign debt, beginning in the period 1694–1711. Quinn (2004) reckons that the Bank dominated the administration of short-term debt by 1706, and Dickson views it as having established a "quasi-monopoly of short-term lending ... by the mid-century" (1967, p. 360). As to long-term issues, the Bank increasingly dominated after 1711 (Bowen 1995, p. 10; Quinn 2004).[3]

---

[3] From a theoretical perspective, the Bank had an incentive to curb default proportional to its anticipated future share of debt flotation fees. Thus, it is not necessary to assert that it had a firm monopoly, before one can predict that it would improve the credibility of debt. A durable and substantial market share suffices.

Broz (1998) views the Bank's monopoly as conferring rents upon it, thereby motivating it to protect the credibility of the debt it brokered. I tell an essentially similar story here.

To elaborate, note that the Bank's compensation for its brokerage services had the following features. First, the Bank charged fees for bond flotations proportional to the total revenue secured. Second, if the government refused to pay its debts, the Bank had no right to share in the revenue gained by repudiation. Third, the Bank did not bear the cost of performance; debt repayments came from the Treasury's accounts, not the Bank's. Thus, the Bank's main interest was to maximize the discounted present value of sales in the market for debt. The Bank was therefore less likely to support default than the Crown.

One might question this line of argument in the case of partial repudiations. If old debts were exchanged for new ones, the Bank might handle the new issue, thus earning additional commissions.[4]

Although the prospect of these "refinancing commissions" did reduce the Bank Directors' incentives to oppose default, the Directors should still have favored performance more than the government. First, bankers and government officials were not identically patient. The government of the day might face war and liquidity crises, greatly increasing its appetite for immediate funds. The Bank of England, a chartered company of great wealth, should have been more patient. Because the pain of future market shrinkage would be felt more keenly by a patient Bank than a desperate government, public creditors could generally expect the Bank to act as a brake on sovereign default. Second, as the size of the haircut grew, the two sides' incentives increasingly diverged. In the extreme of complete repudiation, the brokers would receive no refinancing commissions at all.

How the Bank could Entrench Promises

The literature offers two main explanations regarding how the Bank of England protected the credibility of sovereign debt. One argument is that the Bank's status as monopoly lender increased the penalty it could impose on a defaulting government (e.g., Weingast 1997, p. 231; Broz 1998, p. 232). However, since refusing further loans to the government would hurt the Bank as well as the government, the Bank's boycott threats would have been discounted.

---

[4] Hoffman, Postel-Vinay, and Rosenthal (2000) find the Parisian notaries earned good commissions when refinancing royal debts.

A second argument, on which I focus here, is that the Bank could block the statutes that would be needed to revise or repudiate debt. Since blocking *ex ante* was less costly to the Bank than punishing *ex post*, the Directors should have concentrated their efforts on playing legislative defense.

There were two reasons to expect the legislative status quo could be more easily defended after than before the Revolution. First, new decrees required only the Crown's approval, whereas new statutes required approval by the Commons, Lords and Crown. Thus, when these actors had differing preferences, change was more difficult. This is the argument North and Weingast (1989) originally advanced, as clarified by Stasavage (2003).

The second reason has not been noted in the literature but is arguably as important and not dependent on whether Commons, Lords and Crown disagreed. To explain, we need a detour into the theory of legislatures. The conclusion of that detour can be stated succinctly: legislatures always feature (the possibility of) vote buying, and (the possibility of) vote buying always favors defenders of the status quo.

I'll take the first claim as axiomatic.[5] The second claim is due to Groseclose and Snyder (1996), who devise a model of legislative voting more general than that leading to the well-known median voter theorem. In their model, an actor A introduces a bill, knowing that an actor B may oppose it. Each MP has preferences between the bill and status quo. In addition, however, A may offer side payments to one or more legislators – seeking to buy or solidify their support. Finally, knowing both legislators' preferences and A's inducements, B can offer counter-bribes. MPs then choose how to vote and majority rule determines the outcome.

A key feature of the Groseclose-Snyder model is that the defender of the status quo, B, can search for the weakest supporters of A's proposal and peel off just enough of them to prevent the bill passing. This ability to target the bill's weakest supporters means that B's bribes can be utilized more efficiently than A's. In order to win, A must outspend B by a substantial amount. Indeed, Groseclose and Snyder show that A must outspend B by a factor of two, if all MPs are indifferent between the bill and status quo on the merits.

For present purposes, the main point is that Groseclose and Snyder have identified a very general feature of legislative politics. Defenders of

---

[5] Note that "vote buying" refers not only to illegal exchanges of cash for votes but also to technically legal "side payments."

the statutory status quo can always succeed by prying loose just enough of the least-committed members of any bill's initial supporters. They thus have an inherent advantage in the game of legislative side payments and vote buying.

The Bank of England was a particularly deep-pocketed player and thus well-positioned to exploit the advantages of statutory defense. As explained earlier, the Bank also disliked defaulting on state debts more than any government of the day. Thus, the Bank combined the motivation and means to play an important role in either preventing statutory revisions of the state's debt promises or defending debt-holders' interests when such revisions did occur.

The argument thus far has assumed that, once a promise to repay had been embedded in a statute, with specific funds identified and appropriated to that purpose, the promise could only be revised by a further statute. An early reader of this book asked why the Crown could not persuade a winning coalition of MPs and lords to undo the settlement and then proceed to revise the debt. On this score I will simply point out that, if undoing the settlement meant recreating a Crown that could spend as it pleased, then any promises the monarch made, in order to secure support for repealing aspects of the settlement, would not have been credible.

Limiting Executive Discretion over Repayment

Sovereign promises of repayment differ substantially in the priority they give to promise-holders vis-à-vis other claimants on the government's resources. Relatedly, they differ in the discretion they give to executive officials in deciding which claimant(s) to favor.

In this section, I consider how the nature of the debt promise – whether it conferred a junior or senior claim and how well-funded that claim was – affected the value of England's sovereign debt. Considering this issue helps clarify how my account differs from North and Weingast's. I begin by arguing – per Chapter 4 but contra North and Weingast – that embodying promises of repayment in statutes should *not* necessarily have improved their credibility.

To see why better entrenched promises of repayment were not necessarily more valuable, note that many government loans were either unfunded (no specific funds were legally dedicated to their repayment) or inadequately funded. When tax receipts proved insufficient to pay the principal and interest on a funded loan, the English said that a "deficiency" existed. In such cases, a new statute was required to identify the ways and means to repay the loan; otherwise, bondholders would take a haircut proportional in size to the deficiency. To put it another way, deficiencies meant that the reversionary outcome of the legislative process – that is, what happened if Commons, Lords and Crown could not agree – was partial default. Thus, multiple veto points worked *against* rather than *for* bondholders, because it was they who wanted a new statute.

While Treasury officials might repay un- and underfunded loans with general revenues, they were not legally obligated to repay them with specific funds at specific times. Predictably, this led to substantial delays in the repayment of such debts, which tended to accumulate to crisis proportions before Parliament would deal with them.[6]

Contemporaries recognized that deficiencies threatened public creditors. Daniel Defoe, for example, identified the major reason that English debt lacked value (circa 1700–1710) as "the settling Funds that were in themselves deficient; and making no Provision to supply those Deficiencies" (1710, p. 17). Thus, investors closely examined loan prospectuses to see whether the taxes earmarked to fund a particular loan were likely to prove sufficient.[7]

Realizing this, the Commons undertook a series of technical reforms reducing the expected size of deficiencies. The eventual eradication of deficiencies (on which more later) was a central achievement, because it made repayment the reversionary outcome of the legislative process. That is, absent a new statute specifically repudiating or rescheduling a given debt, it would be repaid in full and on time. In this setting, multiple veto players were obviously advantageous to bondholders.

The main method the English used to combat deficiencies was straightforward: they consolidated funds. For example, when fifteen separate short-term loans proved intermittently deficient by 1697 (see Dickson 1967, pp. 348–349), all were combined into one large fund. This consolidation reduced the probability of gaps, because surpluses in any fund were dedicated to making good deficiencies in others. Only if a net surplus arose in the aggregated funds could Parliament use that surplus for other purposes. Previously, Parliament could use the surplus from any component fund for current expenses.

---

[6] An example is the non-funding of interest payments on various loans, leading to the Deficiencies Acts (8&9 William III, c. 20 and 1 Anne, c. 7). Compare Shaw (1952, vol. 21, p. xxi).

[7] On public creditors' scrutiny of public loans, see Murphy 2013, p. 184. On their preference for legislation that earmarked more revenue streams to fund the national debt and dedicated surpluses to retiring the principal, see "An essay on the sinking fund" (1737) and Dickson 1967, pp. 243–245.

The next major move toward consolidation came with the creation of the Aggregate Fund (1715) and the South Sea Fund (1717). The process culminated in 1752, with Henry Pelham's conversion to consols, and 1787, when all existing public funds were collapsed into one Consolidated Fund. At this point, the probability of a deficiency was essentially zero, since the entire revenue of the state flowed through the Consolidated Fund and payments on the debt were senior to annual expenditures.[8]

Not surprisingly, the Bank of England's directors were prominent in engineering the new system of state credibility. In particular, they pushed the Bank's charter and its monopoly (Broz and Grossman 2004; Murphy 2013, p. 193); bargained for the consolidation of funds and seniority of debt to mitigate the problem of deficiencies (Hill 1971, pp. 407–409); and generally promoted the interests of public creditors (Murphy 2013, pp. 183, 191).

Figure 5.2 presents a quantitative picture of funding and deficiencies over the period 1695–1720. The upward-trending curve shows the fraction of all debts that were funded (per Mitchell 1988).[9]

As can be seen, the practice of earmarking funds to repay particular loans (and stipulating that creditors' claims on those funds would be senior to others) does not emerge all at once after the Revolution. Instead, funding arrives in several steps. There was a steady increase in the 1690s (starting from a base of 0); no change from 1700 to 1710; a sharp increase from 1710 to 1712; and continued growth after 1712 (reaching 92 percent funding by 1720).

The other curve in Figure 5.2 gives total deficiencies, divided by the total debt. Based on four parliamentary reports with reasonably comparable data, we see that before 1711 between 24 percent and 44 percent of the debt could not be paid off by earmarked revenues.[10] The

---

[8] A fiscal common pool problem potentially afflicts parliamentary debt, if individual MPs can propose to repudiate a particular debt in order to finance a particular expenditure. Under the British system, MPs could neither propose to repudiate debts (which would require a money bill, hence ministerial sponsorship) nor propose to spend money.

[9] Some of the short-term loans that Mitchell classifies as "unfunded" did not identify a specific tax dedicated to their repayment. In other cases, payments on the principal were secured on a specific tax but interest payments were not. If one were to count these partially funded loans as funded, then the curve in Figure 5.1 would be considerably higher in the early years – but would still have an upward trend, especially after 1710.

[10] The reports were from 1697 (see Dickson 1967, pp. 353–355), 1699 (*House of Commons Journal*, vol. 12, 4 March 1699), 1710 (Dickson 1967, pp. 64–71), and 1714 (*Calendar of Treasury Books*, vol. 29, 1714–1715, pp. 5–24). These are all the reports I know of that give a comprehensive account of deficiencies as of a given date.

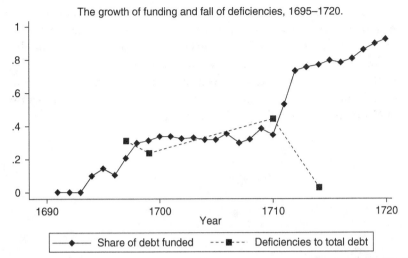

The growth of funding and fall of deficiencies, 1695–1720.

Share of debt funded   ---■--- Deficiencies to total debt

Sources: For the funded and total debt, Mitchell (1988). For deficiencies, see footnote 10. Cox (2015).

FIGURE 5.2. The growth of funding and fall of deficiencies, 1695–1720.

corresponding figure drops dramatically, to 3 percent, by 1714. Thus, deficient funding became rare over a short time period, 1710–1714.

Moreover, after the creation of the Aggregate Fund (1715) and the South Sea Fund (1717), the issue became one of surplus management. The surpluses from the three main funds (General, Aggregate, and South Seas) were swept into the Sinking Fund, which was intended to retire the principal on otherwise unfunded debts. In practice, ministers typically raided the Sinking Fund for current expenses (Dickson 1967, p. 86). This no doubt irritated debt-holders. However, their structural position had still changed considerably for the better, from the days in which the problem had been deficiencies. Now, all debts with a senior claim on one of the three big funds were paid; deficiencies occurred only on "junior" debts (defined as those whose repayment depended on the Sinking Fund actually being used for repayment rather than current expenses).

Conclusion

In my view, constitutional commitment arrived in England later than North and Weingast say. They emphasize the traditional settlement documents, the Bill of Rights 1689 and the Act of Settlement 1701. In contrast, I argue that ministerial responsibility, which emerged 1701–1707, was the capstone constitutional reform.

My account of why constitutional commitment increased also differs from North and Weingast's. They stress "parliamentary supremacy" – and trace it to four specific reforms. I insist on "parliamentary monopoly" and trace it to a rather different set of key reforms.

In the next chapter, I examine what happened to the debt market as monopoly brokerage emerged. In the process, I pit my account against both North and Weingast's and their critics'.

6

The Consequences of Monopoly
Brokerage of Debt

In the previous chapter, I documented the emergence of monopoly brokerage in the loans-for-debts market. Sovereign promises to repay loans became harder to revise or erode, as they became parliamentary and brokered. Such promises also became more valuable, as loan prospectuses increasingly limited executive discretion over the "when" and "how much" of repayment.

In this chapter, I examine the consequences of these reforms, which should have substantially improved the state's expected reversionary repayment. Section 1 considers the volume, variety, and efficiency of trade. Section 2 considers why England lagged behind its continental rivals in the development of long-term debt. Sections 3–6 turn to the evidence on interest rates. Finally, Section 7 reinterprets England's post-revolutionary debt crises, arguing they had little to do with investors' worries that the state would not perform its promises, and much to do with the quality of those promises.

The Volume, Variety, and Efficiency of the
Loans-for-Debts Trade

How did the emergence of monopoly brokerage in the loans-for-debts market affect the volume, variety, and efficiency of trade? Consider each in turn.

England's long-term funded debt stood at zero from 1600–1693, and then increased to £1,200,000 in 1695, £4,100,000 in 1705, and £29,600,000 in 1715 (see Figure 6.1). The structural break in the data is clear; I reconsider the reasons for it later in this chapter.

England's long-term funded debt, by year, 1665–1715.

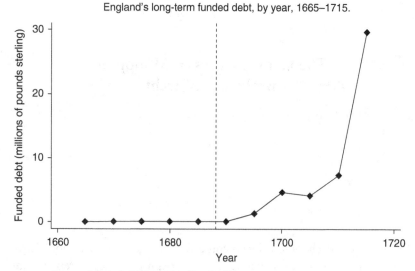

Source: Mitchell 1962, p.401. Cox (2012).

FIGURE 6.1. England's long-term funded debt, by year, 1665–1715.

Short-term debt exhibited no trend from the mid-1630s to 1688, total-ing about £1,000,000 (North and Weingast 1989, p. 822). By Sussman and Yafeh's (2006, p. 922) figures, such debt then increased roughly five-fold by 1695 and was five to ten times the pre-Revolution mean until 1715, declining slightly thereafter.

The variety of products in the debt market increased, too. In addition to introducing England's first long-term funded debt, the post-revolutionary generation experimented with a range of debt and debt securitization schemes much wider than had ever been attempted before (cf. Dickson 1967; Quinn 2008).

The efficiency of the debt market was reflected in the transactions costs involved in arranging sovereign loans. Earlier in the seventeenth century, most loans were connected to the sale of tax farms by the Crown (Brewer 1988, pp. 92–93). Farmers were willing to loan to the Crown because they themselves would collect the tax revenues that would repay them. The monarch would never lay hands on the funds and thus never be tempted to renege. Although tax farming gave the Crown access to credit, complex negotiations were needed to decide which of several com-peting teams would get each farm and on what terms.

Another form of royal borrowing involved installing financiers as cashiers in the collection of the customs or excise taxes (Brewer 1988, pp. 93–94). These loans were credible because the cashier received the funds before the Treasury did. Thus, as with loans from farmers, the Crown had no easy opportunity to renege on repayment. This method of borrowing also required considerable upfront negotiation regarding who would be the cashier and on what terms.

The introduction of the order system in 1665 substantially improved market efficiency. Treasury Orders could be purchased easily; no negotiations were needed. Because repayment did not depend on the personal characteristics of the bearer, moreover, Treasury Orders were easily tradable on secondary markets (Roseveare 1973).[1] These secondary markets grew steadily before the Revolution and then more spectacularly afterward, fueled by the increase in short-term debt. Carlos and colleagues (2013, p. 160) document a "dramatic expansion of the total numbers of individuals holding easily tradable forms of state debt" by the 1720s. By this time, it is clear that individuals with little political clout considered it safe to buy and hold sovereign debt as an investment.

Why Was England a Laggard in Long-Term Debt?

Several prominent scholars argue that England's famed revolution in debt management was primarily administrative, rather than political. Epstein (2000), for example, points out that Elizabeth I and the Stuarts had all been limited to *short-term* loans, while their continental rivals typically issued *long-term* debt. As a consequence, English monarchs paid higher interest rates. Even in the early 1690s, Epstein notes,

the English crown was still having to offer short-term rates of 10 per cent …, when the Dutch Republic could offer [long-term] rates of 3–3.75 per cent, Venice paid 4–5 per cent, France offered 5 per cent, and Hapsburg Austria 5–6 per cent…. [T]he sharp decline in English interest rates after 1700, which North and Weingast ascribe to the benefits of a parliamentary regime, was in fact the effect of a belated catch-up with the Continental European … norm, principally through the introduction of a modern financial system and of its correlate, the consolidated public debt. (2000, p. 25)

Dickson also emphasizes administrative immaturity as afflicting English debt (1967, p. 47).[2] In the opening years of the Nine Year's War

---

[1] Although some royal loans were also transferable, as Brewer (1988, p. 207) noted, the secondary markets for such loans appear to have been much thinner. This makes sense, given that royal loans were Machiavellian, meaning that anyone buying the debt had to have some reason to believe that their political clout or other characteristics would ensure their repayment.

[2] See also Murphy 2012, pp. 56–57.

(1688–1697), he notes, the Commons "insisted ... on trying to finance [the war] by short-term loans," reflecting its "obstinate unwillingness to acknowledge that the war would be long and expensive." Moreover, as English governments had little experience in managing large wartime debts, they often overestimated "the yield of the new taxes imposed to service [new] loans."

I take a quite different view. As shown in Chapter 2, the centerpiece of post-revolutionary parliamentary strategy was to grant taxes for short time periods. When taxes were set to expire automatically, however, one could not secure long-term loans on them. Thus, parliamentarians' insistence on short-term debt stemmed logically from their short-leash strategy on taxes, not their "obstinate unwillingness" to recognize how long the war would be.

As Epstein notes, most continental powers were issuing long-term debt. However, England's failure to match this practice until 1693 was almost entirely a political problem, rather than a technical or administrative one. Only Parliament could fund long-term debt and, as we have seen in Chapter 2, post-revolutionary MPs were in no mood to do so, until they had assured themselves of financial control. As their grip on the purse strengthened, MPs began granting taxes for longer terms. By 1693, the Commons was confident enough to grant certain excise taxes for a term of ninety-nine years. This was the first tax that Parliament had ever granted for a period exceeding the life of the monarch, and its long term made it possible to fund England's first-ever long-term national debt.

As Brewer recounts, the first experiments with long-term debt – in 1693, 1694, and 1697 – were still viewed as temporary and dangerous expedients (1988, pp. 99–100, 146–161). A large block of MPs, hailing from both major parties, were of "the country persuasion." As a general matter, this meant they were especially "suspicious of executive power and committed to the notion of responsible government" (p. 155). More particularly, such MPs opposed both long-term tax grants and long-term debts, because they might allow the Crown to achieve financial independence.

The resistance of "country" MPs to long-term taxes and debts finally subsided in the later 1700s and early 1710s. In my view, the main reason they relented is that the structural credibility of platforms had been transformed by the capstone reform of the Revolution: ministerial responsibility. Once the executive's unfettered legal and constitutional ability to determine how public revenues were expended had been replaced by a parliamentary monopoly on both platforms and taxes, the fear of executive dominance waned and more MPs were willing to grant that which they had previously feared to grant.

The Debate over Interest Rates

Everyone agrees that the amount of English debt increased enormously after the Revolution. Some, however, interpret the run-up in debt as driven mainly by the unprecedentedly large wars that England fought, beginning with the Nine Years' War (1688–1697) and the War of the Spanish Succession (1701–1714). Such scholars prefer to assess the credibility of debt by its price; and I turn to their work in this section.

As noted in Chapter 1, most scholars examining interest rates have concluded against North and Weingast's thesis that English sovereign debt became abruptly more credible after the Glorious Revolution. Let me give four prominent examples.

First, Sussman and Yafeh (2006) show that average interest rates on English debt improved *slowly* and *non-monotonically* after the Revolution, not matching Dutch rates until around 1730. They conclude that North and Weingast's thesis "is not grounded in historical facts" (p. 907).[3]

Second, Murphy (2013) carefully recounts the many efforts of post-Revolution public creditors to force the government to pay its debts. She concludes that "credible commitment was not offered from above by the Glorious Revolution and the subsequent development of the institutions of government; it was demanded from below by the people who invested in the financial revolution." In other words, credibility emerged because creditors got better at lobbying and pressuring the government – a majoritarian argument in tune with Carruthers (1996), Harris (2013), and others.

Third, Stasavage (2003, 2007) shows that British interest rates rose when the Tories became more powerful and fell when they lost ground to the Whigs. In other words, credibility depended primarily on maintaining political support for repayment – another majoritarian argument.

---

[3] This flat disagreement with North and Weingast is not confined to the English case. Where Dincecco (2011) reports that constitutional commitment allowed sharp improvements in debt credibility in nine major European polities, Sussman and Yafeh, based on a study of sixteen countries, argue that "institutional reforms typically do not elicit investor response in the short run, perhaps because a long period of time is needed to establish credibility, or because the very nature of the reform process is gradual and cumulative" (2013, p. 251).

Fourth, Sussman and Yafeh (2013) plausibly argue that wars were the main drivers of British interest rates in the eighteenth century. They show that, as the number of navy seamen went up, so did the yield on British Consols.

Cumulatively, the picture one gets from these studies is pretty clear. There was no "step function" improvement in interest rates at the Revolution, as would be most consistent with North and Weingast's thesis. Instead, interest rates after the Revolution fluctuated with war risks, Whig strength in the House of Commons, and organized lobbying by creditors. The idea that the English state became abruptly better able to commit itself simply is not supported by the data.

Against the studies just discussed, Robinson (2006) has argued that the interest rate evidence is irrelevant. Raising the interest rate only increases a Machiavellian state's incentive to repudiate a debt. Thus, the only rational response to worries about credibility is credit rationing, and the debate focusing on interest rates "has chased red herrings" (Pincus and Robinson 2011b).

In my view, Robinson's account holds only before the Revolution. Because the Crown could unilaterally revise interest rates, its promises to pay high rates were not credible. Thus, investors should have restricted the amount they loaned, rather than demanding high interest payments they would probably never see.[4]

After the Revolution, however, virtually all debt was parliamentary and the Crown could no longer unilaterally revise the terms of repayment. Thus it was no longer irrational for investors to demand higher interest rates and the high post-revolutionary interest rates cannot simply be dismissed as irrelevant.

To put it another way, if North and Weingast are correct, then post-revolutionary debts should have been harder to revise than prerevolutionary ones. But Robinson's model assumes post-revolutionary debts could be as easily revised as prerevolutionary ones. Thus, we have two possibilities, depending on whether Robinson's model is the correct one to explain post-revolutionary debt. If yes, then North and Weingast are wrong by assumption. If no, then Robinson's model cannot defend North and Weingast against their empirical critics.

---

[4] Suppose the Crown offers an interest rate i to investors who can impose a cost Z on the Crown in retaliation for default. In this case, investors would loan an amount L such that $L(1+i) \leq Z$. In other words investors would set a credit limit of $Z/(1+i)$.

In the remainder of this chapter, I explain why the interest rate evidence is consistent with my model. The key point is that England issued a lot of junior and underfunded debt after the Revolution. Thus, even if its commitment to repay its debts as originally promised had been perfect, the face value of its debt was low, implying a high interest rate. I elaborate this argument in the following sections.

Why Interest Rates after the Revolution were Initially High

Recall from Chapter 4 that the improved credibility of English debt was driven by three factors: improved commitment (P), improved seniority (S), and improved funding (E(A)). As described in Chapter 5, each of these factors improved substantially over time, with especially important reforms affecting the credibility of constitutional commitment in 1701–1707, followed by substantial boosts to seniority and funding in 1710–1715.

How does this account of *when* constitutional commitment, seniority, and funding arrived gibe with the evidence marshaled by North and Weingast's critics? I take the main elements of their critique to be that interest rates after the Revolution improved only slowly (Sussman and Yafeh 2006), were sensitive to which party controlled the Commons (Stasavage 2003) and to wartime expenses (Sussman and Yafeh 2013), and exhibited a structural break in 1715, not 1689 (Stasavage 2007).

Yet, each of these observations is consistent with my account. Interest rates should have improved slowly, because it took time to solve the problem of deficiencies (for political reasons explored later). Creditors should have been sensitive to which party controlled the Commons, because curbing deficiencies required positive action by Parliament.[5] War expenses should have made junior and underfunded debts less credible, driving up their fiscal cost. Finding a structural break near 1715 rather than 1689 makes sense, because constitutional commitment benefited bondholders only to the extent that their debts were senior and well-funded, and those conditions emerged mainly in 1710–1715.

---

[5] In contrast, once debts were fully funded, Tory majorities should have posed less of a threat. A Tory government would have to assemble a majority in favor of *rescinding* previous promises or *diverting* previously earmarked funds, a higher bar to clear than merely not agreeing on a painful way to meet prior unfunded obligations.

TABLE 6.1. *Determinants of Fiscal Interest Rates, 1694–1730*

Independent Variable	Model 1 Coefficient (Standard Error)	Model 2 Coefficient (Standard Error)
Constant	9.45***	8.26***
	(.71)	(.71)
Percent of debt funded	-3.61***	-7.44**
	(.95)	(3.49)
Size of Whig majority in the House of Commons (Whigs – Tories)	-	-.003**
		(.0016)
Cumulative war expenditure since 1689	-	.066
		(.040)
Number of observations	37	37
R^2	.33	.51

*** p value < .01; ** p value < .05; * p value < .10.

To explore the determinants of debt credibility after the Revolution more systematically, one can run regressions similar to Stasavage's (2003, p. 80). The dependent variable I use to measure credibility is Y_t, the "fiscal interest rate" in year t. This variable, from Sussman and Yafeh (2006), adjusts the nominal interest rate to take account of the price discounts that England typically had to offer when selling debt. This is an important adjustment, because such discounts were routine and often large.[6]

The independent variables I consider are England's cumulative wartime expenditures from 1689 until year t, the net Whig majority in the House of Commons (Whigs minus Tories) as of year t, and the percent of the debt that was funded as of year t ($PctFunded_t$). The results for the years 1694–1730 are displayed in Table 6.1.

In Model 1, I regress Y_t on $PctFunded_t$ and a constant term. The logic of this specification can be explained as follows. Suppose that all funded debts have the same fiscal interest rate, Y_{funded}; and similarly all unfunded debts have a common fiscal interest rate, $Y_{unfunded}$. In this case, $Y_t \equiv PctFunded_t Y_{funded} + (1 - PctFunded_t) Y_{unfunded}$, and the results of Model 1 imply that unfunded debt carried an interest rate of $Y_{unfunded} = 9.45$ percent, while funded debt carried a significantly lower interest rate of $Y_{funded} = 9.45 - 3.61 = 5.84$ percent.

---

[6] Suppose that an investor pays p for a bond with face value 1 and offering interest i_p. Assuming that all promises are credible, the investor would be indifferent to paying full price and getting a higher interest rate, i_1. Solving the equation $-p + \delta(1+i_p) = -1 + \delta(1+i_1)$ for i_1 reveals the adjusted interest rate. The same exercise can be performed when promises are not perfectly credible.

Because not all funded (or unfunded) debts had a common fiscal interest rate, one cannot take Model 1 too seriously. But the results are consistent with the notion that funding mattered.[7]

In Model 2, I add cumulative war expenditures and the net Whig majority. Fiscal interest rates go up as war expenditures accumulate, albeit not in a statistically consistent fashion. More Whigs in the House of Commons reduce the interest rate, as previously reported by Stasavage (2003, 2007). Controlling for these two variables, the gap between the fiscal interest rates charged on funded and unfunded debts widens, to 7.44 percent, and remains statistically significant.

A better way to assess the differing risks that the market assigned to funded and unfunded debts would take a loan-by-loan approach. For each loan, one would identify (1) whether some specific tax revenues were dedicated to repayment or not (S); and (2) estimate the fraction of face value that the earmarked funds could be expected to repay (E(A)). For fixed P > 0, the interest rate should then decline with SE(A).

Unfortunately, it does not appear possible to calculate either the dependent variable or the independent variable required by this loan-by-loan approach. I know of no source that gives the price discounts paid on each loan, which makes calculating the fiscal interest rate impossible. And I know of no source that allows one to calculate, for each loan, the deficiency it ultimately suffered.

Although one cannot take a loan-by-loan approach statistically, one can approach the data qualitatively. By examining particular events, one can isolate the effects of parliamentary backing (P), seniority (S), and funding (E(A)).

Isolating the Effect of Parliamentary Backing

Treasury Orders were numbered promises to pay the bearer a stipulated amount of money from a specific tax, as soon as collections of that tax had retired all higher-priority (lower-numbered) claims. Some were given directly to tradesmen and contractors in payment for their goods and services. Others were given to the Treasurer of the Navy and other departmental officers, who used them to pay their own tradesmen and contractors. Finally, some were sold to lenders for cash. Only the last type of Treasury Order offered interest payments in addition to "payment in course" of their face value.

---

[7] McDonald (2013) provides similar evidence, plotting the "floating debt as a percentage of free revenues" against the "long-term interest rate" over the period 1690–1725.

Between their debut in December 1665 and the Revolution some Treasury Orders had parliamentary backing, meaning that an act of Parliament identified the tax fund that would be used to pay them off and guaranteed that they would indeed be paid off in numbered order. Most Treasury Orders, however, lacked parliamentary backing. They were sold by royal prerogative, meaning that both the earmarking of the tax fund and the guarantee they would be paid in order were merely royal promises.

Holders of royal Treasury Orders bore greater risks. In the infamous Stop of the Exchequer (1672), Charles II halted payment of orders drawn on several royally earmarked tax funds, while allowing those with political clout to secure payment from stopped funds (Horsefield 1982, p. 512). He thus reneged on both his earmark promise and his order-of-payment promise. Because a royal decree could undo neither Parliament's earmarks nor its guarantee of payment in order, Charles II honored all the outstanding Treasury Orders backed by Parliament.

Those holding significant quantities of stopped orders in 1672, mostly goldsmith bankers who had acquired them on the secondary market, spent many fruitless years seeking payment of their claims. Neither Crown nor Commons rode to their rescue. Even after the Revolution, when their claims were given an extensive hearing in the Committee of Supply, several MPs argued that "it would be a dangerous precedent to accept responsibility for sums borrowed by the crown without recourse to parliament" (Horsefield 1982, p. 518). In the end, the creditors may have got "an average rate of 1½ per cent per annum" on loans that offered 6–10 percent at issuance, along with a hefty capital write-down (Horsefield 1982, p. 523).

Given their greater risks, royal Treasury Orders should either have been refused by the market (credit rationing) or they should have borne higher interest rates and faced more severe price discounts than did otherwise similar parliamentary Treasury Orders. Evidence on interest rates is sparse but three episodes show that credit rationing was a substantial challenge.

First, Roseveare (1973, p. 21 ff) describes the transition from royal Treasury Orders – or their precursors (cf. Wheeler 1996) – to the first parliamentary Treasury Orders authorized by statute in 1665–1669. While other important reforms occurred at the same time, making it hard to attribute all improvement to Parliament's backing alone, it is clear that the Crown's ability to borrow quickly revived. That is, investors who had recently refused to buy otherwise similar royal debts snapped up parliamentary Treasury Orders.

Second, comparing royal and parliamentary Treasury Orders just after the Revolution yields even clearer evidence. Consider, for example, loans anticipating the customs duties. In William and Mary's first year of co-regency, £50,000 was borrowed by selling royal promises to pay when sufficient customs revenues came in. The lender was the Customs Cashier, who was uniquely well positioned to know when the revenues in fact came in. As soon as parliamentary backing was offered (in 2 William & Mary, c. 4), £457,477 was borrowed in the first three months of William and Mary's second year. Looking at a broader range of similar comparisons, Shaw (1931, p. clxxix) marvels at "how poor and unsatisfactory the loans were until the guarantee of parliamentary appropriation intervened and then how instantly forthcoming the required loan money was."[8]

Third, contractors providing goods to the armed forces often had to wait to receive even a formal promise of payment for their deliveries, and they clearly preferred that their promises, when they finally arrived, should be parliamentary rather than merely royal. As Lemire notes, "a mutiny nearly broke out in 1691, when clothing contractors refused to deliver their products when the only security they were offered was the promise of future payment on 'their Lordships' word' " (1997, p. 26).[9]

Isolating the Effect of Seniority and Adequate Funding

Although no systematic data exist, it is not controversial to say that England's more senior and well-funded debt carried lower interest rates than its more junior and less well-funded debt.[10] Often this distinction overlapped with the term of the loan: senior and well-funded meant long term; junior and less well-funded meant short term. In other cases, however, one can hold the term of the debt constant and examine junior and senior claims separately.

For example, several acts of Parliament earmarked funds and guaranteed payment in order but then made no provision at all for the interest

---

[8] It is hard to discount this evidence by arguing that royal demand for loans increased from 1689 to 1690. William III, the Dutch stadtholder, had been at war with Louis XIV for half a year before he became co-regent of England. He clearly had an urgent desire for revenues from day one (cf. Hill 1976, p. 40).

[9] On contractors' preference for parliamentary backing more generally, see Pool 1966, p. 7.

[10] As Brewer puts it, "The practice after 1688 of 'funding' loans through a parliamentary statute which earmarked a specific tax to service a particular debt is usually held to have ensured public confidence in government annuities and stocks" (1988, pp. 88–89). As Coffman points out, such earmarking had begun during the Interregnum and then too investors insisted on it before they would lend (2013, pp. 82, 91).

payments. Lenders thus had two distinct claims on the state. The first was a *senior claim* on a stipulated revenue stream, for the payment of the face amount on their Treasury Order, as soon as their number was reached. In addition, lenders had a *junior claim* for their interest payments. Legally, all this meant is that they had a right to pester the government, in competition with all other junior claimants, for payment out of the government's discretionary revenues.

Promises to repay junior debt were less valuable than promises to repay senior debt. Thus, one sometimes sees the "same" government facing the "same" war getting much different treatment from the markets, depending on the kind of debt promise the government chose to make. To illustrate this point, consider the two largest credit crises that post-revolutionary England faced, in 1697 and 1710–1711.

Although the First Whig Junto (1694–1699) remained in power before, during, and after the crisis of 1697, deficiencies mounted steadily over the first few years of its tenure in office. By the spring of 1697, "deficiencies on short-term tax funds were over £5m, and in April a lottery loan for £1.4m was almost entirely unsubscribed" (Dickson 1967, p. 352). Confronted with an outright refusal of credit, capping a sharp rise in interest rates, the Junto responded with the consolidation of funds known as the First General Mortgage (8&9 Wm. III, c. 20). The ensuing turnaround was, by the autumn of 1697, dramatic (Dickson 1967, p. 357).

One cannot attribute England's improved interest rates and credit access in 1697 to partisan shifts in the Ministry (as the Junto remained) or the Commons (as the 1695 Parliament was not prorogued until July 1698). The main events restoring public faith in English debt were the end of the Nine Years' War (September 1697) and the better funding of the debt (April 1697).

The problem of deficiencies – and the remedy of consolidation – also played leading roles in the crisis of 1710–1711. It is true that the crisis coincided with the accession to power of a new Tory Ministry, whose enemies characterized it as hostile to the interests of public creditors (Defoe 1710). However, the fundamental problem the new Ministry faced was similar to that the Junto faced in 1697: the unfunded debt had gotten out of control (Dickson 1967, p. 64). The remedy was also similar, involving a considerable consolidation of funds, along with a swap of old debts for equity in the South Sea Company. Market reactions were similar, too, with a substantial improvement in credit access and price. All told, the Tory Ministry stayed without much change, the war continued for several more years, yet the value of British debt improved – immediately *after* the South Sea Company came into being and funding of the debt improved dramatically.

Most previous discussions of English debt after the Revolution examine an aggregate measure of its value, such as the fiscal interest rates I explored in Table 5.1. Although presumably everyone would acknowledge that interest rates on funded debts were lower than they were on unfunded debts, this has not been viewed as an independent driver of value. The implicit assumption seems to be that the government of the day issued the best debt it could, in any given year. Thus, the huge compositional change in English debt can be ignored.

My claim is that the market would, at any time, have strongly preferred more over less well-funded debt; and that this was well known. This implies that the government of the day was not optimizing. It was churning out too much short-term unfunded debt, for which it received increasingly meager prices. And it was waiting too long to convert that debt to long-term and better-funded debts on which it would pay lower interest rates and face smaller price discounts. Thus, an important part of the puzzle of English debt is explaining the delay in funding, on some other basis than administrative immaturity, inexperience, or obstinate miscalculation.

Why the Delay in Funding?

In my view, the main reason for the prevalence of unfunded debt in the first five years after the Revolution was Parliament's ongoing drive to force the Crown to accept two central principles: that all sovereign promises about expenditure would henceforth be parliamentary; and that all sovereign promises about repayment of debts would henceforth be parliamentary. The ice of royal resistance to these principles began to crack with the launch of England's first long-term debt (1693–1694), but the Commons could not have viewed these principles as safely enshrined in constitutional practice until the establishment of ministerial responsibility (1701–1707). Once that point was reached, one sees a rapid reconfiguration of sovereign promises: more of them confer senior claims and those claims are on more ample funds.

Figure 6.2 presents an overview of English debt, both as regards quantity and price, consistent with the account just given. Prior to 1707 (marked with a vertical line), the correlation between total debt (given by the higher curve) and the fiscal interest rate is +0.30. After 1707,

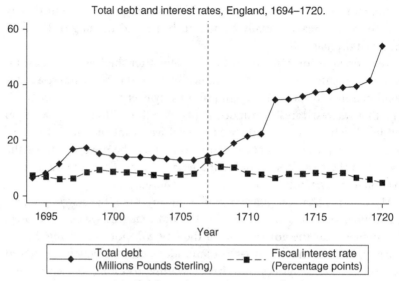

FIGURE 6.2. Total debt and interest rates, England, 1694–1720.

however, total debt increases almost monotonically, while fiscal interest rates decline almost monotonically. The correlation between total debt and the fiscal interest rate (over the period 1707–1720) is −0.86.

My reading of this graph is that the Commons' financial control improved in several steps after the Revolution. Initially, the Commons' lack of trust meant that it relied on short-term debt, completely before 1693 and substantially until 1710. Reliance on short-term debts during wartime in turn meant that junior claims abounded. Thus, wars drove up both the total amount and average cost of debt.

Once the Commons' control solidified with the emergence of ministerial responsibility, debts quickly became more senior and better funded. The wars continued but English debt reached an inflection point in 1707, after which it grew vastly in amount while becoming cheaper at the same time.

Conclusion: Reinterpreting England's Debt Crises

As far as I know, no funded parliamentary Treasury Order (a numbered promise to pay from a stipulated fund) was ever repudiated. No act of Parliament ever repealed the earmark or adjusted the order of payment; nor did Parliament allow executive officials to violate either of these sovereign promises at their discretion. In this sense, much of England's short-term debt was 100 percent credible.

The problems in England's short-term credit operations, which reached crisis proportions in 1697 and 1710, were *not* due to the state failing to perform its statutory promises precisely as stated. Rather, the problem was that the face value of many promises was low.

Many creditors in the war years – such as seamen paid in wage tickets, tradesmen paid in unfunded Treasury Orders, and lenders with unfunded claims for interest – held only junior claims. The government could leave such claims unpaid indefinitely, without violating the letter of the promises the creditors held. Under the press of war, unpaid junior claims accumulated to crisis proportions, until Parliament could ignore them no longer.

The root problem with England's post-revolutionary debt was Parliament's unwillingness to grant the long-term taxes necessary to fund senior long-term debts, and its corollary insistence on issuing mountains of junior short-term debt. The reason for Parliament's unwillingness to grant long-term taxes was the poor credibility of royal platforms. The crucial reforms attacking this root problem all enhanced the credibility of platforms and thus unleashed long-term taxes, as described in Chapter 2.

7

Property Rights

As noted in Chapter 1, North and Weingast's thesis that property rights became more secure after the Glorious Revolution has been disputed by subsequent scholars investigating rates of return on capital assets. In this chapter, I begin by reviewing their evidence.

I then consider when monopoly brokerage of property rights developed, showing that key elements emerged in the thirteenth century. After this point, enforcement of domestic property rights should have been reasonably secure. Thus, unlike North and Weingast, I do not predict an across-the-board improvement in property rights at the Revolution.

That said, some kinds of property were not governed by the system of monopoly brokerage built up around the common-law courts. First, the conciliar courts had long competed for litigation over foreign trading rights (Jha 2012; Harris 2013). Second, rights to develop property had long been conferred in a duopolistic market, with both courtiers and parliamentarians vying for business (Bogart 2005, 2011a; Bogart and Richardson 2011). In each of these markets, the Revolution marked a watershed.

Rates of Return on English Property

To assess North and Weingast's claim that property rights became more secure after the Revolution, Clark argues as follows. First, insecure private property rights tend "to deter investment in capital ... unless the return on capital rises sufficiently to compensate for the enhanced risk" (1996 p. 566). Thus, second, if property rights became more secure after the Glorious Revolution, one should see a decline in the rate of return on capital. But, third, no such decline appears in the historical record.

To establish his third point, Clark examines a large sample of charities' assets – such as land, tithes, houses, rent charges, and private bonds – over the period 1540–1837. Looking for correlations between political events and rates of return, he finds none in the seventeenth century, and concludes as follows: "Secure private property rights existed in England at least as early as 1600, and probably much earlier. As far as most private investors were concerned, nothing special happened in 1688 or, for that matter, in any period between 1600 and 1688" (p. 565).

Quinn undertakes a detailed study of a prominent London banker's portfolio before and after the Revolution. He finds that the Revolution "seems to have raised, not lowered, rates on private debt" (2001, p. 593).

Other scholars have shown that English rates of return on private capital were not low relative to rates elsewhere in Europe until well into the eighteenth century (cf. Homer 1963; Epstein 2000, 2005). Indeed, English rates seem to follow a continent-wide trend from the thirteenth century on, and their eventual divergence comes years after the Revolution (Epstein 2000, p. 62).

North and Weingast fare no better when it comes to qualitative evidence about the security of English property. Julian Hoppit's detailed account of post-revolutionary property confiscation concludes that "property rights became *less* secure after 1688" (2011; p. 94, italics added). Ron Harris' survey concludes that property rights in land "did not develop (between 1700–1850) in a way that the property rights school prescribes as encouraging economic growth" (2004, p. 229). And several scholars (Getzler 1996, pp. 643–646; Harris 2004; Jones 2013, pp. 336–337) view England's inefficient system of transferring title as belying any notion that property rights improved after the Revolution. Indeed, the irrationalities of the English system were so manifest and enduring that they constituted Max Weber's "England Problem" – how to explain "the anomaly of industrialization in an uncertain regime of property title" (Getzler 1996, pp. 644–645).

I do not think the evidence just reviewed can be easily dismissed.[1] But I do think an institutionalist account can accommodate it. In the next

---

[1] Robinson (2006) argues that the rate-of-return evidence can be dismissed. In the case of debt, I do not think so, as I explain in Chapter 6. In the case of property, I again do not think the evidence can be dismissed, but the reason is a bit different than in Chapter 6. Clark (following North and Weingast) implicitly assumes the Crown has poor knowledge of specific properties – presumably because their owners try hard to conceal their

section, I argue that Parliament claimed a monopoly on key decisions regarding how domestic property rights would be litigated in the century after Henry II's legal reforms. By the end of the thirteenth century, a system of monopoly brokerage had emerged. Thus, my account predicts that rates of return should have declined in the thirteenth century and should not have declined after 1688.

Parliament and Domestic Property Rights

The canonical sovereign promise sold to freemen via the royal judiciary was *title* to land. Titles, in addition to authorizing the owner to use his or her property in any of a number of allowed ways, conveyed three implicit sovereign promises. The sovereign promised (1) to provide a fair legal process by which titleholders could defend their usage rights; (2) to exercise the prerogative powers of purveyance and compulsory purchase with reasonable restraint; and (3) to provide a fair legal process by which holders could transfer title.

My conception obviously builds on early institutionalist ideas of property as a bundle of nested rights (e.g., Commons 1968; reviewed by Getzler 1996, pp. 654–655). However, titles are only as good as the legal recourse backing them up. Thus, I highlight the sovereign's role in guaranteeing such recourse – which involves both a general commitment to providing justice between private litigants and more specific commitments to refrain from exploiting the various "loopholes" in private property that exist in all legal systems.

In this chapter, I argue that English landowners sought to deprive the Crown of any legal avenue of attack on private property. They thus wanted each component promise of their titles to be more than a merely royal commitment. Their desires turned, eventually, into demands for parliamentary monopolies on: (1) all decisions relevant to how usage rights in property would be litigated; (2) all decisions about when the powers of purveyance and compulsory purchase would be used; and

---

wealth. The Crown's ignorance turns the threat of royal predation into a statistical one, and Clark's model is appropriate in that case. Robinson, in contrast, assumes the Crown has perfect knowledge of specific properties. In this case, his critique of Clark makes perfect sense. My view is that English property owners concealed their properties' value from a predatory Crown as best they could, and that they succeeded well enough to render the Crown closer to Clark's "blinded" predator than to Robinson's "all-seeing" predator. Thus, I expect that structural reductions in the Crown's capacity to predate should have substantially affected rates of return.

(3) all decisions affecting transfer of titles or usage rights to other private actors. In the next three subsections, I describe these developments.

Legal Recourse

In the first century after the Conquest, landowners who sought legal recourse might have to visit the monarch personally. As van Caenegem describes it, the typical sequence was that A went to the monarch, paid the appropriate fees, talked persuasively about B's depredations, and with luck emerged with a writ that commanded B to surrender the land back to A. Unfortunately, B might then visit the sovereign, pay the appropriate fees, talk persuasively about A's misleading account of events, and with luck emerge with a countermanding writ. After a series of visits from A and B, the monarch might in effect sell the property to the highest bidder (1973, pp. 34–39).

The Crown's inability to commit to its judicial decisions, along with its financial incentive to issue as many countermanding writs as the litigants could afford to purchase, should have lessened landowners' incentives to seek royal justice in the first place. Henry II's famous legal innovations in the Assize of Clarendon (1166) addressed this credibility problem. Royal justices began touring the country on *eyres*, offering their services directly to a mass market. In particular, non-baronial freemen could soon litigate possession and ownership of property before such justices, via an array of new writs (cf. van Caenegem 1973).

The writ of *novel disseisin* offers a concrete example of the new legal recourse available to freemen. It allowed a recently dispossessed property owner to secure a trial by jury of local men. The jurors would render a verdict based largely on specific questions of fact, including whether the plaintiff had occupied the disputed land as of certain dates and whether he had been dispossessed without judgment. The court's verdict would then be enforced by the Crown. Thus, subjects who paid "a moderate fee" (van Caenegem 1973, p. 43) secured a sovereign *promise* of a jury trial before royal justices, with subsequent enforcement of the Court's verdict.

In the earliest years of Henry's system, new kinds of writ (i.e., new forms of action) were authorized at royal pleasure. Because most writs allowed the transfer of cases from local to royal courts, however, local elites sought to regulate their use. In 1215, Magna Carta required baronial permission to transfer some cases to royal courts. In 1258, the Provisions of Oxford stipulated that new kinds of writ could be created only with the sanction of the king's council. By 1285, new writs could be created only with the express sanction of Parliament (per the second Statute of Westminster, c. 24; cf. Maitland 1908, pp. 104–105). Thus, I date the emergence of Parliament's monopoly right to control how usage rights in property would be litigated – via its control over what forms of action could be initiated by common-law writs – to the period 1258–1285.

Purveyance and Compulsory Purchase

After Henry II's reforms, the sovereign's promise to provide fair litigation of property rights between private claimants became substantially more credible. But what if the monarch wished to seize land, or the output of land, for his or her own use? In this section, I consider sovereign promises that seizures of land or output would be undertaken only in the public interest; and landowners' efforts to ensure that such promises would be parliamentary, rather than royal. In particular, I focus on purveyance and compulsory purchase.

Purveyance was the monarch's right to purchase goods at below-market prices. If abused, it could turn into mere expropriation. In early medieval times, only royal promises protected subjects against abusive purveyance. Such promises were often made and just as often belied by experience. Indeed, purveyance for military use became so unpopular that Parliament effectively forced Edward III to discontinue it by statutes enacted in 1340 and 1362 (Jones 1975, pp. 314–315). Thereafter, purveyance was used only to provide the royal household.[2] Three centuries later, at the Restoration, the Crown agreed to discontinue all purveyance and give up various feudal revenues in exchange for half the excise (Aylmer 1957, pp. 90–91). Thus, after 1660, subjects had a parliamentary promise that, if restored at all, purveyance would be used reasonably.

Another potential loophole in English titles, which survives to this day, is compulsory purchase, the British analog of eminent domain in the United States. Landowners distrusted royal promises to exercise this right reasonably, just as much as they distrusted royal promises to use purveyance prudently. Article 39 of Magna Carta mandated that "No free man shall be ... dispossessed ... except by the legal judgment of his peers or by the law of the land."

By "the law of the land," the authors of Magna Carta did not mean decrees issued by prerogative; they meant the common law (and, later,

---

[2] More precisely, "military purveyance [was] entrusted to merchants possessing no special commissions or warrants.... This stipulation represented an effort to transform military purveyors into unofficial buyers, who would be personally liable for their misdeeds" (p. 314).

an act of Parliament). Thereafter, major seizures of land and property, such as Henry VIII's dissolution of the monasteries, had parliamentary authorization.[3] Cole (2007, pp. 155–156), echoing Stoebuck (1972, p. 564), argues that "one prerogative power the crown never possessed, even before the Glorious Revolution of 1688–89, was the authority to take legal title to private land. This power reside[d] in parliament alone." In other words, the sovereign promise to exercise reasonable restraint in compulsory purchase of land was parliamentary well before 1688.

Transfer of Title

By compulsory purchase and purveyance the Crown could potentially expropriate property, or the output of property, for royal use. Even if landowners had fended off these threats of direct expropriation, however, indirect threats remained. In particular, if the Crown could unilaterally grant easements on A's property to B, then the value of titles would obviously be eroded. Thus, landowners wanted to ensure the Crown lacked an unfettered ability to sell rights of way and other easements (much less transfer title *tout court*).

How might landowners fetter the prerogative? One option was to forbid the Crown from awarding easements at all. If a medieval Englishman's property rights "were considered absolutely incapable of infringement by the crown" (Little 1969, p. 186), then presumably this included a prohibition on the sale of easements by prerogative. Certainly this would have been the view taken by advocates of "absolute property" in the early 1600s (Sacks 1994, p. 55).

In the centuries before the Revolution, however, when both royal decrees and royal meddling with the courts were common, the best defense against royal sales of easements might have been the general difficulty of transferring titles. The notion that difficult-to-transfer property rights originated, in part, as defenses against various forms of sovereign predation has been suggested by several scholars. This is how Timur Kuran views *waqfs* in the Ottoman Empire (2011, pp. 110–127); how North, Wallis, and Weingast (2009, pp. 85–86) depict secret conveyances in Tudor England; how John Beckett (2014, p. 39) views strict settlement in seventeenth-century England; and how Joshua Getzler (1996, p. 644)

---

[3] Monarchs could still unilaterally expropriate the property of non-freemen. For example, Edward I expelled and dispossessed the Jews in 1290 (cf. Mundill 2010). Reynolds argues that even freemen suffered expropriation by prerogative in medieval times (2010, pp. 34–46). The examples she considers appear to have involved relatively minor amounts and special pretexts.

interprets "the heavy transaction costs of land exchange and succession" in Stuart and Hanoverian England.

Summary

Blackstone famously concluded that England's "forms of administering justice came to perfection under Edward the first; and have not been much varied, nor always for the better, since" (1979 [1765–1769], Book IV, ch. 33). At least as regards the security of property against royal predation, I have made a similar argument here.[4]

In my view, one of Parliament's chief original purposes was to render landowners' titles to their lands credible by ensuring they were not merely royal promises. Titles conveyed several distinct sovereign promises and titleholders wished to block unilateral royal revision of any of them. First, landowners wanted to solve the "problem of the countermanding writ," whereby the Crown might sell justice to the highest bidder. Henry II's legal reforms were effective in this regard. Second, landowners wanted to protect themselves against royal seizure of their output (purveyance) or capital (compulsory purchase). Magna Carta settled the latter issue in principle, while purveyance was curtailed by statute in 1340 and ended altogether in 1660. Third, landowners wanted to protect themselves against any royal ability to transfer their titles or usage rights to other private actors. Here, the secrecy of English titles, the difficulty of transferring them, and repeated assertions of property's sacred and inviolable character constituted the main bulwarks against royal encroachment.

Lawyers and Domestic Property Rights

Roughly concomitant with the assertion of parliamentary control over property rights, England's legal profession began to take its modern form and to assert monopoly rights over brokering the sale and execution of common-law writs. Efforts to professionalize those pleading cases before the common-law courts began in Edward I's reign – with the first Statute of Westminster, c. 29, of 1275; the London Ordinance of 1280; and the Ordinance "de Attornatis et Apprenticiis" of 1292. These laws, by regulating both admission to practice and conduct before the courts,

---

[4] One's property might, under the new system, still be seized by the locally powerful. North, Wallis, and Weingast, for example, describe a common gambit during the period of bastard feudalism: find a weak claim to some property; physically occupy the property, by force if necessary; bribe or intimidate the local jury called on a writ of *novel disseisin* (2009, p. 97).

established the first form of monopoly brokerage of the law in England. Subsequently, the Crown did not seriously challenge either Parliament's exclusive right to approve writs or the legal profession's exclusive right to broker and execute them.

There were, however, further developments within the legal profession itself. It became increasingly common to purchase writs via solicitors, and the Inns of Court secured a legal monopoly on pleading cases before the superior common-law courts after the decision rendered in *Broughton v. Prince* in 1590. Thus, lawyers trained in the Inns of Court secured exclusive rights both to purchase writs for clients and to execute those writs in court, over the period 1390–1590.

The common lawyers had the usual incentives of monopoly brokers. First, they received fees proportional to the value of the litigation undertaken in the common law courts: "The usual scale was 6 s. 8 d. for every 100 marks claimed" (*Encyclopedia Britannica*, 11th edition, p. 848). Second, lawyers never bore a legal share of the costs the Crown incurred in fulfilling its promises. They did not have to pay the sheriff, for example. Third, if the Crown failed to enforce a court judgment, no solicitor had a right to get some of the cost savings.

Given how they were compensated, lawyers collectively stood to gain by keeping the flow of litigation large. Because nonperformance of writs could only depress future demand for the services of the common-law lawyers who plead those writs, the profession as a whole should have opposed anything that smacked of ex post revision or repudiation of writs.[5]

Limiting Executive Discretion

The Crown also had reasonably good incentives to provide the judicial procedures promised by common-law writs. Most of the costs of the new system were paid by litigants during the course of litigation directly to their lawyers or to the itinerant judges. Other costs were borne by jurors (whose service constituted a sort of labor tax). Thus, the Crown never got its hands on much of the revenue generated by the new judicial process and, thus, could not be tempted to divert it to other uses. Moreover, the revenues that did come the Crown's way arrived only

---

[5] It is true that individual solicitors might benefit, if they could secure the substantive outcome their clients sought by perverting judicial procedures. For example, a solicitor able to pack a jury with shills could dictate outcomes. The Inns of Court, as the peak association of common lawyers, should have had an incentive to deter this sort of abuse.

after each case reached a verdict in the form of fines and forfeitures paid by the losing side. Thus, the Crown wanted the judicial process to reach its conclusion; and it wanted litigants generally to believe that they had received fair justice.

The Consequences of Monopoly Brokerage of Domestic Property Rights

As monopoly brokerage of the market for fees-and-writs emerged over the thirteenth century, the volume, variety, and efficiency of trade improved dramatically. Although annual statistics on the number of writs purchased do not exist, van Caenegem makes clear that sales expanded greatly after Henry's reforms (1973, ch. 2). Sutherland notes that *novel disseisin* was "an outstanding success [which] came to be the most frequently used form of action in the king's court" by the 1260s (1973, p. 43).

The variety of writs also evolved rapidly. Whereas only four original writs existed in 1166, by the mid-1260s the Lullfield Register listed 314 writs, and by 1687 the Registrum Omnium Brevium listed more than 2,500 (Wiener 1972, pp. 499–500). This proliferation in the forms of action meant that the rights titles conveyed became increasingly precise and complex. For example, after the statute *De Donis Conditionalibus* (1285), landowners could create and alienate reversionary rights (North et al. 2009, p. 90). Establishing complex rights would have made little sense, had those rights been merely royal promises.

Finally, market efficiency increased. Relative to their predecessors, Henry's writs could be purchased much more easily (no personal visit to the monarch required) and their legal consequences were substantially clearer (no worries about countermanding writs being issued just because the Crown needed money).

There is also some rate-of-return evidence that property rights became more secure after the establishment of monopoly brokerage. Figure 7.1 displays Clark's (2009) estimates of the rate of return on capital in the English economy from 1200 to 1860. As can be seen, rates of return decline substantially in the century after 1258, when the Provisions of Oxford restricted the Crown's ability to authorize new kinds of writ. Since most of Europe shows a similar decline in the late medieval era, it is hard to attribute the decline in England to uniquely English events. Nonetheless, had the data shown no change, this would have counted against my thesis.

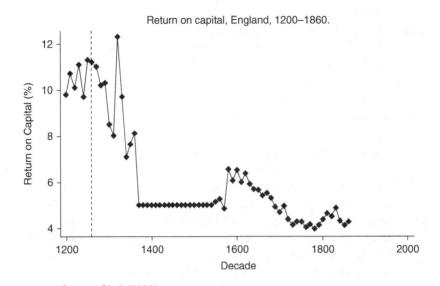

Return on capital, England, 1200–1860.

Source: Clark (2009).

FIGURE 7.1. Return on capital, England, 1200–1860.

Foreign Trading Rights and the Act of Settlement

Additional evidence of the importance of monopoly brokerage can be gained by considering the stark difference between rights in domestic and foreign property. Prior to 1660, the admiralty courts, which operated under civil rather than common law and were supervised by the Privy Council, often regulated English subjects' foreign assets (Jha 2012, pp. 27–28). Moreover, the right to trade internationally was typically granted by royal charter. Among other things, the dominance of decretal law in creating and regulating foreign property meant that the Crown could predate upon joint stock companies' profits. For example, the Crown could and did raise customs charges on specific items in which trade was booming, and it could and did revoke charters in order to reallocate profits (Jha 2012, p. 28).

After the Restoration, trading companies continued to face several threats. First, the monarch could extract concessions by threatening to revoke royal charters. This threat to company profits waned after *Phillips v. Bury* (1694) established that only an act of Parliament could alter corporate charters (Lamoreaux 2009, p. 14).

Second, the monarch could threaten to veto statutory re-charterings. This risk abated when ministerial responsibility emerged, after which the monarch could threaten to veto re-chartering Acts only on advice.[6]

Third, the monarch retained vast legal prerogatives in foreign affairs and the right to dismiss common-law judges at pleasure. Profitable companies might well have feared vigorous assertion of the Crown's prerogative rights before such judges. This threat to company profits abated after the Act of Settlement (1701) established that judges would serve "during good behavior" rather than "at royal pleasure." Two similar statutes had previously been rejected by William III or blocked by his parliamentary allies. By inserting service "during good behavior" in a bill that the Crown otherwise strongly favored, advocates of judicial reform extracted the king's grudging assent. Klerman and Mahoney (2005) show that shares in English trading companies experienced abnormal positive returns, when the amendment stipulating service "during good behavior" was introduced. Evidently, investors believed that English companies would bring home a larger share of their foreign profits, once judges were more independent of the Crown.

Questioning Commitment

The account just given might seem to conflict with that of Harris (2013). He seeks to explain why the pre-revolutionary market in corporate charters did not simply collapse in the face of royal opportunities for revision and repudiation. He thus highlights (1) considerations that would restrain even a Machiavellian prince's actions; and (2) constitutional features that constrained the Crown's actions, even before the Revolution.

Harris' arguments that the Crown faced constitutional constraints before the Revolution are similar to arguments (reviewed in Chapter 6) that sovereign debt had already undergone significant changes before the financial revolution. One can accept them, without bringing into question the assertion that commitment to charters improved sharply after the Revolution.

Harris' main assertion is that, "even if not fully independent, the common-law courts in late Tudor and early Stuart times could constrain the crown's power to revoke charters through a number of channels" (p. 28). Thus, the judiciary could enhance the credibility of sovereign promises.

---

[6] More generally, I explain the fact that the last royal veto occurred in 1708 in terms of ministerial responsibility. Ministers should have worried that they would be held accountable for vetoes, just as much as for other actions taken under the prerogative.

To explain the Crown's inability to simply sweep aside judicial niceties, Harris cites the growing popularity of parliamentarian and common-law theories of the English constitution. If enough elite actors were willing to defend the principle that "the judiciary was independent and could not be dismissed by the crown for enforcing the law against the crown's interests" (p. 30), then this would constrain the king even if "service at pleasure" was still the formal rule. One can accept this line of argument, yet still believe that getting service "during good behavior" onto the statute books (1701), and getting a precedent denying any prerogative right to alter corporate charters onto the case books (1694), would further enhance the credibility of rights granted by charter.

The Market for Development Rights

Entrepreneurs seeking to build turnpike roads, bridges, or canals faced the daunting task of cutting through a maze of existing property rights. Negotiating with all rights holders was typically too costly and so developers sought either royal patents or private acts of Parliament to confer the needed development rights. In either case, they paid an array of fees to obtain their rights.

Prior to the Revolution, with both royal courtiers and MPs offering to procure development rights, the duopolistic market did not operate well. Part of the problem was that the Crown could and did revoke royal patents. For example, Charles I revoked the Earl of Bedford's charter (for a drainage project) after the latter sided with the parliamentary opposition (Bogart 2011, p. 1080). The risk that royal patents would be revised should have depressed demand for them.

Might the Crown simply authorize higher tolls in order to tempt investment? One answer is that higher tolls might just increase the Crown's incentive to renege later, in which case royal promises would lack credibility (Robinson 2006). If the Crown could credibly promise higher tolls, then such promises would attract greater local opposition to the project, to which the Crown might be responsive. All told, then, higher tolls were no surefire solution to the Crown's credibility problems.

Might investors simply avoid a royal patent in favor of the greater security of an act of Parliament? Investors should always have preferred acts to patents, all else equal. However, all else was not equal. In particular, it took substantial time to push a private bill through Parliament and, prior to the Revolution, Parliament met infrequently and for short sessions. In contrast, the royal court was always open for business. Thus, before 1688 the chance of obtaining an act was considerably lower than the chance of obtaining a patent.

Moreover, the problem was even worse than just suggested. The Crown decided when to call Parliament, and investors who could not get an act might seek a patent, thereby increasing Crown revenues. For example, when James I pursued a strategy of not calling Parliament in the 1610s, he "awarded a patent to Jason Gason giving him powers over any river improvement in England" (Bogart 2011, p. 1079). In essence, James I farmed out the sale of river improvements.

After the Revolution, Parliament was always open for business. Investors thus flocked to the House of Commons. As Bogart notes, "only one river improvement proposal was made directly to the crown between 1689 and 1727 compared to more than 100 bills introduced to parliament" (p. 1086). Parliament had achieved a de facto monopoly.

Arguably, it soon achieved something like a de jure monopoly as well. After the emergence of ministerial responsibility, no royal patent for development rights could have been issued except on advice of ministers, and those ministers had to worry about their parliamentary support. Since the collective interests of backbench MPs were very much to ensure their own control of the market for development rights, one suspects that any ministerial forays into this market would have been unpopular. This may explain why ministers qua ministers were rarely involved in development issues.

Brokers

After the Revolution, the private bills committees of Parliament quickly emerged as the monopoly "sales force" for development rights. Both backbench MPs and a new species of parliamentary solicitors handled the emerging business (cf. Rydz 1979).

If MPs could discover a private actor willing to pay, they classified a bill as "private" and extracted an array of fees (Rydz 1979, p. 3). Otherwise the bill was "public" and MPs' compensation depended on their being placed on boards of directors, offered shares of stock, or otherwise cut in on the deal.[7] In both cases, MPs' compensation was roughly proportional to the value of the rights purchased.

If the Crown failed to enforce the terms of a private act conferring development rights, no individual MP or parliamentary solicitor had a

---

[7] See Eggers and Hainmueller (2009) for a study of MPs' compensation in more recent times.

legal right to share in the cost savings. Similarly, neither MPs nor solicitors bore direct personal costs of performance.

Thus, as with other species of monopoly broker, unofficial MPs and parliamentary solicitors wanted the market, and hence their fees, to expand. This required increasing the predictability and efficiency of private bill legislation (see later in this chapter) and avoiding coercive revisions of rights after they had been granted. The development rights conferred after the Revolution should have been more secure than those conferred before – and they were. Prior to the Revolution, 33 percent of river undertakers suffered *ex post* revision of their rights; afterward, the corresponding figure fell to 6 percent (Bogart 2011, pp. 1087–1088).

Limiting Executive Discretion

Because development rights – rights of way, rights to collect tolls, and the like – were conferred by statute after 1688, officials in the executive branch could neither legally revise nor easily erode them. In other words, the threats of unilateral executive revision or erosion of entrepreneurs' rights substantially abated, leaving only the "absolute despotic power" of Parliament to worry about.

Consequences

The consequence of establishing Parliament's monopoly, empowering the brokers, and limiting executive discretion was that the market for local development rights boomed. Bogart, exploiting a new and comprehensive database of investments in roads and rivers, reports as follows (see Figure 7.2): "The difference in completed investment before and after the Glorious Revolution is striking. Approximately the same amount was completed in the fifteen years from 1695 to 1709 as in the previous 85 years from 1604 to 1688 ... [A]verage investment was £11,600 from 1689 to 1749 which is more than double the average of £5,000 from 1660 to 1688" (2011, p. 1090). Formal statistical tests confirm that a structural break occurred in the 1690s.

Complementing these data on total investments, Albert shows that the number of acts creating turnpike trusts was nil during every year of the Restoration save one, but that almost no year goes by without a turnpike act after the late 1690s (with the running average below five until mid-century) (1972, pp. 202–203). Examining the broader category of "acts pertaining to property rights," Bogart and Richardson (2011) show the number of such acts increased sharply after the Revolution.

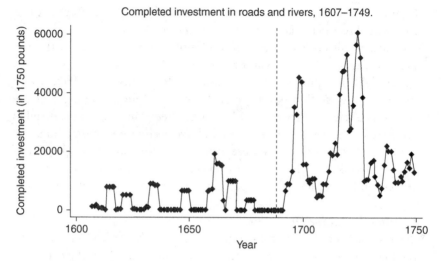

Completed investment in roads and rivers, 1607–1749.

Source: Bogart (2011), Figure 1. Bogart (2011).

FIGURE 7.2. Completed investment in roads and rivers, 1607–1749.

Figure 7.3 displays the total miles of turnpike roads in each year from 1690 to 1830 in England and Wales, using data compiled and maintained by www.turnpikes.org.uk.[8] The data show exponential growth in turnpike road miles in the first eighty years after the Glorious Revolution. Indeed, a simple exponential curve explains 96 percent of the variance in the data over this period.[9]

As to the efficiency of trade, Hayton's examination of all legislative initiatives – based on Hoppit (1997) – shows a (slowly declining) decadal success rate at or below 30 percent throughout the Restoration, jumping to 44 percent in 1690–1700 and then to 59 percent in 1701–1715. MPs, with a little practice, doubled the chance of a legislative deal being done (2002, p. 385).

Conclusion

In this chapter, I have told three stories about English property rights. The first story is that titles to land were the first kind of sovereign

---

[8] The figures represent lower bounds on the total mileage. First, I exclude some roads from the analysis for which turnpikes.org did not list a year in which the road first opened. Second, turnpikes.org did not update the mileage of the roads it documents, when the trust was reauthorized (and such updates would have been upward).

[9] The estimated equation is ln(Turnpike Miles) = −113.6 + .069*[year−1690].

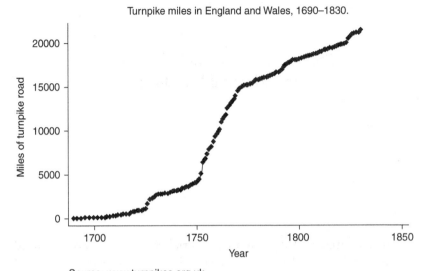

Turnpike miles in England and Wales, 1690–1830.

Source: www.turnpikes.org.uk.

FIGURE 7.3. Turnpike miles in England and Wales, 1690–1830.

promise in English history to become parliamentary, rather than royal. Landowners were determined to close off each and every avenue by which a cash-strapped monarch might encroach on their rights. Through a combination of legal reforms, military victories, and solemn pronouncements, they won the day. That is, there were no obvious de jure ways by which the Crown could unilaterally relieve freemen of their property.

The second and third stories concern types of property over which the Crown's prerogative rights were much more formidable: foreign trading rights and development rights. In these cases, I argue that the Crown continued to milk the system for revenues. Although some early legal impediments to such milking were raised, before 1688 foreign trading and development rights often relied on merely royal promises. After the Revolution, in contrast, several reforms – *Phillips v. Bury* (1694), judicial service "during good behavior" (1701), and ministerial responsibility (1701–1707) – converted trading and development rights from royal to parliamentary promises. The markets for both kinds of right showed immediate increases in the volume, variety, and efficiency of trade.

8

From Constitutional Commitment
to Industrial Revolution

North has argued that Britain's Industrial Revolution was explained by "a combination of better-specified and enforced property rights and increasingly efficient and expanding markets" (1981, p. 166). If property rights became significantly more secure due to the Glorious Revolution, then a strong link is suggested between the changes in England's politics after 1688 and the changes in Britain's economy after 1780. While North and Weingast (1989, p. 831) were circumspect in drawing this link, others have asserted it more emphatically. For example, Olson observes that "individual rights to property and contract enforcement were probably more secure in Britain after 1689 than anywhere else, and it was in Britain, not very long after the Glorious Revolution, that the Industrial Revolution began" (1993, p. 574). More recently, Acemoglu and Robinson (2012) entitle one of their chapters "The turning point: How a political revolution in 1688 changed institutions in England and led the way to the Industrial Revolution."

Sceptics, however, have questioned whether England's political reforms led to Britain's economic success. Mokyr observes that "the precise connection between the events of the Glorious Revolution and the Industrial Revolution that followed more than half a century later remains murky" (2008, p. 27). Allen wryly notes that "it was a long stretch from the excise tax on beer ... to Watt's invention of the separate condenser" (2009, p. 5). Jones points out that "a link has not been established between supposedly greater security of property under William III and industrialization a century later" (2013, p. 328). Findlay and O'Rourke doubt that "British success can really be attributed to superior institutions, put in place by the Glorious Revolution" (2007, p. 349), while Rodger remarks that "it seems less and less plausible that parliamentary government could have been the essential factor in Britain's economic success" (2010, p. 9).

In this chapter, I consider three specific causal mechanisms that might have connected the two revolutions. My aim is to show these paths make good sense and are supported by prima facie evidence, rather than to attempt conclusive tests.

The first path connects the Glorious to the Transportation Revolution, per Bogart (2011), and then connects the Transportation to the Industrial Revolution, per Szostak (1991). The initial political reforms that set England on this path had nothing to do with enhancing the security of property rights; rather, they improved the transferability of property and thus landowners' ability to bargain among themselves.

The second path connecting the Glorious to the Industrial Revolution hinged on the increased contestability of *new* rents. The seventeenth-century Crown could and did cut deals with special interests pursuant to essentially private negotiations. A panoply of sinecures (Harling 1996) and mercantilist rents (Nye 2007) resulted. The eighteenth-century Parliament was, by comparison, much more transparent. When a group sought to embody new rents for itself in statutory law, its elite opponents would have fair warning – since any bill had to be "read" several times to all MPs and proceed through a legendarily long legislative process. The fair warning the statutory process afforded meant that new statutory rents were more contestable after 1689 than new decretal rents had been before.[1] Their greater contestability meant that new statutory rents imposed lower external costs on groups capable of marshaling opposition in Parliament than had new decretal rents before the Revolution. Eventually, as a wider array of business interests gained parliamentary influence, the most egregious forms of protectionism waned. Beginning in the 1780s, a substantial reduction of sinecurism, mercantilist rents, and other inefficiencies ensued, which dramatically transformed British politics by the 1830s and 1840s.

The third path from the Glorious to the Industrial Revolution went through the fiscal-military state's wartime expenditures. War produced huge government demands for the necessities of warfare: ships, guns, uniforms, and rations. The result was that technological knowledge ratcheted up with each new war in those sectors sustaining the military effort.

---

[1] The Crown could of course promise not to grant new rents, except after some long process of vetting had been conducted by the Privy Council. But the monarch remained legally free to renege on such promises when that seemed expedient.

Politics, Transportation, and Industry

Following Bogart (2011), Chapter 7 argued that the Glorious Revolution led directly to eighteenth-century Britain's boom in infrastructural investment. By 1770, before the traditional starting date for the Industrial Revolution (1780), Britain possessed "the best transport system in Europe, and thus the world" (Szostak 1991, p. 49). Britain's advantages, moreover, were not small. France, for example, had one-third the waterway density in 1815 (Szostak 1991, p. 55), one-half the density of paved roads in 1840 (Bogart et al. 2010, p. 89), and roadway travel speeds one-half as fast in 1760 (Szostak 1991, p. 70).

Szostak (1991) argues that Britain's Transportation Revolution had two important effects. First, it created a truly national market for consumer goods for the first time. Second, it sparked a massive reorganization of production: as transporting capital and labor inputs became cheaper, large factories became more efficient than the putting-out system.

Szostak (1991) also argues that an increasingly large national market, combined with increasingly large firms, led to increasingly rapid regional specialization and technological innovation – constituting the Industrial Revolution. His account thus echoes Adam Smith's classic assertion "That the Division of Labour is Limited by the Extent of the Market."

Secure versus Negotiable Rights

The causal path from the Glorious to the Industrial Revolution that previous scholars have typically considered runs from "more secure property rights" to "better incentives to invest and innovate." That is not the argument I am making here. As explained in Chapter 7, I do not think domestic property rights became "better-specified and enforced" after the Revolution.

To clarify the difference between North's (1981) argument and mine, consider the following observation by Allen: "property rights were at least as secure in France ... as in England. Indeed, one could argue that France suffered because property was too secure: profitable irrigation projects were not undertaken in Provence because France had no counterpart to the private acts of the British parliament that overrode property owners opposed to the enclosure of their land or the construction of canals or turnpikes across it" (2009, p. 5).

While agreeing with Allen's observation, I would go further. Not just France but French landowners suffered due to the over-security of property rights.

A title's value depends both on the titleholder's right to use the property and on his/her right to rent (or sell) usage rights to others. Thus, one might decompose the value of a given title as follows:

$$V_{title} = V_{use} + V_{sale} (1)$$

Let's consider each component, V_{use} (which represents what I called the face value in Chapter 1) and V_{sale} (which represents the transfer value), in turn.

Suppose John Jones owns farmlands that, when he works them himself, produce corn worth £c per year, net of all input costs. Suppose also that Jones views a pound received one period in the future as equivalent to δ pounds received immediately. In this case, were Jones and his heirs to use the land themselves in perpetuity, the discounted present net value of such use would be $V_{use} = c + \delta c + \delta^2 c + \ldots = \dfrac{c}{1-\delta}$.

Now consider the value of Jones' right to rent or sell his property, V_{sale}. This component, I claim, depends on landowners' ability to bargain efficiently when profit-making opportunities arise that can only be seized by combining the usage rights of multiple owners.

My claim might rankle those who believe owners of private property can routinely bargain to efficient outcomes at low cost. But there is no sound theoretical reason to expect private actors in early modern Europe should have been successful when bargaining over complex projects affecting many landowners. One might appeal to the Coase Theorem (Coase 1960). But this theorem holds only when none of the standard causes of bargaining failure exist; and such causes – for example, commitment problems, informational asymmetries – abounded in early modern Europe.

Empirical evidence that early modern bargainers in fact failed to reach efficient deals is provided by Rosenthal's (1990) study of irrigation in Provence. As he explains, the power of eminent domain was highly fragmented throughout eighteenth-century France. For example, canal builders wishing to provide irrigation from the river Durance might need separate grants of eminent domain from several local actors, such as the Estates of the *Comtat Venaissan* and the villages of the *Terres Adjacentes*. As Rosenthal shows, the multiplicity of local veto players was a recipe for free-riding and holdups (1990, pp. 625–630). Although returns on Provençal canals were attractive throughout the eighteenth century, actually building them awaited the French Revolution's centralization of control over eminent domain and the end of the Napoleonic wars. A similar picture emerges in Rosenthal's (1992) account of drainage projects in Normandy 1700–1860. Improvements, despite their likely profitability, were blocked because competing rights holders could not reach agreement among themselves.

Let's return to the value of Jones' right to alienate his property, V_{sale}. Let P be the probability that entrepreneurs will propose a project – for example, a road or canal – that requires combining some of Jones' usage rights with rights held by other landowners. Let Q be the probability that a proposed project will secure the legal authorizations it needs to go forward, either by private negotiations or eminent domain. Finally, let U be Jones' expected net benefit from a legally authorized project. U might be negative, if eminent domain is abused to enrich the monarch's cronies and Jones has little clout at court.

With this notation, we can express the value of Jones' rights of alienation as follows:

$$V_{sale} = V_{bilateral} + \frac{PQU}{1-\delta} \tag{2}$$

Here, $V_{bilateral}$ represents the discounted present value of the Jones family's right to sell its property in the future, in a bilateral transaction with a single other private actor; $\frac{PQU}{1-\delta}$ while is the discounted present value of the family's right to participate in multilateral negotiations over complex projects.

If there are lots of profitable projects (P is high), then landowners should be interested in strengthening eminent domain in order to increase Q, the likelihood of assembling the needed package of rights. However, they will obviously worry that abuse of eminent domain might lower both V_{use} and U.

From a generic landowners' perspective, the optimal system of property rights would be one in which the central government granted eminent domain but was constrained to honor two sovereign promises: (1) that eminent domain would be invoked only to help landowners reach mutually beneficial deals among themselves; and (2) that owners of seized property would be given fair compensation. Were these two promises of "reasonable use" credible, then eminent domain could be deployed to overcome unreasonable holdouts (raising Q) while preventing confiscation (ensuring U > 0). In other words, lowering the security of property – by centralizing eminent domain – can, under certain circumstances, raise its value.[2]

---

[2] Reforms that centralize eminent domain and impose "reasonable use" constraints will still depress V_{use}. Thus, the effect on V_{title} will be positive only when P is large enough; the increment in Q is large enough; and U (given reasonable use) is large enough.

Because absolutist rulers could not credibly promise reasonable use of eminent domain, landowners insisted on maintaining veto players whose assent would be necessary before rights of way and other easements could be granted. In France, the veto players were local actors – provincial estates, courts, villages. In England, the veto players were national actors – Parliament and the common-law judiciary.

Where eminent domain was regulated by decentralized veto players, as in France, the system offered too little eminent domain and too much protection to individual usage rights. Improvements that could be attained only by orchestrating contributions from a variety of stakeholders often did not happen. Investments in transportation infrastructure suffered as a consequence.

Post-Revolution Great Britain, alone among its major competitors, combined centralized eminent domain with a credible – because parliamentary – commitment to reasonable use. This was an important reason that the Transportation Revolution occurred first in England, Wales, and Scotland.[3]

Credible Restraints on Eminent Domain Elsewhere
Great Britain's European imitators appear to have appreciated the importance of centralized, yet credibly constrained, eminent domain. Indeed, the first written constitutions of all major west-central countries promised landowners that the government would exercise eminent domain in the public interest and with compensation.[4] Consider two early examples:

France 1791, Article 17: Property being a sacred and inviolable right, no one can be deprived of it, unless a legally established public necessity evidently demands it, under the condition of a just and prior indemnity.

Spain 1812, Article 172(15): The King may not take the property of any individual or corporation, nor disturb them in the possession, free use, and benefit thereof; and in any case, if it should be necessary, for an object of recognized public utility, to take the property of an individual, that person shall be indemnified, and given a fair sum according to the judgment of upright men.

---

[3] Bogart (2011b) shows that British juries could be "biased" in favor of landowners and that this discouraged some investment on the margin. But, as he notes, the speed and finality of the juries' compensation decisions contrasted sharply with procedures in France. While litigation could go on for decades in France without producing a clear resolution, a private act in Britain often took only a year or two and was completely authoritative.

[4] Putting aside classical precedents, the idea that eminent domain should be exercised in the public interest and with compensation went back at least to Grotius and had been reiterated by many eighteenth-century thinkers, including Pufendorf, Montesquieu, Wolff, and Vattel (see McNulty 1912).

TABLE 8.1. *Constitutional Regulation of Eminent Domain in Europe*

Country	Year in which Eminent Domain was Constitutionally Regulated
England	1689–1707
France	1791 [Article 17]
Netherlands	1795 [Article 5]
Sweden	1809 [Article 16]
Spain	1812 [Article 172(15)]
Portugal	1822 [Article 6]
Belgium	1831 [Article 11]
Piedmont	1848 [Article 29]
Prussia	1848 [Article 8]
Austria	1849 [Article 29]
Denmark	1849 [Article 87]

Table 8.1 provides a more complete list of countries, along with the dates on which they promulgated constitutional provisions regulating eminent domain (all quite similar to those just quoted).

Some absolutist regimes had earlier promised to compensate those whose property they confiscated. For example, France adopted a rule in 1705 requiring compensation when houses, timber lands, and vineyards were taken by the state (McNulty 1912, p. 555); and Prussia adopted regulations requiring compensation in 1794 (James 1913, p. 202). However, such promises were merely royal, and Borchard and Stumberg (1931, p. 222) opine that eminent domain in *ancien régime* France amounted to "virtual confiscation followed by a problematical indemnity." It is clear from the dates at which the new eminent domain rules came in that absolutist rulers were reluctant to surrender their powers.

After the Napoleonic wars ended, the new system of centralized-yet-constrained eminent domain facilitated increased investment in transportation infrastructure across continental Europe. All the countries listed in Table 8.1 experienced transportation revolutions in general, and railway booms in particular, by mid-century.

It is true that the Russian Empire also built many miles of railway, without granting a similar constitutional protection until 1906. However, there had never been local or central veto players capable of blocking an imperial grant of eminent domain in Russia. The czar could grant rights of way to roads and railways at will.

If we focus just on European states in which landowners had earlier erected bulwarks against unilateral crown exercise of eminent domain, then the following generalization holds: no such state laid many miles of railway track before constitutionally regulating eminent domain. The vast bulk of their railway booms came after they constitutionally regulated eminent domain.

The Contestability of Rents

Many scholars have pointed out how venal English MPs were in the eighteenth century and how rife politics was with factionalism, patronage, and rent-seeking (e.g., Brewer 1988; Harling 1996; Zahedieh 2010). But compare rent-seeking before and after the Revolution.

During the Restoration era, favors might be had by anyone who could get access to the monarch (or the relevant Crown officials). Moreover, contemporaries often lacked a clear idea of who was proposing what to the Crown (Weiser 2003, ch. 3). The non-transparency of royal deal-making meant, among other things, that rent-seekers faced relatively weak pressures to ensure their rents imposed the least external costs on others.[5]

After the Revolution, one needed a statute to get important rents. Securing an act of Parliament, however, was a much more public affair than catching the ear of the monarch. Any group promoting a bill had to expect those harmed by the bill would organize against it (Brewer 1988, pp. 237–238). Thus, they had more reason to achieve their rents in the most efficient manner possible (cf. Becker 1983). To illustrate how the seed of greater contestability eventually bore the fruit of greater intra-elite efficiency, consider mercantilist rents.

Mercantilist Rents

It is well known that mercantilist rents declined dramatically in the later eighteenth century. As Mokyr puts it:

Many special interest groups ... found themselves on the defensive as the eighteenth century wore on and the more free-market ideas of the Enlightenment began to sink in. It was a very different parliament in 1774 that tossed out the Calico Act – a shameless piece of special interest legislation benefitting the wool and silk industry – from the one that had passed it in 1721 (Mokyr and

---

[5] There were royal institutions in place to vet rent-seeking claims prior to 1688 (see, e.g., Weiser 2003, ch. 5, on the Board of Trade under Charles II). However, their activity levels were spotty, and the Crown remained free to ignore or bypass them.

Nye, 2007). After 1780, parliament increasingly used its powers to make selected dents in the rent-seeking machinery of the ancient regime under the platform of making the economy more efficient and streamlined. (Mokyr 2008, pp. 30–31)

In the remainder of this section, I suggest two paths by which the greater contestability of rents made it more difficult to sustain tariffs on intermediate and finished products. (Raw products were not at issue, as even mercantilists did not seek to block their entry into the country.)

Intermediate Products

The economic cost of tariffs on intermediate products (such as calico) should have increased as the Transportation and Industrial Revolutions gathered steam. To illustrate, consider an industry in which each firm converts a single input x into an output $q(x)$, delivering its product at an average transportation cost $c(r)$ to all consumers within a radius r of its production site. The production function $q(x)$ is an S-shaped curve. That is, there are increasing returns to scale in producing q over some initial range of inputs x. Transportation costs increase exponentially with distance, taking the form $c(r) = \lambda e^r$.

Prior to the Transportation Revolution, suppose λ was so large that each firm served only a local market. In this case, each firm would produce only a small amount and, thus, would not exploit the economies of scale potentially available in the production technology. After the Transportation Revolution, in contrast, suppose λ fell so much that some firms sought to produce a large amount for the national market. In this case, such firms would be able to exploit the available economies of scale in production (or invent new methods of production that exhibited scale economies).

With this scenario in mind, consider the costs a tariff imposed on imports of x. Prior to the Transportation Revolution, such a tariff will cause small declines in production and small deadweight losses. The costs will fall on many small producers unlikely to have much parliamentary clout. After the fall in transport costs, however, the same tariff will cause larger declines in production and larger deadweight losses. Moreover, the costs will fall on larger firms more likely to wield parliamentary influence.

The observations just made may shed light on why the Calico Act was repealed in 1774. By this time, the spinning jenny had been in use for a decade. Entrepreneurs would thus have appreciated the potential to expand production, if restrictions on the importation of calico could be repealed. By 1774, moreover, the old system of transporting cloth by packhorse teams had largely given way to more efficient transportation on canals and turnpikes. Thus, the domestic market was larger, something entrepreneurs would also have appreciated. In any event, business leaders in Manchester lobbied for repeal, and repeal was followed by a burst of investment in labor-saving technology by large firms using various kinds of calico as inputs.

Finished Products

In the case of finished goods, domestic manufacturers promoting import tariffs had a clear organizational advantage over the consuming public who paid higher prices as a consequence. As Britain's transportation and communication networks expanded, however, consumers' interests should have been better defended before Parliament.

To see why, note first that lobbying tactics changed substantially over the course of the eighteenth century. While nationwide petitioning campaigns had been mounted as early as the 1690s, they became more and more frequent. Moreover, where lobbies' propaganda campaigns had targeted MPs and Crown officials in the 1690s, with a premium on face-to-face lobbying, after 1730 they typically targeted public opinion via broadsheets, pamphlets, and newspapers (Brewer 1988, pp. 231–243).[6]

This shift in communication tactics was produced by competition. Whichever side was losing the battle in private lobbying of MPs could go public. As the cost of going public declined due to improvements in transportation and communication, the frequency of public debates about tariffs and taxes increased.

In an abstract competition between an organized special interest seeking rents and an unorganized public bearing costs, the technology of communication matters. The special interest has all the advantages when face-to-face private communication is the main technique of lobbying and reduced advantages when the debate is conducted largely through mass media. Thus, the reduced success of British trade groups seeking protectionist tariffs was partly due to the greater contestability of rents awarded by the new parliamentary regime.

Mercantilism's Effect on Economic Growth

Beginning with Adam Smith, many economists have argued that mercantilism retarded economic growth throughout Europe. Yet, an equally long

---

[6] Tilly's (1995) study of "contentious gatherings" in England between 1758 and 1828 shows that social movements increasingly adopted a similar strategy of pressuring Parliament via petitions and appeals to public opinion.

line of observers have argued that, in some cases, protecting infant industries from foreign competition may be essential in inducing entrepreneurs to make the large fixed investments necessary for them to become globally competitive. Parthasarathi (2011) makes such an argument regarding eighteenth-century Britain's textile industry, which he views as needing protection against cheaper Indian competitors in order to become the innovative sector it eventually became.

My argument is orthogonal to the debate over the net effects of mercantilism. Whether protecting infant industries was good economic policy or not, the long-run trend was for those harmed by import tariffs – the larger and more diffuse groups of potential manufacturers and consumers – to gain political power relative to the concentrated beneficiaries of such tariffs. This shift in political power enabled the cost-bearers to reduce tariffs, regardless of what the net economic merits of those tariffs were at any given time.

The Ratchet of War

A third path by which the Glorious Revolution connected to the Industrial Revolution was the ratchet of war: spikes in government demand sparked innovations, which then diffused after the war ended. Let me first describe the ratchet of war from a global perspective, before focusing on the United Kingdom in particular.

Prior to the Industrial Revolution, European economies did not outperform their strongest competitors elsewhere in Eurasia. However, as Hoffman shows, the Europeans did excel in one sector: the development of guns, ships, forts, ordnance, and military technology more generally. Indeed, beginning in the Middle Ages, total factor productivity in Europe's military sector grew at unprecedented rates (2015, ch. 2). By the early modern era, the Europeans had left all their competitors far behind – which explains why they conquered the world.

As Hoffman argues, endemic capital-intensive warfare drove Europe's precocious development of military technology. Europeans fought each other continually and victory belonged to whichever side could build bigger ships armed with more cannons, field and feed larger armies, and provide troops with faster-firing guns, more mobile artillery, and better organization. Effectively, Europe engaged in an episodic continent-wide arms race from the Middle Ages onward, which drove innovation in military technology, logistics, and organization (McNeill 1982; Hoffman 2015).

British Military Invention between the Nine Years' and Napoleonic Wars

In the century after the Glorious Revolution, the ratchet of war can be observed in all the main sectors to which Britain's fiscal-military state looked for supplies – metals and metallurgy (for armaments and ship construction), textiles (for uniforms), agriculture (for rations), and transportation (for getting all of these goods to London). Let's consider each in turn.

Government demand for armaments and ships increased enormously during the frequent wars in which the English (and then the British) engaged. John (1955) shows how these wartime spikes in government demand motivated technological experimentation, which led to a series of innovations in mining and metallurgy – such as the reverberatory furnace (1688–1698), the Savery steam engine (1698), the use of coal in making iron (1708), the Newcomen engine (1712), and the development of coke pig iron suitable for wrought iron manufacture (1748).

Wartime demands also accelerated investment in capital equipment, with the sums dwarfing those in the civilian economy. In the early eighteenth century, for example, Brewer reckons that "the fixed capital in one of the largest sectors of the nation's most important industry [woolens] was ... a mere eighteen per cent of the fixed capital required to launch the British [fleet]" (1988, pp. 34–35). Moreover, as Rodger notes, "much naval capital expenditure went on advanced technology, and much running expenditure went to sustain the enormous and complex industrial enterprises of the dockyards, each of them many times the size of any private firm" (2010, p. 13). Those managing the naval-industrial complex thus "faced the challenges of large-scale industrial organization more than a century before they began to affect private businesses" (p. 16).

The state also had a huge wartime appetite for uniforms to clothe soldiers and sailors. Lemire argues that "the injection of ever-larger measures of government funding ... [led to] expanding economies of scale" (1997, p. 11). The innovations capturing these economies of scale could then be redeployed for civilian use. The Hudson's Bay Company, for example, relied on the same network of contractors as the government (pp. 10–11).

Soldiers and sailors also had to be fed. By the early eighteenth century, the navy's Victualling Board "was buying a fifth of all the products traded on the national agricultural market" (Rodger 2010, p. 14). As the largest single purchaser, it "was at least influential, and possibly critical, in the growth of a sophisticated and integrated national ... agricultural market" (Rodger 2004, p. 307). In any event, Britain's famous Agricultural Revolution occurred, for the most part, after the vast post-1688 expansion of the Victualling Board's budget.

The wartime state also had a substantial demand for transportation. Materials to build ships had to get to the shipyards. Supplies for each ship had to get onboard, usually in London. Thus, it is no accident that the exponentially growing turnpike road system centered on London, connecting it to key industrial areas. Nor is it accidental that transportation investments clustered in war years: "There is, for example, a marked concentration of turnpikes Acts on the northern coalfield in the years 1746–8, and the considerable number of road improvements in Kent during 1756–8 coincided exactly with the extensive building of men-of-war by private and government owned shipyards in these years" (John 1955, p. 334).

The state did not directly finance the construction of roads and canals in England and Wales. However, entrepreneurs seeking to maximize their tolls would obviously have taken careful account of how goods purchased by the government would be transported. Thus, an important root cause of the burst of road and canal building in eighteenth-century Britain was entrepreneurial anticipation of the government's wartime demand for transport.

British Military Invention during the Napoleonic Wars

During the Napoleonic Wars, we see yet another episode of immense government expenditure, inducing rapid technological-logistical-organizational advance. McNeill, for example, notes that "the men who built the new coke-fired blast furnaces in previously desolate regions of Wales and Scotland would probably not have undertaken such risky and expensive investments without an assured market for cannon" (1982, p. 211). Once their investments were sunk, however, "British ironmasters [had] extraordinary incentives for finding new uses for the cheaper product their new, large-scale furnaces were able to turn out." Effectively, McNeill argues that wartime government demand was essential in motivating investments at the technological frontier of metallurgy, where entrepreneurs faced large fixed costs. As Neal puts it, the Industrial Revolution "occurred precisely during and because of the Napoleonic Wars" (1990, p. 218).

Many theorists of "poverty traps" argue that large fixed costs, or other sources of large increasing returns to scale, prevent poor countries from entering certain industries and thereby keep them poor (see Azariadis and Stachurski 2005 for a review). McNeill and Neal can be viewed as making such an argument about the Industrial Revolution. The Napoleonic conflicts were the largest and most capital-intensive wars that had ever been fought. The British state spent vastly larger sums waging those wars than any single state had ever before spent. These expenditures induced investments that would never otherwise have been profitable. Once the increasing returns hurdles had been cleared, however, modern economic growth – at least in the sectors serving the state – was possible. Indeed, the Industrial Revolution was largely confined to iron smelting, textiles, and transportation for the next half century.

The Incentive to Innovate

Why did the Napoleonic Wars not induce an industrial revolution in France? The novel capital investments British entrepreneurs undertook looked profitable only because *all* the crucial inputs – (1) coal; (2) skilled mechanical labor; (3) experience in managing large enterprises; (4) scientific and engineering expertise; (5) reliable and cheap transportation – were available to them and, in addition, (6) they faced huge and predictable government demand.

French entrepreneurs were broadly comparable to their British counterparts in their managerial experience, as well as in their access to scientific and engineering expertise. However, by 1789, British entrepreneurs enjoyed advantages on all other fronts. Coal was cheaper (Allen 2009). Britain's mechanical workers were significantly more skilled (Kelly, Mokyr, and Ó Gráda 2014). Transportation was clearly superior (see earlier in this chapter). And the British government's ability to sustain vast expenditures over the long haul was a much safer bet.

The greater availability of coal deposits in the British isles than in France cannot be attributed to Britain's superior political institutions. Nor does the greater skill of Britain's mechanical workers circa 1790 seem mainly due to political institutions. First, there was a substantial exodus of Huguenot clock and instrument makers to England when France revoked the Edict of Nantes in 1685, and this brain drain obviously put a "plus" in the British column while constituting a "minus" in the French column (Landes 1983). Second, the share of military expenditures that went to food and clothing was higher in army-centered France than in navy-centered Britain. The proportionately larger capital expenditure of the British on dockyards, ordnance, and shipbuilding implied proportionately more work for skilled mechanical workers of all specialties.

Britain's remaining advantages, however, were primarily institutional. I have already traced Britain's superior transportation to her unique handling of eminent domain, coupled with the government's steady demand for transport (see earlier in this chapter). Similarly, I have already traced the British state's ability to spend so much and so consistently to the credibility of her platforms (Chapters 2–3) and debt (Chapters 4–6).

I would add that the post-1688 state should have been better able to commit to awarding state contracts on economic merits, rather than to those with court connections. This in turn should have improved the incentives of those lacking royal connections to undertake research. Consistent with these observations, British eighteenth-century inventors seem more often to be from non-elite families than their French counterparts.[7]

All Great Britain's advantages interacted. For example, cheaper coal raised the value of building roads to transport it, but better roads made more mines profitable. Thus, I am not arguing that the Anglo-French political differences were all that mattered. However, I think a strong prima facie case exists that the improved credibility of the post-Revolution state was an important root cause of its precocious industrialization.

The Scientific Revolution

Continual wartime expenditure fueled technological, logistical, and organizational innovation throughout post-medieval Europe (McNeill 1982; Hoffman 2015). Yet, if the story were simply one of Europeans learning how better to wield deadly force, then it would be hard to explain the continuation of modern economic growth in the second Industrial Revolution and beyond. As Mokyr notes, "the true question of the Industrial Revolution is not why it took place, but why it was sustained beyond, say, 1820" (2002, p. 20). Here, the development of the scientific method – rules by which research and development could most efficiently be conducted, together with standards by which progress should be communicated – must surely be given pride of place.

The importance of more abstract and efficient mathematical notation, shared across a community of scholars, can be appreciated by considering

---

[7] Compare the list of eighteenth-century French inventions and discoveries in chemistry with the list of eighteenth-century English inventions and discoveries in the same field. Using the lists on Wikipedia, I find that 12.5 percent of the English inventions are due to members of elite families, versus 50 percent for France.

the respective shelf lives enjoyed by Aristotle's *Physics* and Newton's *Principia*. Aristotle's ideas about motion dominated thinking in much of Eurasia for more than a millennium. Newton finally knocked Aristotle off the reading list of those seeking state-of-the-art knowledge. Yet, such was the pace of scientific discovery that Newton himself was knocked off the reading list within a century (Guicciardini 2005, p. 85). The pace of discovery has since tended to increase further, and the endogenous development of scientific and technological knowledge is still driving world economic growth (cf. Mokyr 2002, 2009).

To this account of how "modern" rates of economic growth emerged I would simply add that efforts to invent better gunpowder drove advances in chemistry, efforts to invent better ordnance drove advances in metallurgy, and so on. To develop the scientific method required building a sufficiently large network of inter-communicating scientists. We can think of scientific journals and societies as constituting an early "platform," with mathematical notation being an early "programming language." As more and more brilliant minds plugged into the Europe-wide platform, and as methods of communication became more efficient, rapidly increasing scientific knowledge resulted. As with other network goods, science could become profitable only with large enough initial investments, and Europe's fiscal-military states were the single most important venture capitalists.

Conclusion

Most scholars responding to North's (1981) argument that "better-specified and enforced property rights" were key to Great Britain's Industrial Revolution have denied that such rights changed at the Glorious Revolution and argued that over-secure rights could in any event hinder development. By and large, I believe the critics have successfully impugned the most obvious interpretation of North's thesis. I have suggested three alternative paths – plausible enough to merit further investigation – by which the Glorious Revolution might have sparked the Industrial Revolution.

First, by ensuring that Parliament was in session annually, the Revolution allowed a much greater use of the private bill process to structure bargains among local stakeholders. In effect, this meant that local landowners could harness the power of eminent domain to clinch deals among themselves, without much worry of expropriation by Crown officials. The result was a boom in infrastructural investment, especially in transportation. As Szostak (1991) argued, Britain's Transportation Revolution greatly expanded the size of the market, thus sparking Smithian specialization.

Second, the Revolution changed the nature of rent-seeking. New rents were more contestable and thus became more efficient within the parliamentary elite, especially when more firms began to exploit production technologies featuring economies of scale. Compounded over the half-century 1780–1830, the greater contestability and cost of protectionist rents led to a dramatic net reduction of mercantilist rents and other inefficiencies.

Third, the Revolution established a fiscal-military state that could extract much larger taxes and secure much larger loans than ever before. This generated strong incentives to innovate in the sectors supplying the military effort. Thus, one observes a ratcheting up of innovative effort during wars in the supply sectors, intensifying a process that had been going on in Europe since the Middle Ages.

9

Summarizing the Revolution

In Chapters 2–7, I argued that England's constitution underwent crucial reforms after the Glorious Revolution enhancing the credibility of several kinds of sovereign promise. In this chapter, I first summarize what the "crucial reforms" were. My account differs from North and Weingast's (1989) and Acemoglu and Robinson's (2012), as I explain by reference to a weakest-link theory of executive constraint.

This chapter also summarizes the consequences of constraining the executive. For each kind of sovereign promise, I review when parliamentary monopolies emerged, when monopoly brokers appeared, and when sales boomed. In each case, I attribute market expansion to the creation of monopoly brokerage in the respective markets, and explain why alternative theories of sovereign credibility fail to provide a persuasive account of market expansion.

I then reconsider the role of preferences in sustaining sovereign credibility. I argue that, once Parliament had a monopoly in a given area of law, the tactics promise holders used to secure performance shifted. Promise holders could abandon their efforts to extract performance from a Machiavellian state, in favor of optimizing the state's reversionary performance. This shift in strategy (and the state's anticipation of it) meant inter alia that all sovereign promises to deliver private goods became transferable. Transferability in turn led to the emergence of brokers and secondary markets, both of which played key roles in assuring that preferences were structurally biased toward performance. Thus, state promises became simultaneously more liquid and more reliable.

I close the chapter with some preliminary comments on the exportation of English parliamentarism to other countries. Many countries have sought to achieve Britain's outcomes – in particular, its military and economic success – by imitating its constitutional design. Only a few have succeeded and it is important to consider why.

What Happened Constitutionally?

When scholars summarize the Revolution's reforms, they stress either parliamentary supremacy or executive constraints. Here are three typical examples:

- "First and foremost, the Revolution initiated the era of parliamentary 'supremacy'" (North and Weingast 1989, p. 816).
- "The Glorious Revolution limited the power of the king and the executive, and relocated to Parliament the power to determine economic institutions" (Acemoglu and Robinson 2012, p. 102).
- "[T]he Glorious Revolution ... consolidated parliamentary ascendancy, limited royal prerogatives and secured private property" (Allen 2009, p. 5).[1]

What specific rules underpinned parliamentary supremacy or constrained the executive? In both the literature on the Revolution and the broader literature on executive–legislative relations, the answer to this question turns into a list of powers, with the sum of powers determining the legislature's aggregate power or, on the flip side, the executive's aggregate constraint.

Consider legislative power first. Fish and Kroenig's (2011) recently published work is a comprehensive and useful characterization of contemporary legislatures. They identify thirty-two legislative powers, code each country's national assembly as possessing or lacking each power, and produce an overall score by adding up the number of powers possessed. Many other scholars have taken a similarly additive view of legislative power.

Next consider executive constraints. Both North and Weingast (1989, pp. 815–816) and Acemoglu and Robinson (2012, p. 191) list what they view as the key constraints on royal power introduced after the Revolution. The Polity IV measure of executive constraint (Marshall, Gurr, and Jaggers 2014), widely used by political scientists and economists, also rests on a list of constraints.

In this book, I have insisted on a stronger condition than parliamentary supremacy, dubbed parliamentary monopoly. Relatedly, I take a non-additive view of executive constraint, elaborated in the next section.

---

[1] Here, Allen summarizes what he takes to be North and Weingast's view.

A Weakest-Link Theory of Executive Constraint

"[T]he contest, for ages, has been to rescue Liberty from the grasp of executive power. Whoever has engaged in her sacred cause ... has struggled for the accomplishment of that single object." – Daniel Webster, speech to the U.S. Senate, 7 May 1834.

To prevent unilateral executive revision of sovereign commitments, English MPs had to block all of the imaginable legal vehicles by which the Crown might revise an existing law – decrees issued by royal prerogative, statutes enacted by a rubber-stamp Parliament, decisions rendered by pliant judges. Thus, preventing unilateral executive legislation entailed fashioning a chain of constraints, each of whose links limited the executive, and whose aggregate strength depended on the weakest link.

To elaborate in the context of an abstract polity, let p_d denote the probability that the executive *cannot* revise sovereign promises by decree, p_s the probability that the executive *cannot* turn Parliament into a rubber stamp (e.g., by appointing its members), and p_c the probability that the executive *cannot* dictate judicial decisions (e.g., by exploiting service "at royal pleasure"). Define the aggregate constraint imposed on the chief executive as the probability p that s/he cannot unilaterally revise sovereign promises. If the executive has only one shot at revision, then s/he will seek to revise by whatever means – decree, statute, court decision – offers the highest chance of success.[2] Thus, in this case

$$p = \min\{p_d, p_s, p_c\} \tag{1}$$

In words, the weakest constraint on the executive determines the overall constraint.

Alternatively, if the executive can simultaneously seek to revise promises by multiple means (with independent chances of success), then constraint takes a multiplicative form:

$$p = p_d p_s p_c \tag{2}$$

In words, all component constraints must bind, else the executive will be free to unilaterally revise sovereign promises by at least one legal avenue.

For my purposes, the difference between Equations (1) and (2) is not important. The main point is that neither formula is anything like the additive indices suggested in the literature, which would look like $p_d + p_s + p_c$. In what follows, I focus on the weakest-link formula given by Equation (1).

---

[2] Here, I assume the executive would prefer to revise the promise. That is, the benefits of revision exceed the costs that promise holders can impose in retaliation.

TABLE 9.1. *Synopsis of Constitutional Reforms After the Revolution*

I. Defending against absolutism
    A. Regulate standing armies (Mutiny Act, Bill of Rights)
    B. Prevent packing of parliamentary corporations (2 W&M c. 8)
    C. Limit royal influence in Parliament (Act of Settlement)
    D. Judges serve "during good behavior" (Act of Settlement)

II. Promoting parliamentary monopoly
    A. Sun-setting taxes (via the "for longer time" clause of Bill of Rights)
    B. Preventing issuance of royal platforms (via the rule of 1706)
    C. Preventing issuance of royal debts
    D. Preventing issuance of royal patents for development rights

---

Constraining the English Crown

The model of executive constraint just sketched has guided my interpretation of what the key reforms of the Revolution settlement were. In this section, I recap the discussion in previous chapters.

Table 9.1 lists (under the heading "Defending against absolutism") the most important de jure reforms in post-Revolution England that prevented unilateral revision of sovereign promises. To help prevent rule by decree, Parliament regulated the raising and maintenance of standing armies. To help prevent the creation of a rubber-stamp Parliament, MPs hindered the packing of parliamentary corporations and limited the Crown's ability to bribe MPs with places of profit. To help prevent judicial decisions dictated by the Crown, MPs ensured that judges would serve "during good behavior" rather than "at royal pleasure."

Table 9.1 also lists (under the heading "Promoting parliamentary monopoly") the most important reforms preventing unilateral erosion of sovereign promises. The two key accomplishments were preventing the Crown from collecting taxes in anticipation of parliamentary reauthorization (via the "for longer time" clause of the Bill of Rights); and preventing the Crown from offering royal platforms to the Commons (via the "rule of 1706").

These reforms – regulating taxes and platforms – entailed further restrictions on the royal prerogative. Consider first how the Crown's unilateral ability to issue royal debt disappeared. The Commons exploited its short-term taxes to secure royal acquiescence to an unprecedented burst of appropriation, thereby depriving the Crown of the funds on which royal loans could be secured. After the development of ministerial responsibility, moreover, the decision to borrow had to be on the advice of ministers, who had to avoid parliamentary censure. Thus, unilateral royal borrowing, just like unilateral royal vetoing of bills, became unconstitutional, even if both remained technically within the prerogative.

Consider next how the Crown's ability unilaterally to issue royal patents conferring development rights disappeared. Because the Commons granted mostly short-term taxes and enacted only annual budgets, it assured frequent sittings. As entrepreneurs preferred the greater security of an act of Parliament, the main reason for seeking royal patents – the infrequency of parliamentary sittings – was thus removed. After the development of ministerial responsibility, moreover, the decision to issue a royal patent had to be on the advice of ministers, who had to avoid parliamentary censure. Thus, unilateral royal patents too became constitutionally contestable.

In their constitutional battles, I do not need to insist that either the Crown or the Commons farsightedly pursued a consistent strategy. Many historians caution against such a conclusion, as regards both prerevolutionary struggles and post-revolutionary developments.[3] While the post-revolutionary strategy of putting the Crown on a short leash was widely articulated and appreciated (cf. Roberts 1966, 1977), it is fine for my purposes if the prerevolutionary struggle was myopic and intermittent. All I insist on is that, when push came to shove, the Crown's lack of credibility was the root problem; that royal non-credibility led to the syndrome of prerevolutionary dysfunctions plaguing the Stuart regime; and that resolving the underlying credibility problem logically required a lengthy chain of constraints on executive action, with all links in the chain in good working order.

Was there Really a de jure Change?
Throughout this book, I have tried to identify the specific reforms key to establishing parliamentary monopolies in various markets. In the process, I have plumped for a view of the Revolution as a watershed in constraining the executive, rather than "just another step."

It is possible to hold that the chain of executive constraint had been forged mostly in the period 1640–1660, or that the most important links had then been forged, with only the final links hammered out after 1688. This view would remain consistent with my main argument, as long as it

---

[3] For example, Horwitz comments that "it would be misleading to read into the developments of the first three years of [William and Mary's] reign a clearly conceived or fully conscious constitutional design" (1977, p. 88).

acknowledged that the pre-1688 chain had failed to constrain, because it possessed weak links that the executive duly exploited. The Revolution would be a watershed in the sense that it completed the last few links in the chain, which brought non-incremental improvements in executive constraint.

My own view is that several links in the chain were properly forged only after the Revolution. For example, I stress the "for longer time" clause of the Bill of Rights, the conventions of ministerial responsibility, and the rule of 1706 as novel and important reforms.

In any event, it is only after the Revolution that all the links in the chain of executive constraint were strengthened simultaneously. Thus, if the "treatment" to which the body politic was subjected was "executive constraint," one can reasonably say that England got low doses all the way to 1688, followed by an abruptly larger dose thereafter, which reached full strength with the rule of 1706.

The Rule of Law and Monopoly Brokerage

One way to summarize the reforms of the Revolution is to say that they established the rule of law in England, capping it with monopoly brokerage. By the rule of law, I mean no more and no less than I do by parliamentary monopoly: Only a statute could authorize the sale of a certain kind of promise, and all avenues by which the executive might unilaterally revise that promise were closed off. This is close to some notions of the rule of law in the literature, especially those viewing it as primarily a constraint on the executive. However, most view the rule of law as a global characteristic of a polity or its constitutional order, whereas I view it as a characteristic of a specific market or even a specific promise.

The role that monopoly brokerage plays in my analysis is to mitigate common-pool, free-riding, and rent-seeking problems. In the case of platforms, ministers have a monopoly right to propose expenditures. In the case of debts, the Bank of England has a monopoly flotation right. In the case of writs, the Inns of Court have a monopoly on pleading. In each case, the monopolist internalizes the damage that would be done to the market in the future, were commitments repudiated today. The argument is abstractly similar to others in the literature on budgets (e.g., Hallerberg, Strauch, and von Hagen 2010), debt (e.g., Broz 1998), and labor-management bargaining (e.g., Katzenstein 1985). My account differs in placing more emphasis on the efficiency gains due to monopoly brokerage, as opposed to just the mean shifts (e.g., greater fiscal discipline, debt credibility, and wage restraint).

The Rule of Law and Trade in Sovereign Promises

A central claim of the present book is that, once the rule of law and monopoly brokers came to govern a given market for sovereign promises, that market expanded. For example, the improved credibility of platforms (sovereign promises to expend revenues in particular ways) vastly expanded the House of Commons' willingness to grant taxes. Increased tax receipts, along with the improved credibility, seniority, and funding of debts (sovereign promises to repay loans), vastly expanded England's access to credit. The increased frequency of parliamentary sessions, along with the superior credibility of parliamentary "restraints" (sovereign promises to exercise eminent domain in the public interest), vastly expanded demand for development rights.

In addition to evidence that sales expanded after the rule of law and monopoly brokerage emerged in a given market, there is also cross-sectional evidence. When royal and parliamentary debts coexisted (1665–1688), investors viewed the former as less credible and either refused to buy them or sought price discounts (a form of credit rationing). When royal (Civil List) and parliamentary (all else) platforms c-existed (1689–1830), MPs viewed the former as less credible and were less willing to expand their purchases. When both royal patents and parliamentary acts were available to confer development rights, entrepreneurs bought only the latter.

Competing Explanations

In this section, I consider whether punishment or majoritarian theories of sovereign credibility can explain the various market expansions documented in earlier chapters. When the sale of writs boomed, for example, did this coincide with an improved ability of property owners to punish the Crown for predatory acts, or to the emergence of a new majority in favor of enforcing property rights, rather than to the emergence of the rule of law and monopoly brokerage?

Let's start with punishment theories. They can in principle explain abrupt improvements in credibility, if promise holders' ability to boycott abruptly increases. One might interpret the Bank of England as creating a force that could help organize lenders' boycotts, similar to Root's (1989) analysis of France. However, the Bank seems much better designed to help creditors *prevent* default than to *punish* it. The Bank could be trusted to lobby for better funding and seniority of debts and to oppose efforts to rewrite the terms of repayment. After a default had occurred, however, the Bank would have been keen to reestablish the market quickly, so that its flow of flotation fees would recommence. Thus, the Bank was far from the best agent to deliver threats of a long boycott in order to extract concessions from the government.

A punishment account seems even less plausible for the other markets studied here. For example, should we understand the increasing sale of common-law writs after 1166 as reflecting litigants' improved ability to settle out of court, thus forcing royal courts to provide better justice in order to attract business? While logically possible, there is no evidence that litigants' ability to settle out of court changed enough to explain a sevenfold increase in the number of writs from 1166 to the mid-1260s. Moreover, if out-of-court settlements had in fact become easier, then the credibility of all courts would have been enhanced. Litigants would have had no need to flee the baronial courts and flock to the royal courts, as they did.

What about majoritarian theories? They can in principle explain abrupt improvements in credibility, if new majorities emerge at critical junctures. However, no one has argued, nor does it seem plausible, that changes in preferences explain why the sale of common-law writs, supply bills, and development rights boomed at the particular times they did.

In contrast, there is a majoritarian explanation on offer for debt. Stasavage (2003, 2007) and Pincus and Robinson (2011) explain the increased credibility of England's debt after 1688 in terms of the emergence of a mercantile majority at the Revolution, followed by the entrenchment of that majority in 1715. As explained in Chapter 6, however, I do not think the balance of party forces was the key driver of the state's access to credit or the price it paid. In the next section, I point to some further evidence against a majoritarian explanation.

How the Rule of Law Affected Promise Holders' Tactics

Was the enhanced credibility of the various promises just described due mainly to the preferences of those making political decisions? Did parliamentary monopoly simply change the risk promise holders faced from "the monarch may decide to revise our promises" to "a majority of MPs may decide to revise our promises"? Should we conclude, with the majoritarian theorists (e.g., Stasavage 2003; Lamoreaux 2011), that promise holders needed to constantly tend to their majority alliances? In this section, I argue that introducing the rule of law changed the tactics that

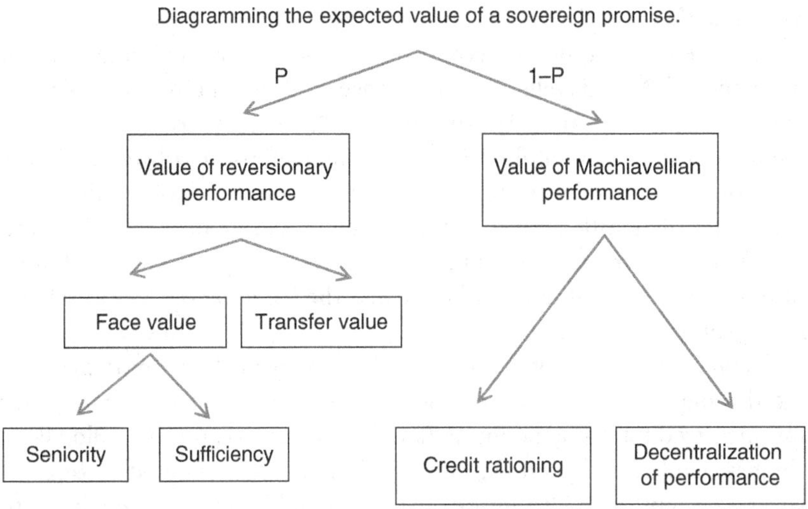

Diagramming the expected value of a sovereign promise.

FIGURE 9.1. Diagramming the expected value of a sovereign promise.

promise holders used to secure performance, and that the new tactics resulted in structural biases in favor of performance.

Choosing Tactics

In Chapter 1, I distinguished between a promise holders' reversionary performance – what s/he could expect if the original promise legally bound the government – and his or her Machiavellian performance – what s/he could expect if the original promise did not legally bind the government. Equation (1), repeated here, expressed the overall value of a sovereign promise (E(V)) as depending on both the expected value of the state's reversionary performance (E(V_r)) and the expected value of its Machiavellian performance (E(V_M)), weighted by the probability (P, 1 – P) of each event:

$$E(V) = PE(V_r) + (1 - P)E(V_M) \tag{1}$$

Figure 9.1 diagrams Equation (1), showing the factors that influence the value of the state's reversionary and Machiavellian performance.

If the government is likely to be unconstrained (P ≈ 0), then investors should focus on improving the state's Machiavellian performance. If, instead, the government is likely to be constrained (P ≈ 1), then investors should focus on improving the state's reversionary performance. Let's consider each of these polar cases in turn.

Machiavellian Tactics

Prior to 1688, royal debts were made credible by two main devices that presupposed Machiavellian performance and sought to maximize its value. First, most loans were structured so that the Crown never got its hands on the money until such time as the creditor had been paid. The creditor directly collected the taxes (tax-farming) or was installed as a cashier legally entitled to receive the revenues before their transmittal to the Treasury (Brewer 1988, pp. 92–94). Either way, the non-credibility of royal promises did not matter because the lender never had to rely on such promises.

Second, if lenders were promised repayment from monies flowing through the Treasury, then they followed two principles. First, they rationed credit, lending no more than their ability to punish would allow. That is, lenders followed the canonical advice of economic theories of sovereign debt (as in Robinson 2006). Second, lenders sought ways to enhance their ability to punish default. For example, those providing valuable political services to the Crown could lend more, to the extent that withdrawal of their services would be painful and hard to remedy.

The first tactic, which I label "decentralization of performance" in Figure 9.1, was used to enhance the credibility of many other royal promises too. For example, the main profits of justice arrived in the Exchequer only after the writ had been performed (see Chapter 7). Purchasers of monopolies (prior to the Statute of Monopolies) never struck a deal in which the Crown collected the monopoly rents and then gave them an agreed share; only the reverse would do. Feudal taxation to finance warfare was an entirely decentralized labor tax; the Crown never received a large mass of fungible resources that it might be tempted to divert to other purposes.

The second tactic, labeled "credit rationing" in Figure 9.1, was also widespread. For example, Chapter 2 noted that the grant of taxes prior to 1688 should theoretically have been, and empirically was, rationed. The willingness of entrepreneurs to pay upfront fees for royal charters conferring trading rights was also limited. And, of course, the Crown faced credit rationing in the market for royal debt before the Revolution.

Rule-of-Law Tactics

Debt is the most obvious example in which English investors turned their attention from the state's Machiavellian to its reversionary performance. After 1665 some debts, and after 1688 virtually all debts, became parliamentary. Thus, after the Revolution, investors no longer relied on the old tactics of dealing with a Machiavellian monarch. Instead, they sought to optimize Parliament's promises. I have discussed promise holders' demand for senior and well-funded claims in previous chapters. Here, I focus on another characteristic of promises that investors universally valued: transferability, the ability to sell their debts easily, quickly, and cheaply on secondary markets.

Transferability was generally hard to devise for royal debts. Consider two examples. First, the main security for repayment that tax farmers and cashiers had was their legal right to intercept revenues before they reached the Treasury. If farmers sold their debts, could the new debt holder establish a legal claim to the revenues the farmer would have used to repay the debt had he kept it? Second, after 1665, the Crown issued royal Treasury Orders that promised impersonal transferability. Yet, these debts almost immediately showed grave imperfections in their impersonality; after the Stop of the Exchequer, only those with court influence were paid.

In contrast, transferability was straightforward to devise for parliamentary debts. Debt holders needed no particular characteristics to ensure repayment, except those explicitly required in the statute. While Parliament could have confined eligibility for repayment to certain social classes, or left repayment to the discretion of executive officials, such stipulations would only have shrunk the market back toward its Machiavellian size. Thus, all parliamentary debts were made transferable.

Another example of how transferability of sovereign promises followed, soon after they became parliamentary, is title to real property. Chapter 7 described the emergence of a parliamentary monopoly over common-law writs 1215–1258. Soon thereafter, *De Donis* (1285) substantially improved the transferability of certain usage rights.

Patents of monopoly provide a third example of sovereign promises that were hard to transfer when royal but became alienable once they were parliamentary. Especially before the Statute of Monopolies, the recipients of "unearned" monopolies never, as far as I know, sought to sell them to another group. To do so would have been tricky. Could the purchasers extract a comparable Machiavellian performance from the Crown? If they were politically uninfluential, then the Crown would simply rescind their privileges and sell them to someone else. Thus, the logic of Machiavellian performance hindered transferability. In contrast, once royal evasions of the Statute of Monopolies had been rendered unlikely after the Revolution, it became perfectly sensible to purchase patents regardless of one's influence at court.

My discussion here echoes North, Wallis, and Weingast's (2009) seminal discussion of impersonality. The main differences are that I focus on transferability, rather than the broader concept of impersonality, and view the extent of transferability as hinging on the legal nature of the state's promises. Machiavellian promises were hard to transfer because performance depended on the holder's ability to punish. Rule-of-law promises were easy to transfer because performance, in equilibrium, did not depend on the holder's ability to punish (and was highly likely).

The demand for transferable sovereign promises facilitated the emergence of vibrant primary and secondary markets, along with brokers to manage them. As argued in several previous chapters, the brokers structurally biased the political process toward performance. One might say the same about the secondary markets, where prices could render swift judgments on government pronouncements relevant to future performance.

Summary

When England's sovereign promises were Machiavellian, promise holders insisted on decentralized performance, imposed strict credit limits when performance was centralized, and found it hard to transfer their claims to other investors. After sovereign promises became parliamentary monopolies, promise holders preferred centralized performance, relaxed their credit limits, and found it easy to transfer their claims.

These sea changes in promise holders' tactics provide further evidence that investors after the Revolution actually relied on state promises. In terms of Equation (1), they assigned a high value to P. Their change of tactics makes sense only given such a belief.

Cumulatively, investors' new tactics meant that the state was – all else equal – less exposed to liquidity crises. Although the English quickly ensured that all else was not equal by taxing and borrowing at much higher rates than ever before, the improved flexibility and resilience of public finances was still an important achievement.

Consequences and Causes of Institutional Reforms

The central claims I make in this book concern the *consequences* of particular political reforms. At various points, however, I also assert that actors pushed those reforms with an eye to securing their consequences. In this section, I consider these "functionalist" assertions about the origin of political reform.

To convincingly explain why particular reforms were instituted at particular times would require much more argument and evidence than I provide in this book. Among other things, one would wish to consider who supported and opposed particular reforms, what each side said about their likely consequences, and so forth. I do none of that. Thus, my comments about the causes of political reform remain speculative.

That said, the bigger the effects of a particular reform *ex post* and the clearer the reasons to expect them *ex ante*, the more plausible it is that someone pushed the reform in order to secure its anticipated effects. As regards the central reform on which I focus – the establishment of a parliamentary monopoly (aka the rule of law) in some domain – the effects were quite large and contemporaries might well have anticipated the reasons for those effects.

In particular, I believe those pushing Magna Carta, the Provisions of Oxford, and the second Statute of Westminster wished to protect property, thought the various clauses cited in Chapter 7 would help, and pushed them for that reason. Similarly, I believe those pushing ministerial responsibility (see Chapter 2) sought the effects it in fact had (and here Clayton 1966 provides considerable relevant evidence). Finally, I believe that the European business elites promoting annual budgets with shut-down reversions (see Chapter 10) viewed them as essential to improving their control over state expenditures, and demanded them for that reason.

Some other reforms I consider are less directly related to my central concerns, and I have less at stake in my speculations about their causes. For example, I suggest that regulation of placemen was relaxed in 1706 in part because ministerial responsibility offered a superior bulwark against royal misbehavior, and I suggest the Calico Act was repealed in 1774 because the deadweight losses it imposed had grown by then. I think these ideas merit further investigation but their truth or falsity touches the main thesis of the book only indirectly.

Exporting British Parliamentarism

At this point, it is useful to consider briefly why it might be hard for other countries to imitate the Glorious Revolution and get similar results. One answer has to do with the difficulty of implementing a comprehensive enough reform. Fashioning a chain with no weak links is not easy. Moreover, countries that adopt many but not all the constraints of the English system may achieve a much lower level of executive constraint, because overall constraint is determined by the weakest link. Thus, reforms in imitation of Great Britain, even if sincere, may fail because the dose of reform they administer is too small.

Another reason that imitators of British parliamentarism may not experience large fiscal responses has to do with the regime from which they are starting. Pre-1688 England had two important characteristics that helped increase its response to the dose of reform administered at the Revolution. First, England was a divided fiscal regime with active ideological disagreements about what the state should do. Thus, its pre-revolutionary tax revenues were substantially depressed and the increase in taxation from before to after 1688 larger than it might have been, had the prerevolutionary regime been less gridlocked. Second, England had a unified tax regime, with the central government able to set tax rates for the entire nation and possessed of a bureaucracy able to collect them. Thus, when the state's credibility problem was solved, the full potential of its unified tax regime could be realized relatively quickly.[4] Imitators of Britain sometimes lacked one or both of these pre-reform conditions. Their response to improved credibility could thus be considerably smaller and slower. In the next three chapters, I explore the British constitutional diaspora more systematically.

---

[4] The importance of unified tax regimes has been urged, and documented, by Epstein (2000), O'Brien (2002), and Dincecco (2011), among others.

PART II

THE ENGLISH CONSTITUTIONAL DIASPORA

10

Exporting the Revolution – The
Early Adopters

"He who ... reduces the budget to such a point that the whole business of government comes to an end, is only fit for a madhouse." – King Wilhelm I of Prussia, 1863 (quoted in Bismarck 1899, p. 336).

The Glorious Revolution is perhaps the single most important seedbed of Western constitutionalism. As other European nations pondered Great Britain's military and economic successes, they adopted features of what they took the Revolution settlement to be. This chapter investigates the earliest adopters of English parliamentarism – the major states of west and central Europe in the late eighteenth and nineteenth centuries – focusing on how they sought to control public expenditures.

The first step toward imitating English fiscal practices was to require that national budgets – plans or promises of expenditure to be made in the coming year – be annually approved by Parliament. Yet, annual statutory budgets were not enough. Much depended on what happened if MPs refused their support – or on what I call the budgetary reversion. The English made sure that (a) the executive's legal authority to *collect* revenues automatically lapsed or (b) the executive's legal authority to *spend* public revenues automatically lapsed or (c) both. Thus, a budget deal had to be done or parts of the government – including the military – would be forced to "shut down."

As I will show, not all nineteenth-century imitators of Britain's constitution mandated shutdown reversions. If no agreement could be reached with Parliament, some allowed the executive to carry on with the previous year's budget, while others allowed the executive simply to promulgate the budget by decree. Both of these alternative budgetary reversions avoided the madhouse situation King Wilhelm I decried, but in the process they substantially undercut Parliament's bargaining leverage. To explore how annual budgets coupled with differing budgetary reversions affected state revenues, I rely on the data assembled by Dincecco (2011; Dincecco, Federico, and Vindigni 2011).

The English Budget

As noted in Chapter 2, English MPs used two basic methods to punish the Crown should it spend appropriated revenues contrary to statutory intent. The earliest method was to ensure that the Crown's legal authority to collect certain taxes lapsed after a certain date.[1] Thus, if the Crown misappropriated revenues, MPs could retaliate simply by allowing revenues to lapse.

A second method, which the American colonists enshrined in their constitution of 1787, was to ensure that authority to expend public revenues automatically lapsed. The appropriation clause of the U.S. Constitution effectively required a "government shutdown" should the annual appropriations bill for one or another part of the government machinery not be enacted.[2]

Because either tax or expenditure authority would lapse every year, forcing portions of the government to "shut down," parliamentarians were assured the Crown would seek a new budget every year, whereupon they could bargain for attainment of their various goals. As Madison put it, "This power over the purse may ... be regarded as the most complete and effectual weapon with which any constitution can arm the immediate representatives of the people, for obtaining a redress of every grievance, and for carrying into effect every just and salutary measure" (2009 [1788], p. 298).

Montesquieu had earlier stressed the complementary point that disabling the power of the purse risked tyranny: "If the executive power enacts on the raising of public funds without the consent of the legislature,

---

[1] Redlich notes that, even in the twentieth century, the Commons continued to insist that a few important tax grants should automatically expire (1908, vol. III, p. 126).

[2] There were only two ways to avoid this result. First, Congress might explicitly provide for temporary funding, via what eventually came to be called a continuing resolution. Second, Congress might provide for what were effectively "permanent appropriations," as for example in the Anti-Deficiency Act. As long as Congress did not offer a permanent appropriation that was too generous, its bargaining position was similar to the English Parliament's. In particular, mere congressional inaction would cause a painful contraction of expenditure.

there will no longer be liberty, because the executive power will become the legislator on the most important point of legislation" (1989 [1748], pp. 164). In other words, the legislature's right to deny the funds requested by the executive was essential to ensure it could check and balance the latter's ambitions. As the Whig leader Charles James Fox put it, writing a few years before Madison, "To withhold the demanded funds is the most powerful of all weapons ... [and] makes the difference between a free people and the slaves of an absolute monarchy" (1784, quoted in Stourm 1917, p. 385).

A Typology of Budgets

Before investigating whether early imitators of British fiscal practices took Fox's maxim to heart, consider the wider menu from which they might have chosen. Budgetary processes can be divided into categories, depending on who has the de jure right to (1) set the budget; (2) levy the taxes needed to fund the expenditures in the budget; and (3) execute and, if necessary, revise the budget. Let's consider each stage in order.

Setting the budget means deciding the *planned* expenditures for the coming fiscal year. The plan, once decided, can be given legal force either by decree or by statute. In the latter case, the statute can be enacted either under ordinary legislative procedures (in which case I call the statute "parliamentary") or under special procedures that advantage the executive (in which case I call the statute "executive-dictated"). In practice, these three options – setting the budget by decree, by executive-dictated statute, and by parliamentary statute – exhaust the possibilities.

Once the budget – that is, the plan of expenditure – is set, the question of ways and means is raised.[3] The authority to collect taxes, in order to fund planned expenditures, can be granted either by decree or parliamentary statute. In practice, these exhaust the possibilities (as executive-dictated statutes are not used to grant taxes).

Finally, once the budget plan has been set and the taxes necessary to fund it voted, the executive may wish to make changes. If the budget was set by decree, then the government-of-the-day can unilaterally

---

[3] Of course, some taxes are permanent, so not all the taxes required to fund a particular annual plan of expenditure need be raised anew. I shall assume permanent taxes do not suffice to fund the expenditures that the executive would typically desire. Where this is not the case – and permanent taxes are ample – the legislature's position is even weaker than in the scenario I consider here.

TABLE 10.1. *A Typology of Budgeting Processes*

Type of Budgeting Process	Stage 1 Expenditure Plan Set by ...	Stage 2 Taxes Set by ...	Stage 3 Actual Expenditures Constrained by Plan?
Absolutist	Executive decree	Executive decree	No
Machiavellian	Executive decree	Parliamentary statute	No
Rechtsstaat	Executive-dictated statute	Parliamentary statute	Yes
Rule-of-law	Parliamentary statute	Parliamentary statute	Yes

order any impoundments or virements it might desire by a new decree. In this case, actual expenditures are legally unconstrained by the original expenditure plan. Otherwise, if the budget was set by statute (whether executive-dictated or parliamentary), then the government-of-the-day cannot unilaterally impound or vire, in which case actual expenditures are legally constrained by the original budget.

A budgetary process consists of rules stipulating how the budget is set, how taxes to fund the budget are levied, and whether the executive is constrained by the budget or not. Table 10.1 displays the four most commonly observed combinations of these three variables in European history.

First, if the executive sets the budget by decree, levies taxes by decree, and revises the budget at will, then the budgeting process is "absolutist." Second, if the executive sets the budget plan by decree, Parliament votes the taxes after hearing that plan, and the executive then spends without being legally constrained by the original plan, then budgeting is "Machiavellian."

A third possibility is that the executive largely determines the budget plan but it is then placed in a statute. This ideal type – of executive-dictated statutory budgets – can be approximated by (a) making the executive's proposal the budgetary reversion and (b) allowing the executive to veto amendments. After seeing the executive's proposed budget, Parliament votes the taxes. When it actually disburses funds, the executive is constrained by the originally announced plan (because it is statutory). In this case, we have what I call a *Rechtsstaat* budget. The logic of such a budget is that the executive will remain fully in control of setting the plan of expenditure but will then be constrained to honor the promises contained in that plan (or at least more constrained than it had been when budgets were purely royal documents).[4]

Finally, in a rule-of-law budgeting process, only Parliament can set the budget, levy taxes, or revise the budget. This was the system the English set up after the Glorious Revolution.

In general, I define the "rule of law" to mean that use of the state's monopoly on coercive force can only be authorized by parliamentary statutes. This excludes absolutist and Machiavellian monarchs, who had the power to authorize the use of force by royal decree. Even though the German word *Rechtsstaat* often translates into English as "rule of law," *Rechtsstaat* rulers did not authorize force exclusively through parliamentary statutes either. For example, some *Rechtsstaat* rulers could issue decrees that immediately obtained the legal force of statutes and retained that force until explicitly rejected by Parliament. These provide another example of what I call "executive-dictated statutes" in Table 10.1.

In Chapters 2 and 3, I examined what happened to English revenues when England transitioned from a mostly Machiavellian budgeting process before 1688 to a mostly rule-of-law process thereafter. In this chapter, I examine a panel of European states, some of which made the same transition, and some of which transitioned from Machiavellian to *Rechtsstaat* budgets. Even the latter polities made important structural improvements in the credibility of their budgets vis-à-vis the *ancien régime*. These improvements, which stemmed from annual publication and statutory entrenchment, can be explained as follows.

Under the *ancien régime*, the publication of budgets was a rare event. In Prussia, for example, "only five budgets were published between 1815 and 1847" (Tilly 1966, p. 491); and in pre-1790 France there was just Necker's "Account to the King" of 1781. Once annual budgets commenced, subjects had a substantially clearer idea of what expenditures the state had promised to undertake in the coming year. Thus, the sovereign promises contained in the budget could be more effectively monitored for compliance.

In addition, embedding budgets in statutes made it harder for a government to legally revise its budgetary promises. In the *ancien régime*, the Crown could engage in impoundment (the refusal to spend funds for the purpose originally promised) or virement (the expenditure of funds, originally earmarked for one purpose, for another instead) at will. Few would

---

[4] I call this a *Rechtsstaat* budget because it seems to fit with the limited aims of German liberalism, as described, e.g., in Mork (1971), Hahn (1977), and Flynn (1988).

even know of these royal changes, because the budget had never been published in the first place. Once budgets became annual and statutory, unilateral virements and impoundments by the executive became either technically illegal or, at least, politically contestable.[5]

Although *Rechtsstaat* budgets clearly improved the credibility of sovereign promises about how public revenues would be spent, they fell short of what could be attained in rule-of-law processes. In particular, because the budgetary reversion gave the government great discretion in setting the budget, it could not make credible commitments about future budgets. Thus, a version of the credibility problem afflicting Machiavellian processes persisted.

All told, the credibility of a state's commitment to expend public revenues as promised in the state's budget clearly improved as it moved from absolutist or Machiavellian budgets to *Rechtsstaat* budgets, and improved further with a move to rule-of-law budgets. In this chapter, I investigate whether MPs became more willing to authorize tax increases when the government could better commit to spending the resulting revenues in specific ways.

The Early Imitators

In important work, Dincecco has examined the revenue consequences of limited government in Europe. He counts a government as becoming "limited" in the "year that parliament gained a stable constitutional right to control the national budget on an annual basis" (2011, p. 28).

To give a flavor of his findings, Table 10.2 shows the mean pre- and post-reform revenues (measured in grams of gold per capita) in each of eleven cases for which data exist to make the calculations.[6] As can be seen, mean revenues per capita consistently increased after annual statutory budgets were introduced. Moreover, Dincecco has shown that this basic finding persists in panel regressions, on which more later.

---

[5] Countries vary in how clearly they forbid unilateral impoundment and virement. As late as the 1970s, President Richard Nixon pushed the United States' constitutional envelope by impounding funds against the wishes of Congress's Democratic majority. His actions led eventually to the Congressional Budget and Impoundment Control Act of 1974.

[6] The table excludes Belgium, Denmark, and Italy because Dincecco has no data on revenues for these countries prior to their adoption of annual statutory budgets (in 1831, 1848, and 1861, respectively). It excludes England because it adopted limited government long before the period on which I focus here (1790–1913). It adds Piedmont from Dincecco et al. 2011.

TABLE 10.2. *Per Capita Revenues in Eight European Polities*

Country	Date of Limited Government (Dincecco 2011)	Prior to the Onset of Limited Government		Average Per Capita Revenue[a]	
		Did Parliament Approve Taxes?	Were Taxes Set Centrally?	Before Limited Government	After Limited Government
Austria	1867	Yes	Yes	5.50 (1848–1866)	14.64 (1867–1913)
France	1870	Yes	Yes	11.11 (1790–1869)	30.19 (1870–1913)
Netherlands	1848	Yes	Yes	10.88 (1806–1847)	13.82 (1848–1913)
Piedmont	1848	?	Yes	4.60 (1835–1847)	6.34 (1848–1859)
Portugal[b]	1851	Yes	No	0.73 (1768–1850)	2.60 (1859–1913)
Prussia	1848	Yes[c]	Yes	3.77 (1806–1847)	12.40 (1848–1913)
Spain	1876	Yes	Yes	2.44 (1845–1875)	3.74 (1876–1913)
Sweden[d]	1866	Yes	Yes	2.89 (1750–1860)	9.85 (1866–1913)

[a] The figures are in grams of gold per capita. The figures for Piedmont are from Table 4 of Dincecco et al. (2011). All other figures are from Dincecco's (2011) posted data set.

[b] Note that the comparison in the last two columns is between the period 1768–1850, when Dincecco codes Portugal as absolutist and decentralized, and 1859–1913, when he codes Portugal as limited and centralized.

[c] This is a qualified "yes." See Tilly (1966, p. 488).

[d] Note that the comparison in the last two columns is between the period 1750–1860, when Dincecco codes Sweden as absolutist and decentralized, and 1866–1913, when he codes Sweden as limited and centralized.

The magnitude of the revenue increases was remarkable. Over the half century from 1850 to 1900, mean revenue extraction in west-central Europe doubled on a per capita basis. By the turn of the century, the rate of extraction had reached historically unprecedented levels (and continued to increase during the twentieth century).

Do the results just noted support the expectations laid out in the previous section? They do in part, because Dincecco's judgment of when Parliament "gained a stable constitutional right to control the national budget on an annual basis" largely coincides with my judgment of when annual statutory budgeting began. However, my approach requires examining not just whether Parliament must approve the national budget but also whether non-approval entails a government shutdown. The dose of credibility-enhancing reform that governments received when they first allowed Parliament to annually approve the budget should have depended substantially on the budgetary reversion. Where the reversion was a government shutdown, the response should have been larger. Where the reversion favored the executive, revenues should have grown less robustly.

To explore these predictions, I first consider the cases of Denmark, Spain, and Prussia in some detail. I then turn to panel regressions in the next section.

Denmark's Provisional Period

Like many other European polities, Denmark adopted a liberal constitution in the aftermath of the revolutions of 1848 (and Dincecco accordingly counts its government as "limited" thereafter). Two years after losing Schleswig and Holstein to Prussia, however, Denmark adopted the Revised Constitution of 1866. Article 25 of this charter gave the king recess decree powers. Although recess decrees had to be presented to Parliament at its next sitting, the latter had little chance to reject them, because any resolution by the *Folketing* had to be sanctioned by the king before attaining legal force (Article 24).

In 1875, Jacob Estrup became prime minister of Denmark, leading a minority conservative party at a time when debates over military preparedness dominated domestic politics. In 1877, after failing to secure support in the *Folketing*, Estrup convinced the king to issue the budget as a provisional law under Article 25.

Although elements of the opposition called for a retaliatory "taxpayer revolt," others took a more pragmatic approach. For the next few years, they made sure that Parliament passed the budget, typically after severe cuts to the military budget (Woodhouse 1974, pp. 207–209). By the mid-1880s, however, disputes over military preparedness hardened and Denmark embarked for ten years (1885–1894) on the so-called *provisorietid* [provisional period]. As Woodhouse describes it, "for nine Rigsdag sessions from 1884/85 through 1892/93, the Folketing's rejection of the government's proposed budget was followed, every April 1, by a Provisional Finance Act" (p. 212). Moreover, whereas Estrup had confined the budget of 1877 to areas of agreement between the two chambers of Parliament, during the *provisorietid* no such niceties were observed (p. 211). In particular, massive fortifications protecting Copenhagen were built.

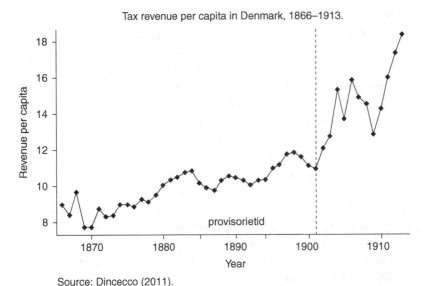

Source: Dincecco (2011).

FIGURE 10.1. Tax revenue per capita in Denmark, 1866–1913.

During the *provisorietid*, then, parliamentary refusal to support the government's budget led simply to the promulgation of that budget by decree. In other words, the budgetary reversion was the executive's choice.

After Copenhagen's fortifications were *faits accomplis*, the government and opposition reached the settlement of 1894, under which budgets were again approved by Parliament. When the conservatives suffered electoral losses in 1901, the king finally appointed a left-wing government and publicly accepted the so-called *systemskifte* [change of system]. Although the principle would not be formally incorporated in the constitution until 1953, henceforth the king lacked the right to promulgate the budget by decree (pp. 216–217).

With this brief vignette in mind, consider Figure 10.1, which presents Dincecco's data on tax revenues per capita in Denmark. Two features of the data merit comment. First, in the period 1866–1900, revenues grew at an average annual rate of 0.094 grams of gold per capita. In contrast, after the onset of parliamentarism, revenues per capita grew at an annual rate more than four times as fast (0.427). Second, during the *provisorietid*, there was no revenue growth at all. Thus, per capita revenue growth in Denmark was closely tied to how parliamentary the sovereign promises embedded in the budget were.

Spain's Budgetary Reversion

Dincecco finds a relatively small increase in Spain's tax revenues after the onset of limited government, which he dates to 1876.[7] I would highlight two features of Spain's 1876 constitution that substantially weakened the *Cortes'* fiscal control, relative to the English benchmark. First, Article 53(7) gave the king full power of intra-departmental virement and (by implication) impoundment. Second, Article 85 ensured that "If the budget cannot be voted before the first day of the next fiscal year, that of the previous year shall remain in force."

Article 85 meant that, if the Deputies refused to approve a budget, then the consequences would not be anything like the immediate shutting down of key parts of the government. Rather, the government could carry on with the previous year's budget, reallocating funds (per Article 53(7)) as it saw fit within very broad budget categories. The bargaining position of the Congress of Deputies under Spain's Constitution of 1876 was thus markedly inferior to that of the House of Commons after the Glorious Revolution.

If the *Cortes'* de jure grip on the purse was debile under the Constitution of 1876, might its de facto grip have been stronger? This seems unlikely because Spanish governments had a history of prolonging budgets by decree. Under the Constitution of 1845, which did not explicitly define the budgetary reversion, ministers nonetheless "frequently recurred to governmental decrees to prolong" the budget. Moreover, "some governments ... abused the extensions" (Comín 2010, p. 228).

Spain did not institute a budgetary reversion favorable to the *Cortes* until the brief Second Republic, for which I have no data on taxation. After that, Spain operated under fiscal absolutism until 1978, when the *Cortes'* control over taxation was restored and a budgetary reversion closer to England's was finally adopted. In Figure 10.2, I plot the available data on Spanish tax revenues per capita from 1965–2005. Before 1978, revenue per capita grew at rate of 0.02 per annum. Afterward, revenues grew more than ten times faster (0.27 per annum).

Bismarck's Prussia

King Friedrich Wilhelm IV of Prussia granted a liberal constitution in 1848, revising it somewhat in 1850. Both charters mandated annual statutory budgets and Dincecco accordingly counts Prussia's government as limited beginning in 1848.

---

[7] Dincecco's coding gibes with the Polity IV project's, which rates executive constraint in Spain at the highest level, 7, over the period 1876–1922.

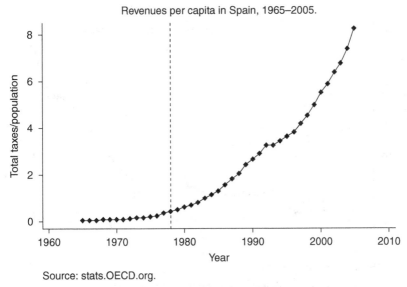

FIGURE 10.2. Revenues per capita in Spain, 1965–2005.

When Otto von Bismarck became Prussia's Minister-President in 1862, the *Landtag* refused to accept the national budget, pressuring Bismarck to change his initially announced policies. The Minister-President responded by observing that the constitution said nothing explicit about what should happen when a budget was not approved and arguing that his responsibility was to keep the government running. Accordingly, he submitted the budget directly to the pliant *Herrenhaus*, which approved it.[8] Prussia's budgets continued to be enacted in this fashion through 1866 (Stourm 1917, pp. 21–22).

After securing military victories against Denmark (1864) and Austria (1866), Bismarck extended an olive branch to Parliament. The government returned to a more regular budgetary process. In return, Parliament enacted an Indemnity Bill that retroactively legalized the state budgets from 1862 to 1866 and indemnified state officials (Mork 1971).[9]

Bismarck continued to push executive prerogatives thereafter. After a dissolution of Parliament and a fervent appeal to patriotism, he succeeded in extracting the first of a series of *Septennats* – seven-year military budgets – from the *Reichstag* in 1874 (Mork 1971). I take this date

---

[8] The Crown appointed the members of the *Herrenhaus* (per Articles 65–68).
[9] The text of the Indemnity Act can be found at *germanhistorydocs.ghi-dc.org*.

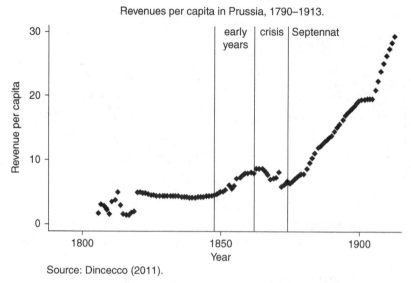

FIGURE 10.3. Revenues per capita in Prussia, 1790–1913.

as ending the period during which mainstream German liberals actively fought for the principle of annual budgets.

The *Reichstag* was not merely a rubber stamp thereafter. It frequently amended government bills; it temporarily blocked a *Septennat* in 1885; and it made trouble on taxes right up to World War I (Mork 1971; Flynn 1988; Berman 2001). However, Prussia differed substantially from the English model. The military budget – which constituted 90 percent of federal expenditures after unification – was typically voted every seven years, not annually. Budgets were proposed by ministers who were not meaningfully responsible to the *Reichstag* (Hahn 1977). Moreover, given the ambiguity of the Prussian and Imperial constitutions, future governments might have resorted again to budgets enacted by one chamber or promulgated the budget by decree.[10,11]

Figure 10.3 displays Prussian revenues per capita from 1790 to 1913. As can be seen, revenues declined gently from the 1820s to the dawn of

[10] Although King Wilhelm I promised in 1866 not to pass budgets only with the *Herrenhaus*' consent again (Stourm 1917, p. 22), the Imperial Constitution of 1871 did not address the ambiguity that Bismarck had exploited in the Prussian constitution. This failure to clarify Parliament's right to deny supply must have represented a victory for those who advocated multiyear budgets and executive control.

[11] The Prussian Constitution (Article 63) afforded recess decree powers that approximated those in Denmark.

the constitutional era in 1848. In the early years of the new constitutional regime, per-capita revenues grew by 0.3 grams of gold per year. During the period of constitutional crisis under Bismarck (1862–1874), revenues *declined* by 0.2 grams per year. After Bismarck established a precedent for seven-year military budgets in 1874, revenues grew by 0.6 grams of gold per year. Indeed, revenues grew so fast that, by the eve of the Great War, the government's ability to secure further grants from the *Reichstag* was increasingly questionable (Berman 2001).

Revenue Growth in Nineteenth-Century European Polities

In this section, I examine revenue growth in Dincecco's sample of European countries more systematically.[12] I sort the countries into three classes, based on how large a dose of fiscal reform their constitutions administered at the onset of stable annual budgeting. France, the Netherlands, and Sweden took large doses, combining annual budgets with shutdown reversions and thus implementing rule-of-law budgets. Austria, Denmark, Portugal, Prussia, and Spain took smaller doses, counteracting the effects of annual budgets by opening the possibility of budgets by decree (Austria,[13] Denmark, Portugal,[14] Prussia) or authorizing the automatic extension of the previous budget (Spain). Meanwhile, Belgium, England, and Italy experienced no constitutional change during the period for which the data set contains observations on their revenues.[15]

---

[12] The only countries that do not have revenue data for the full period (1790–1913) are Austria (1818–1910), Belgium (1831–1913), Denmark (1864–1913), Italy (1862–1913), and the Netherlands (1803–1913). In the latter case, there are data for 1790–1795, followed by a gap 1796–1802. I include only the contiguous block of years in the analysis here.

[13] Finer, describing Austria's "extraordinary Article 14," which conferred recess decree powers similar to Denmark's, notes that "this power was used extensively to sail right over the head of the *Reichsrat* at the emperor's pleasure" (1999, vol. III, p. 1605). I would simply add that Article 14 explicitly allowed decisions to spend public revenues to be taken during recesses.

[14] The Portuguese Constitution of 1826 gave the Crown exclusive control of the armed forces (Article 116) and imposed a broad and vague mandate to use them as the Crown saw fit to protect public safety (Articles 75(4) and 75(15)). In addition, it conferred substantial emergency powers (Article 145(34)). In essence, then, the Crown had a sort of "blank check" to spend money to maintain internal order, even if not envisaged in the budget.

[15] Dincecco's revenue data for England do go back before the Glorious Revolution but my analysis here focuses on the years after 1790. Although England did reduce the Civil List in 1830, I do not count this as a significant enough reform to alter its coding for purposes of this analysis.

To explore the consequences of these different doses of limited government, I use ordinary least squares with panel-corrected standard errors
(Beck and Katz, 1995), as did Dincecco. The specification is

$$R_{jt} = \alpha_j + \beta_1 Annual_{jt} + \beta_2 Shutdown_{jt} + \beta_3 Centralized_{jt}$$
$$+ \{controls\} + error \qquad (1)$$

Here, R_{jt} denotes per capita revenues (in grams of gold) in country j at
time t; α_j is a country-specific fixed effect; $Annual_{jt}$ is Dincecco's variable
indicating the onset of annual budgeting; $Shutdown_{jt}$ is a new variable
indicating that, when annual budgeting began, it was combined with a
shutdown reversion; and $Centralized_{jt}$ is a dummy variable indicating
that the national government could set uniform tax rates for the entire
country. In Model 1, I use Dincecco's battery of control variables – which
focus on warfare, urbanization, and changes in the global gold stock.
Model 2 adds a time trend to the list of controls. The error includes a
common AR1 term and adjusts for both contemporaneous correlations
and panel heteroscedasticity.

Table 10.3 presents estimates of both models. Among the control variables, the most important driver of revenues was warfare, measured by
the population of the alliance against which a country was fighting (if
any). One way to summarize the effect of warfare is to say that the major
powers – those involved in more and bigger conflicts – extracted substantially more revenues per capita, holding constant their constitutional
structures. Circa 1900, for example, Austria and Prussia had much higher
revenues per capita than Spain and Portugal, while England and France
had much higher revenues than Sweden and the Netherlands.

The centralization of taxation does not show large effects in the
post-1790 sample. Most countries centralized before they adopted limited government, so estimating the effect of centralization is substantially
affected by truncating the pre-1790 data.

The other control variables show results similar to those Dincecco
reported. After warfare, the most important control is for changes in the
global gold stock. The rate of urbanization is also important (in Model 1)
but washes out in the presence of a time trend (Model 2).

Since revenues were trending upward across the continent, I focus on
Model 2 here. As can be seen, the onset of regular annual budgeting
boosted per capita revenues by about 0.81 grams of gold, while annual
budgeting combined with shutdown reversions boosted per capita revenues by 0.81 + 1.69 = 2.50 grams of gold. In other words, taking a full

TABLE 10.3. *Panel Regressions Explaining Per Capita Revenues*

Independent Variable	Model 1 Coefficient (Standard Error)	Model 2 Coefficient (Standard Error)
Annual budgets	1.41*** (0.33)	0.81* (0.34)
Annual budgets with shutdown reversions	1.72*** (0.61)	1.69*** (0.61)
Centralized taxation	0.01 (0.31)	−0.53 (0.33)
War deaths	0.08 (0.12)	0.08 (0.11)
Enemy coalition size	0.15*** (0.05)	0.15*** (0.05)
Mercenary dummy	−0.40 (0.23)	−0.37 (0.23)
Internal war dummy	−0.15 (0.13)	−0.10 (0.13)
Urbanization rate	20.03*** (6.96)	1.69 (7.28)
Change in gold stock	0.31*** (0.05)	0.16*** (0.06)
Trend	-	0.09*** (0.02)
Country dummies	Yes	Yes
Number of observations	1138	1138
R^2	0.27	0.27

*** p value < .01; ** p value < .05; * p value < .10.

dose of reform produced more than three times the fiscal response on average as taking a limited dose.

A Difference-in-Differences Approach

A somewhat different approach is to examine pairs of similar countries just before and after one of them introduces fiscal reforms. An example is provided in Figure 10.4, which displays revenues per capita in France and Prussia ten years before and after the Franco-Prussian War of 1870. Both states exhibited gently declining revenues per capita 1860–1869 and gently inclining revenues 1870–1879. The big difference is that French revenues step up by more than 60 percent in 1870, when Emperor Napoleon III fell from power and the Third Republic was instituted, while Prussian revenues show no response in that year.

France's fiscal response in 1870 might of course have been due to losing the war and paying reparations. We cannot observe the counterfactual world in which Napoleon III remained in power, in order to see whether he would have been able to boost revenues in a comparable fashion. We can, however, run a panel regression including both year and country fixed effects. To the extent that countries share a common trend in revenue growth, this difference-in-differences approach should estimate the causal effect of annual budgeting with shutdown reversions, based on a series of comparisons similar to that illustrated in Figure 10.4.

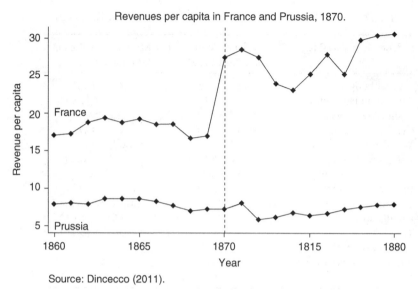

Source: Dincecco (2011).

FIGURE 10.4. Revenues per capita in France and Prussia, 1870.

I have run such regressions, including the same controls for warfare and gold supply as in Table 10.2. The results are very similar. Introducing annual statutory budgets boosts revenue, but the boost is significantly larger when shutdown reversions are also implemented.

Discussion

My interpretation of the results presented earlier is that they support a weakest-link view of executive constraint. While the monarchs of Austria, Denmark, Portugal, Prussia, and Spain did accept annual statutory budgets, their constitutions offered them avenues of escape, either clearly (Austria, Spain) or debatably (Denmark, Portugal, Prussia) within their legal rights to take should bargaining with MPs become too difficult. The existence of these potential avenues of escape eroded MPs' ability to control expenditure. Thus, MPs in these countries should – all else equal – have been more reluctant to authorize higher taxes than their counterparts in more fiscally limited monarchies. The evidence suggests they were.

Why were Annual Statutory Budgets Instituted?

But why did particular countries institute annual statutory budgets when they did? Relatedly, if annual budgets boosted credibility and hence revenues, why did rulers wait until the nineteenth century to imitate British practices?

When an absolutist monarchy granted annual budgets, the Crown was trading its ancient de jure right to control public expenditures, in order to secure financing for projects that it could not swing on its own. For example, in England after the Glorious Revolution (see previous chapters), in Piedmont before the *Statuto Albertino* of 1848 (see Dincecco et al. 2011), and in Prussia before the Constitution of 1848 (see Tilly 1966), business and commercial elites convinced the Crown that substantial new fiscal-military investments could be made if and only if Parliament were granted a more credible role in state finances. The reason for fiscal reform was to carve out a credible enough role for Parliament to clinch a mutually profitable deal.[16]

If commercial elites lobbied for those reforms, then why not say that the rise of the commercial elite was the root cause, at least in these cases? Even if we posit that a united front among business elites caused annual statutory budgets to be instituted in some particular cases, there are still two possibilities as regards the effect of such reforms. One is that the fiscal reforms had no further significant effect on the credibility of state budgets, above and beyond the increase in credibility one would expect from the appearance of a united business elite. In this case, it might be reasonable to say that the rise of the commercial elites was the fundamental cause. However, another possibility is that the fiscal reforms had some significant additional effect. In this case, the rise of commercial elites drove the reforms but those reforms were important, even crucial, in enhancing credibility – which is why the business elites demanded them.

My view is that English, Prussian, and Piedmontese business leaders knew what they were doing. They could have allowed the Machiavellian budgetary process to continue, hoping that their united front would allow them to punish repudiations by the Crown more severely. Instead of taking the Machiavellian option, however, business elites sought fiscal reforms. They presumably realized that their ability to punish repudiations would require constant organization and that, even then, they would need to carefully calculate the Crown's "credit limit."

With fiscal reforms, business elites could secure two kinds of more permanent and secure advantages. First, statutory budgets would be harder

---

[16] In the smaller German states prior to unification, leaders similarly "viewed constitutions and parliaments as assuring a 'bargain' to ease the process of taxation," although here the aim was more to ease the burden of past war debts than to gear up for new wars (Ziblatt 2006, p. 117).

to change and thus more reliable. Second, annual budgets with shut-down reversions would effectively give Parliament the right to control public expenditures. To the extent that business elites were confident of their influence in Parliament, they could then protect themselves against unwanted future changes of budgetary course.

In other words, entrepreneurs investing in fiscal-military states, just like venture capitalists investing in private corporations, wanted control rights to protect themselves against *ex post* opportunism (Bolton and Dewatripont 2005, p. 527). They thus made fiscal reform the sine qua non of their cooperation. Once in place, the reforms deeply affected the credibility of state budgets, quite independently of how they came into being. In that sense, the story told here is a thoroughly institutional one.

That said, the account just offered also suggests the effects of fiscal reform will not be the same in all polities. If the business elite's ability to both withhold taxes absent reform and grant taxes with reform is key to convincing the Crown to cede power, then polities that lack business elites with this ability would never adopt the reforms. Moreover, if rule-of-law budgets were somehow introduced – say when a colony becomes independent – one would not expect them to generate additional revenues. Rather, one would expect the executive to quickly rescind them, since doing so would restore full power over expenditures without much damaging the ability to raise revenues.

Why Not Sooner?

If Europe's absolutist rulers could not achieve high per-capita tax revenues by force or Machiavellian deals, then why did they wait so long to improve the credibility of their expenditure plans? The problems were several.

The Crown's Reluctance to Trade

Absolutist rulers were trading away control rights whose value they knew well. Indeed, the right to dispense public revenues was the foundation of their power. Such rulers, moreover, would have understood that granting annual statutory budgets, much less shutdown reversions, would permanently reduce their ability to control expenditures. Given the immense and durable value of the control rights they were trading, monarchs needed a very good reason to alienate some of that power. Thus, one answer to "why not sooner?" is simply that historical circumstances had to arise in which the Crown so desperately wanted immediate financing for a valuable project that it was willing to sacrifice slices of de jure power to get it.

In the weaker Iberian regimes, imperial collapse after the Napoleonic wars forced the Crown to deal, as the price for staying in power. In the healthier absolutist regimes, such as Piedmont and Prussia, the opportunity for railway-led industrialization – in imitation of Britain, the world's first industrial nation and global hegemon – finally convinced the Crown to deal.

Commitment Problems and the Instability of the Rechtsstaat Monarchies

Even when a compelling reason to alienate control over expenditure presented itself, however, commitment problems plagued bargaining. In particular, a version of the old credibility deficit plaguing the *ancien régime* remained in the *Rechtsstaat* monarchies.

To illustrate, consider a polity in which the government can promulgate the budget by decree if it fails to secure parliamentary support. After a fiscal shock, suppose the executive and Parliament reach a deal on a package of new taxes and expenditures. Can the entire deal be implemented within a single year? If not, then Parliament must either ensure that the taxes expire annually or trust that the executive's future budgets will continue to implement whatever deal has been struck. But the executive can effectively dictate future budgets and secure their passage against the will of mere parliamentary majorities. Thus, any promises it makes about future budgets are not credible.

The inability of the Crown in *Rechtsstaat* monarchies to make long-term budgetary commitments should have complicated bargaining and raised the risk of fiscal stalemate. When actual stalemate arose, however, governments would face a choice: Should they do nothing and live with the structural risk of stalemate? Should they end stalemate by repressing Parliament's fiscal rights? Or should they end stalemate by accepting ministerial responsibility and a parliamentary monopoly over both taxes and expenditures?

The trilemma just noted was inherent in states with *Rechtsstaat* budgets. They had merely replaced a Machiavellian crown under the *ancien régime* with a monarch who could make credible but short-term promises about expenditure. Thus, the risk of inefficient executive-legislative stalemate remained significantly higher than in the benchmark case of Britain.

The Fiscal Common Pool

A final reason that absolutist monarchs may have resisted reforms to improve the credibility of their expenditure promises concerns the fiscal common pool. Advocates of royal power might have thought that giving Parliament the right to decide state expenditures would set up an even worse system. Instead of executive moral hazard, with kings chasing military glory at the taxpayers' expense (Hoffman 2009; Cox 2011), one might have a special interest feeding frenzy, with MPs funding pet projects at the taxpayers' expense. I return to this issue in the final chapter.

Conclusion

Per-capita tax revenues grew in those European states that, in imitation of Great Britain, adopted annual statutory budgets. However, these countries differed substantially in how much de jure bargaining leverage they gave to their post-reform legislatures, and their revenue growth varied accordingly. Some polities gave their parliaments little leverage and experienced meager revenue growth: Portugal and Spain. Others also gave their parliaments little leverage but got more out of them: Austria and Prussia. Finally, a handful of countries gave their parliaments better leverage and, on average, experienced the greatest revenue growth: France, Netherlands, Sweden, and (after 1901) Denmark.

The process of fiscal reform constituted a trade, in which the Crown gave away some of its constitutional rights in exchange for future tax revenues. Because all crowns greatly valued their de jure rights to control the expenditure of public revenues, they were willing to trade those rights only for sufficient recompense. Parliamentary elites made the following offer: we will grant higher taxes if and only if we are given greater control rights over state expenditures. This was a credible offer that crowns eventually took, albeit only when historical conjunctures arose at which they particularly craved the additional revenues that only Parliament could help them get.

11

Exporting the Revolution – The Late Adopters

After the first wave of English parliamentarism had washed over nineteenth-century Europe, subsequent waves – mediated mostly by colonization – swept the globe. The vast bulk of these late adopters' constitutions mandated an annual statutory budget. Yet, the resulting budgets have often been little more than executive promises. In other words, the first step England took to limit the executive has not been taken by many of its inheritors and imitators worldwide.

To avoid the trammels of legislative bargaining, executives have pursued the same three strategies Stuart monarchs used – but with more success. First, some rulers have reached power by militarily crushing their political oppositions. Such rulers, when they issue annual budgets, do not subject them to meaningful legislative approval. Second, some rulers have established one-party states in which the legislature is no longer independent. Legislative approval in these cases is a foregone conclusion. Third, some rulers have defanged their legislatures, reducing their de jure control over state expenditures.

Because violence and one-partyism are both well-recognized routes to autocracy, I focus here on the last and least obvious tactic of executive control: removing the legislature's de jure fiscal rights. Although some constitutions, such as Saudi Arabia's, confer no power on the legislature at all, most confer an incomplete set of rights, leaving gaps the executive can exploit. In particular, many constitutions have created executive decree powers at least as strong as those conferred by Denmark's Revised Constitution of 1866, while others have mandated budgetary reversions no less favorable to the executive than Spain's Constitution of 1876. Even when these provisions have not been actively exploited, their mere existence has undermined the legislature's bargaining position vis-à-vis the executive and, accordingly, lessened the extent to which national budgets are parliamentary promises.

To elaborate these points, I proceed as follows. Sections 11.1 and 11.2 discuss what I call executive-favoring budgetary reversions (or EFRs). Section 11.3 shows that the world's constitutions, over the period 1875–2005, have increasingly opted for EFRs. Sections 11.4–11.6 examine some consequences of EFRs. In particular, I explore how they affect tax revenues in a cross-section of sixty-seven democracies; and the duration of democracies over the period 1875–2005.

Can Polities Live with Persistent Threats to Shut Down the Government?

When the French finally imitated British practice, mandating a shutdown reversion in 1870, they feared cataclysm: "if the year were to open without the budget having been voted, the bondholders could not get their interest; nor the pensioners their pensions; the tradesmen would beat in vain at the gates of the Treasury; the officials would work without salaries; the schools would be closed; the Army would be deprived of its pay ... [and] the activities of the country would be paralyzed" (Stourm 1917, p. 381). Seven years later, cataclysm loomed when the legislature sought to force a ministry out of office by denying funds. Fears of armed conflict arose, partisan animosities were on full display, and an actual shutdown was averted only at the last moment (Stourm 1917, pp. 387–388).

The French example highlights an obvious problem with shutdown reversions. If denial of funds is to be its "most complete and effectual weapon," then the legislature must sometimes threaten to deny funds. Since inter-branch bargaining may fail, actual shutdowns may occur – as in the United States in 1995 and 2013. But shutdowns are extremely disruptive and unpopular, even when they do not reach the cataclysmic proportions feared in the Third Republic. Thus, whenever bargaining in a country with a shutdown reversion fails, citizens naturally ask how such shutdowns can be avoided in future.

The parliamentary method of avoiding shutdowns is simple. Governments that cannot pass a budget typically resign, lest they be ousted via a vote of no confidence. Parliament itself then dictates what sort of temporary financial arrangements will be made until a new (non-caretaker) government forms that can pass a budget. The ability of

Parliament to remove the ministry at will ensures that the government never actually shuts down, even if the constitution requires closure in the absence of funding approved by Parliament.[1]

In presidential and semi-presidential regimes, various reforms have been proposed to avoid shutdowns. One kind of reform seeks to ensure the assembly's preferences coincide with the executive's. In the extreme, this leads to a one-party regime in which the president controls legislative nominations.

Another kind of reform seeks to reduce the assembly's ability to veto the budget. In the extreme, a country's rulers might wholly abrogate the legislature's fiscal powers. However, outside periods of rule by military juntas, this is rare: the vast bulk of contemporary constitutions endow their legislatures with the right to approve taxes, loans, and the state budget.[2]

A much more common method of reducing the legislature's power to deny funds has been to institute an EFR. EFRs come in two types – one in which the budget reverts to the executive's proposal, and one in which the budget reverts to a modified version of the previous year's budget. Let's consider each in turn.

Executive-Favoring Reversions

Reversion to the Executive's Proposal

Article 44.4 of Chile's Constitution of 1925 stipulated that, if no new budget had been adopted by the beginning of the new fiscal year, the executive's proposal would automatically come into force. To see the effect of this clause, suppose that a cohesive legislative coalition, controlling majorities in both chambers of Congress, disliked the president's proposal. What could such a coalition's members do?

They could reject the proposal – but then the reversion (the executive's proposal) would come into force. If they amended the proposal,

---

[1] On rare occasions, the government shuts down in bicameral parliamentary regimes when the two chambers cannot reach agreement. An example is Australia in 1975: http://www.washingtonpost.com/blogs/worldviews/wp/2013/10/01/australia-had-a-government-shutdown-once-it-ended-with-the-queen-firing-everyone-in-parliament/.

[2] According to the Institutions and Elections Project data set (http://www2.binghamton .edu/political-science/institutions-and-elections-project.html), legislative approval of the budget (resp., taxes) was required in 93 percent (resp., 95 percent) of the country-years covered (167 countries, 1972–2005). A survey by the International Parliamentary Union and the World Bank Institute found that the legislature approved the state budget in 92 percent of the fifty-two countries responding (Pelizzo and Stapenhurst 2004, p. 7).

the president could veto the amended budget.[3] If the coalition lacked the two-thirds majority needed to override, no new budget would be enacted by the beginning of the fiscal year, again triggering the reversion. Thus, only a legislative coalition large enough to override a veto could amend the president's budget. To put it another way, the Chilean president could dictate any budget, subject to one constraint: not producing a rebellion in Congress so widespread as to create opposition majorities more than two-thirds in both chambers.

How did such a fiscally impotent assembly come to be established in Chile? Nineteenth-century Chilean legislators clearly viewed EFRs as important threats to their authority: "[T]he Revolution of 1891 originated in a deadlock over the budget. In January 1891, as the Chilean parliament refused to approve the budget ..., President José Manuel Balmaceda decreed that the previous year's budget would remain in effect, thus openly violating constitutional provisions. Parliament proceeded to impeach him and the revolution broke out" (Santiso 2004, p. 14).

The congressional forces triumphed in 1891 and continued to wield the power of the purse thereafter. Congressional majorities would often delay passage of the budget as a bargaining tool, in order to extract policy concessions or force ministers to resign (Guerra 1929, p. 237). In the view of contemporaries favoring a stronger executive, the results were disastrous: budgetary interruptions, shifting legislative majorities, and unstable governments (Guerra 1929, p. 22). The solution, implemented in the new Constitution of 1925, was to break Congress's power of the purse by establishing the executive's proposal as the budgetary reversion (Guerra 1929, p. 268). Henceforth, proponents said, Congress would be able to *approve* the executive's proposed state budget, but could neither delay nor reject it.

Reversion to Last Year's Budget – as an EFR

Reversions to last year's budget also favor the executive in most of the world's constitutions, because the executive can either impound funds or transfer them across budgetary categories under the reversion. In other words, the reversion is not simply "last year's budget." Last year's budget merely establishes some spending caps, with the executive then able to reduce line items or transfer spending across budget categories at will.

---

[3] Some question whether the president can veto the budget under the 1980 constitution (see Siavelis 2002). But there were no questions about the 1925 constitution (see Guerra 1929).

Thus, the reversion is *foreseeably* better for the executive than for his/her legislative opponents, which significantly erodes the latter's bargaining position.[4]

Reversions to last year's budget also favor the executive when they are combined with prohibitions on legislative amendment of the executive's budget proposal. Banning legislative amendments enables the executive to make a take-it-or-leave-it offer on the budget, which is obviously a potent source of influence (Cheibub 2007, p. 103).[5]

Reversion to Last Year's Budget – as Approximating a Government Shutdown

Some countries allow reversionary spending according to last year's budget *but only for a few months*. If no new budget had been approved by the end of this grace period, the government shuts down. Obviously, these time-limited EFRs approximate government shutdowns more and more closely as the grace period shrinks. Other countries allow reversionary spending according to last year's budget *but only in a few specified areas*. These too approximate government shutdowns (more closely as the areas in which spending is allowed to continue shrink). In what follows, I classify EFRs that are subject to strict time or scope limits as government shutdowns.[6]

Summary

All told, two types of EFR exist – reversions to the executive's proposal, and reversions to last year's budget with neither scope nor time limits (and weak regulation of impoundment and virement under the reversion). There are also two types of government shutdown – those that

---

[4] The general importance of regulating the executive's powers of impoundment and virement is widely recognized – see, e.g., Stourm 1917; Wilmerding 1943; Stith 1988. What has been less widely recognized is how impoundment and virement in reversionary budgets erode the legislature's bargaining position.

[5] The prohibition on congressional amendment of the budget is such a potent power that it can reverse the legislature's preferences regarding the reversion. In particular, as Romer and Rosenthal (1978) show, a more extreme reversion is better when one can make a take-it-or-leave-it offer.

[6] More specifically, if a reversion to last year's budget entails a government shutdown within *six months* after the beginning of the new fiscal year, I classify it as an effective government shutdown. In practice, reversions to last year's budget with grace periods between six and twelve months are quite rare. The cutoff of six months thus provides a natural dividing line between those with stringent grace periods (mostly four months or shorter) and those lacking any provisions for an eventual government shutdown. I also classify reversions with scope limits (which are rarer) as effective government shutdowns. An example is Germany under its 1949 constitution.

are immediate and comprehensive; and those with grace periods and/ or scope limits.[7] These four categories exhaust the empirically observed reversions. Henceforth, I usually focus on the binary distinction between EFRs and government shutdowns.

Trends in Budgetary Reversions, 1875–2005

In this section, I exploit an original data set that codes the constitution-ally stipulated budgetary reversions in 165 countries over the period 1875–2005. Countries often have statutes that further elaborate their budgetary reversion (e.g., the United States' Anti-Deficiency Act), but here I focus on constitutionally mandated reversions.

The sample covers every country in the world from the first year in which it operated as a sovereign state under a written constitution until 2005, excluding (a) countries that did not have a population exceeding 500,000 by 1990 (or its last year of existence, if it ceased to exist before 1990); and (b) years before 1875. The starting point of 1875 is a con-venient date after both Italian (1861) and German (1871) unification. Moreover, there are only three spells of democratic government (as coded by Boix, Miller, and Rosato 2012) before 1875, so almost nothing is gained for present purposes by considering the pre-unification state system.[8]

Figure 11.1 displays the number and percentage of constitutions containing EFRs in each year from 1875 to 2005. Where only eleven constitutions stipulated such an EFR in 1875, the number grew almost monotonically, reaching ninety-one in 1982, before falling back to eighty by 2005. The overall percentage also grew, from 31 percent in 1875 to 67 percent in 1982, falling back to 52 percent by 2005. Thus, for most of the twentieth century, the world experienced a striking growth in EFRs.[9]

Figure 11.2 illuminates what has driven the increase in EFRs, by divid-ing the full sample of 165 countries into five quarter-century cohorts.[10] While the first two cohorts exhibit some growth in EFRs over time, most

---

[7] In practice, there are no cases in which scope and time limits are lacking and yet there exist strict regulations of impoundment and virement.

[8] I include the United Kingdom in my sample (as possessing a written but unconsolidated constitution), as well as several cases in which Basic Laws are taken to be the constitution.

[9] Reversions to the executive's proposal increased from 3 percent (1875) to 27 percent (1982), before falling back to 8 percent (2005). EFRs involving a reversion to last year's budget were fairly steady: 28 percent, 30 percent, 28 percent over the same years.

[10] The figure starts plotting each cohort in the year following the period defining it. Thus, the 1875–1899 cohort begins plotting in 1900, the 1900–1924 cohort in 1925, and so on. The exception is the last cohort (1975–2005), which begins plotting in 1990.

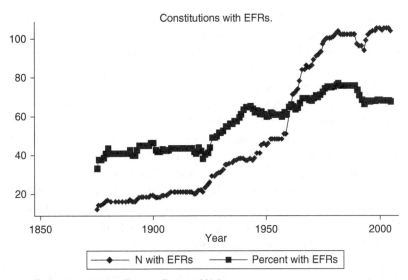

Source: Legislative Powers Dataset V4.2

FIGURE 11.1. Constitutions with EFRs.

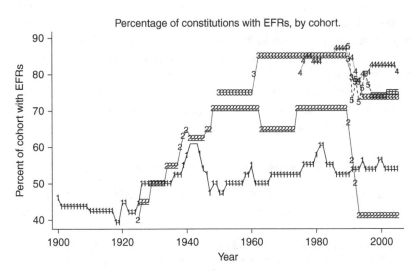

Note: The first cohort is represented by the series of connected 1s, the second cohort by the connected 2s, and so forth.

FIGURE 11.2. Percentage of constitutions with EFRs, by cohort.

of the overall growth is explained by differences between the cohorts.[11] The predilection for EFRs is particularly striking in the last three cohorts, composed largely of countries emerging on the scene after World War I (the 1925–1949 cohort), World War II (the 1950–1974 cohort), and the Cold War (the 1975–2005 cohort).

The extent to which new countries drive the growth in EFRs can also be seen by considering the 160 new EFRs documented in the data set. Of these, 11 (7 percent) are in place as of 1875, 76 (48 percent) arise because a founding constitution mandates an EFR, and 73 (46 percent) correspond to conversions from government shutdowns to EFRs.

A caveat in interpreting the results presented thus far is that some constitutions do not contain *explicit* provisions regarding what happens should no budget be approved by the beginning of the new fiscal year. These cases were coded according to their implicit provisions.[12] Whatever errors exist in these codings, they do not affect the conclusions suggested by Figures 11.1–11.2. Constitutions have been increasingly clear about the budgetary reversion: the percent with explicit clauses increases almost linearly from 22 percent in 1875 to 70 percent in 2005. Looking only at constitutions with explicit clauses, the trends in Figures 11.1 and 11.2 are similar.

What does the upward trend in EFRs just documented mean? There are several ways EFRs might be safeguarded. My view, however, is that they invite further encroachment. To chain the executive is difficult; and EFRs weaken a very important link. From this perspective, we should expect countries with EFRs today to have difficulty raising tax revenues (like nineteenth-century Spain before them) and to be at risk of further moves toward autocracy (as Montesquieu predicted). In the next several sections, I explore these ideas.

Budgetary Reversions and Tax Revenues circa 2005

As argued in Chapter 10, EFRs should erode the credibility of the executive's long-term commitments regarding annual expenditures. Thus, one

---

[11] The decline in EFRs in the second cohort is driven by the democratization of Bulgaria and Poland, along with the restoration of sovereignty to the Baltic republics.

[12] The coding rules were as follows (see the Web appendix for a fuller explanation). If the constitution does not confer the traditional powers of the purse, then the reversion is classified as the executive's proposal. If the constitution confers the right to approve the budget (and possibly also taxes and loans) but opens loopholes (e.g., recess or emergency decree powers) that allow the executive to spend money without explicit legislative approval, then the reversion is classified as favoring the executive. Otherwise – powers conferred, no loopholes – the reversion is classified as favoring the legislature.

expects that more taxes should be granted and collected when platforms are more credible (due to shutdown reversions) than when they are less credible (due to EFRs).[13]

The taxes-for-platforms market should also operate more efficiently, when expenditure promises are more credible. When political entrepreneurs seek to finance new projects, they can more easily assure prospective purchasers (MPs) that the revenues really will be spent on the proposed project. Thus, the transaction costs of financing public projects decline – which should also boost taxes (in regimes with shutdown reversions relative to otherwise similar regimes with EFRs). In this section, I explore the connection between budgetary reversions and tax receipts in contemporary democracies.

Cross-sectional Evidence

In this section, I consider sixty-seven democratic countries circa 2005 – all those for which the World Bank's World Development Indicators provided data on tax revenues as a percent of GDP. As Model 1 of Table 11.1 shows, there is a significant bivariate correlation between tax revenues and shutdown reversions. The twenty democratic countries that lacked such reversions collected taxes that amounted to 14.3 percent of their respective 2005 GDPs. In contrast, the forty-seven democracies with shutdown reversions collected an additional 5.8 percent of GDP in taxes, for a total of 20.1 percent.

This bivariate correlation remains largely intact, as can be seen in Models 2–7, when one controls for whether the regime is parliamentary, an index of legislative powers, polity's democracy score, polity's executive constraints index, whether the country had an English common-law legal heritage, or GDP per capita. The first five control variables offer alternative ways of coding whether the executive is constrained or not. Two of them – whether the regime is parliamentary and whether the country has a common-law heritage – are based on purely de jure information. The other three, however, reflect coders' judgments about how

---

[13] Giving the executive long-term expenditure authority, as with Prussia's *Septennats*, does not solve the problem. Long-term authorizations mean the executive can violate the spirit of any expenditure promise with relative impunity, given the long lag until Parliament will have an opportunity to retaliate. Moreover, specifying everything in the letter of the appropriation is infeasible. Assemblies do try to reduce executive discretion, by multiplying line items in the budget. But even in the United States, where line items abound, legislators facing a president not of their own party are often dissatisfied with their ability to control executive branch expenditures and behaviors and react by underfunding agencies, among other tactics (McCarty 2004).

TABLE 11.1. *Tax Revenues as a Function of Shutdown Reversions*

Independent Variable	Model 1	Model 2	Model 3	Model 4	Model 5	Model 6	Model 7
Constant	14.3***	13.7***	17.1***	0.81	-3.8	13.6***	13.6***
Shutdown reversion	5.8***	4.8**	6.5***	3.6*	3.8*	5.0***	4.0**
Parliamentary regime	-	2.1	-	-	-	-	-
Legislative Powers Index	-	-	-4.9	-	-	-	-
Polity score	-	-	-	1.7**	-	-	-
Executive constraints index	-	-	-	-	3.0**	-	-
Common law heritage	-	-	-	-	-	4.6**	-
GDP per capita	-	-	-	-	-	-	0.00
N	67	67	67	67	67	67	66
Adjusted R^2	0.11	0.11	0.11	0.18	0.18	0.18	0.13

***p value < .01; **p value < .05; *p value < .1.

TABLE 11.2. *Tax Revenues in Brazil and Venezuela*

Country	Average Taxes as Percent of GDP in Four Years before Reform	Average Taxes as Percent of GDP in Four Years after Reform
Brazil	12.5% (1997–2000)	16.0% (2002–2005)
Venezuela	14.3% (1995–1998)	11.9% (2000–2003)

politics in a particular country play out de facto. It is interesting that whether a country's constitution mandates a shutdown reversion has an effect, even controlling for other variables meant to capture aspects of executive constraint.

As for the final control, GDP per capita, this has a systematic effect when included as the sole predictor: taxes are higher in richer democracies. However, once one includes an indicator for whether the budgetary reversion mandates a government shutdown, the effect of GDP per capita washes out.

Brazil and Venezuela

Among the countries studied earlier, only two democracies changed their constitutionally stipulated budgetary reversions near the middle of the period for which the World Development Indicators provide tax data (1995–2005). Brazil moved from an EFR to a shutdown reversion in 2001 (when it curbed executive decree power) and Venezuela introduced a formal EFR when the Bolivarian constitution was promulgated in 1999.

Table 11.2 presents tax revenues as a percent of GDP in these two countries, averaged over the four years before and after their respective reforms. As can be seen, tax revenues in Brazil increase, from 12.5 percent before the reform (introducing a shutdown reversion) to 16.0 percent after. Meanwhile, tax revenues in Venezuela decline, from 14.3 percent before the reform (entrenching an EFR in the constitution) to 11.9 percent after.[14] Thus, while there is not much over-time evidence to consult in this particular data set, what there is gibes with the theory's expectations.

Are EFRs Compatible with Democracy?

EFRs were part of a global pattern of constitutional reforms intended to strengthen executive power. A wave of such reforms swept interwar

---

[14] Venezuela already had a statutory EFR prior to 1999. Thus, one might have expected the effect of the reform to be small.

Europe under the banner of *parliamentarisme rationalisé* (Lavaux 1988; Huber 1996), and similar reforms were undertaken at various times in Latin America's presidential systems (O'Donnell 1994; Shugart 1998).

EFR proponents argued that a fiscally powerful president was compatible with democracy, because the president would be directly elected. They believed, in other words, that the executive's increased accountability to voters (via direct elections) would make up for any reduction in accountability to legislators that EFRs entailed (e.g., Guerra 1929; Debré 1957, 1959).

There are reasons to expect, however, that EFRs might undermine electoral democracy. Indeed, a standard worry in early modern Europe was that executives would extract rents from the state budget and use those rents to undermine the electoral process;[15] and similar worries seem apt in more recent times. After all, a parliamentary majority must approve the budget when the reversion is a shutdown but only a parliamentary minority must approve it under an EFR. Thus, it should be easier to pass budgets under EFRs that redistribute income to the leader and his/her supporters. Moreover, private transfers become a more efficient means of building coalitions, relative to public goods provision, as the size of the required coalition declines (Cox 1987; Bueno de Mesquita et al. 2003). All told, EFRs both better enable the incumbent executive to redistribute income to his/her core supporters and make such a strategy more attractive.

Incumbent leaders can also use the rents that EFRs confer to buy MPs' support for reforms, such as lifetime presidencies or waivers of term limits, that entrench themselves in power. Alternatively, leaders can use EFR-sourced rents to bias elections in their favor. When incumbents in initially democratic regimes succeed in such efforts, democracy dies. One can characterize the cause of death as an "auto-coup."[16]

Not every EFR plausibly threatens to undermine democratic governments, however. In particular, if the legislative majority can remove the

---

[15] English parliamentarians, even after they had implemented a shutdown reversion, introduced a series of "place bills" limiting the Crown's ability to offer official positions and pensions to legislators; as well as a series of acts seeking to reduce the Crown's ability to influence elections (Foord 1947; Kemp 1957).

[16] Some use the term "auto-coup" narrowly, to refer to clearly unconstitutional, or even violent, actions taken by an incumbent to consolidate power. Here, I use the term broadly, to encompass any successful effort to create a regime in which either (a) the incumbent is insulated de jure from electoral competition; or (b) the electoral process is significantly biased in the incumbent's favor by the usual techniques of "electoral authoritarianism" (Schedler 2002; 2006). My "auto-coups" are close to Maeda's (2010) "endogenous terminations."

executive from office at will, then the latter should be much less able to exploit any EFR. I call an EFR "safeguarded" when the executive can be immediately removed by a legislative majority.[17] Such a threat clearly does *not* exist in presidential regimes. At the opposite extreme, some – but by no means all – parliamentary constitutions give a government no option but to resign when it loses a vote of confidence. In between these extremes, many constitutions allow an assembly majority to vote no confidence but do not then require the government's immediate resignation. While these intermediate cases vary widely in terms of the executive's ability to cling to power after a vote of censure, here I classify them all as giving the executive some ability to remain in power and thus giving it some ability to exploit any EFR that may exist.

In the remainder of this chapter, I contrast democracies that have operated under either shutdown reversions or safeguarded EFRs with those that have operated under unsafeguarded EFRs. I investigate whether these systems differ in their durability and, when they die, their cause of death.

The Durability of Democracy under EFRs

One can find cases that seemingly comport with either the optimistic or pessimistic view of EFRs' compatibility with democracy. Post-authoritarian Chile and France V both have unsafeguarded EFRs, yet one might argue their presidents have nonetheless remained electorally constrained and have not abused their fiscal powers.[18] In Francophone Africa, in contrast, one might argue that democratically elected presidents with EFRs have faced weak electoral constraints and accordingly have abused their fiscal powers.

In this section, I investigate the compatibility of democracy and EFRs more systematically. Were EFRs, as Montesquieu might have opined, invitations to tyranny? Or, as advocates of executive power argued, were EFRs strong medicine whose administration would save rather than endanger democracy?

---

[17] I code an executive as subject to immediate removal if (a) a majority in the lower chamber of the assembly appoints the government and can vote no confidence in the government; and (b) the government must resign when the lower chamber votes no confidence.

[18] See Siavelis (2002, pp. 96–100) for a discussion of why post-authoritarian Chilean presidents have not overtly exploited the EFR reestablished in 1980; and Baldez and Carey (1999) for an analysis that emphasizes how well the president nonetheless does. See Huber 1996, ch. 6 for a detailed case study of the electoral constraints French governments faced in budgetary politics.

To address these questions, I investigate all democratic episodes occurring between 1875 and 2005, as identified by Boix, Miller, and Rosato (2012). For example, by their criteria, Chile was a democracy in 1909–1924, 1934–1972, and 1990–2005. It thus experienced three democratic episodes, lasting fifteen years, thirty-eight years, and fifteen years respectively (with the last being right-censored).[19]

I then identify the budgetary reversion in force at the beginning of each democratic episode. All told my sample includes thirty-two democratic episodes beginning with a reversion to the executive's proposal, thirty-four beginning with a reversion to last year's budget (but approximating a reversion to the executive's proposal), and eighty beginning with a reversion to a government shutdown (or a reversion to last year's budget approximating a shutdown).

Figure 11.3 presents box-and-whisker plots to illustrate how long each democratic episode lasted, as a function of the budgetary reversion in place at the beginning of the episode.[20] As can be seen, democracies tend to survive longer when, at the beginning of their life, the budgetary reversion is a government shutdown. Indeed, fully 25 percent of the democracies that begin with government shutdowns as their reversions have survived longer than the longest-lived democracy that has ever debuted with an EFR.

Do the apparently life-prolonging effects of shutdown reversions disappear when one controls for other factors that affect democratic stability? To explore this matter, I use a parametric survival model to predict the length of each democratic episode. Following recent precedents (Svolik 2008; Reenock, Staton, and Radean 2013), the analysis controls for five variables often cited as important determinants of democratic survival: real income per capita,[21] economic growth, presidentialism,[22] previous breakdowns,[23] and initial quality of democracy (as measured

[19] A few cases in my data set are left-censored at 1875, but those cases have been fixed by using Boix, Miller and Rosato's data set, which extends further back in time.

[20] In my sample, only 5 percent of democracies ever change the reversion with which they begin life.

[21] Przeworski and colleagues documented that higher per capita incomes were good predictors of whether democracy, once it emerged, would stabilize in a particular country. Indeed, they famously observed (2000, p. 98) that "no democracy has ever been subverted ... in a country with a per capita income higher than that of Argentina in 1975: $6,055 [in constant 1985 dollars]."

[22] Linz (1990) famously argued that presidentialism generated a series of incentives that led to democratic breakdown. Cheibub (2007) has since shown that no evidence favors the particular causal mechanisms Linz suggested.

[23] Poole and Londregan (1990) documented that political violence is strongly auto-correlated.

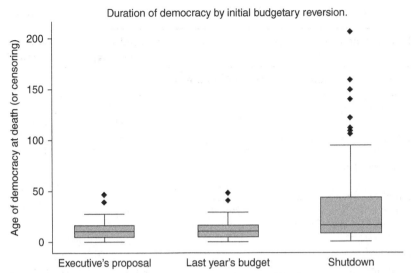

FIGURE 11.3. Duration of democracy by initial budgetary reversion.

by the country's Polity 2 Score).[24] In addition, I control for the decade in which each episode began. The Web appendix provides sources for each variable and summary statistics.

Table 11.3 displays the results based on a Weibull specification with errors clustered by episode.[25] Model 1 focuses on the full sample (146 democratic episodes, 1875–2005) and shows – not surprisingly – that democratic episodes last longer in richer countries with better growth records. More important for present purposes, the model also shows that democracies with shutdown reversions last longer than those with EFRs. For example, a parliamentary regime with no previous breakdowns and income per capita in the second quartile would expect to survive twenty-five years longer, if it began with a shutdown reversion rather than an EFR. Given that the median length of democratic episodes in the sample is fifteen years, this is a substantial effect.

[24] The Polity 2 score, which ranges from −10 (full autocracy) to +10 (full democracy), is a widely used indicator of the quality or level of democracy. See www.systemicpeace.org/ polity/polity4.htm.

[25] Although I present only the Weibull results here, the results do not change significantly when one uses other common distributional assumptions (Gompertz, log-normal, log-logistic). Plotting the cumulative hazard against the Cox-Snell residuals, as Blossfeld, Golsch, and Rohwer recommended (2007, pp. 218–222), reveals a reasonably good fit for any of these models.

TABLE 11.3. *Democratic Death as a Function of the Budgetary Reversion*

Independent Variables	Model 1 (1875–2005)	Model 2 (post-1914)
Budgetary reversion is a government shutdown at t_0	−0.78** (0.36)	−0.95** (0.41)
GDP per capita at t_0	−0.30*** (0.11)	−0.21 (0.18)
Economic growth rate at t	−5.78** (2.67)	−4.90 (3.33)
Non-presidential regime at t_0	−0.15 (0.33)	−0.66 (0.61)
Number of previous democratic breakdowns at t_0	0.04 (0.21)	0.37 (0.37)
Polity Score at t_0	−0.05 (0.04)	−0.12 (0.09)
Decade dummies?	Yes	Yes
Constant	−3.66*** (0.83)	−17.13*** (1.27)
ln(p)	0.03 (0.08)	0.22** (0.10)
Number of observations	3,607	1,063
Number of episodes	146	72
Number of failures	66	32
p value, Wald χ^2	0.0000	0.0000

***p value < .01; **p value < .05; *p value < .10.

Notes: Dependent variable: Time to death (by any cause).

Negative coefficients indicate that increasing the variable in question decreases the risk of death.

t_0 indicates the year in which the democratic episode began. The variables measured at t_0 are time-invariant. The only time-varying variable is the economic growth rate.

Model 2 replicates Model 1 for a subsample of the data: all seventy-two countries outside of Western Europe attaining independence after 1914. As can be seen, the main finding remains the same. Controlling for income per capita, economic growth, regime type, previous breakdowns, initial quality of democracy, and decade of birth, non-Western democracies that begin life with shutdown reversions survive significantly longer than those that begin with EFRs.[26]

---

[26] Although the effects of income and growth are no longer statistically significant in the post-1914 sample, one cannot reject the null hypothesis that the effects are the same in the post-1875 and post-1914 samples. If one drops economic growth from the specification, the number of countries that can be included in Model 1 (resp., Model 2) increases to 157 (resp., 79). The main result, however, remains the same.

Presidentialism?

Presidential democracies are well known to survive for shorter periods on average than their parliamentary counterparts (Linz 1990; Cheibub 2007). Thus, a natural question is whether the results just reported reflect regime type – parliamentary versus presidential – rather than budgetary reversion. The obvious response to this worry is that the analysis in Table 11.3 already controls for regime type.

If one adds an interaction between regime type and the budgetary reversion, one finds that shutdown reversions prolong the life of parliamentary democracies somewhat more than they prolong the life of presidential democracies. To put it another way, democracies that attempt to combine Parliament's right to remove ministers with executive-favoring reversions – such as Austria 1920, Cuba 1940, Peru 1980, Bangladesh 1986, or Thailand 1975, 1983, 1992 – do not survive long.

In Table 11.4, I explore the relationship between regime type, budgetary reversion, and democratic duration further. When one includes nothing but an indicator for parliamentary regimes (Model 1), one recovers the conventional finding: presidential democracies are more prone to lapse into authoritarian rule. This conventional finding persists when one controls for initial GDP per capita and annual economic growth rates (Model 2). However, when one adds an indicator for shutdown reversions (Model 3), the effect of regime type is much reduced and no longer statistically significant. These results suggest that *presidential democracies have shorter lives mainly because they are more likely to have EFRs* (indeed, 65 percent of presidential democracies begin life with EFRs, versus 24 percent of parliamentary democracies).

Such a claim might seem to conflict with Cheibub's (2007) analysis. He argues that presidential democracies have shorter lives mainly because they are more likely to arise in countries with histories of military rule. So, which is it – budgetary reversions or military legacies?

Historically, executive-favoring budgetary reversions and military rule are deeply intertwined. In seventeenth-century England, the threat of military takeover was addressed precisely by ensuring that most of the military budget reverted to zero at the end of each fiscal year. In the Latin American countries that Cheibub identifies as having military legacies, in contrast, the military budget was often protected by EFRs, expansive emergency powers (Loveman 1993), or both. In other words, shutdown reversions have been used to deter military rule and military rulers have scrupulously avoided shutdown reversions.

TABLE 11.4. *Democratic Death and Regime Type*

Independent Variables	Model 1	Model 2	Model 3
Non-presidential regime at t_0	-0.73**	-0.67**	-0.23
	(0.30)	(0.33)	(0.34)
GDP per capita at t_0	-	-0.27***	-0.30***
		(0.09)	(0.10)
Economic growth rate at t	-	-5.38**	-5.48**
		(2.62)	(2.64)
Budgetary reversion is a government shutdown at t_0	-	-	-0.92***
			(0.36)
Decade dummies?	Yes	Yes	Yes
Constant	-4.90***	-4.40***	-3.79***
	(0.78)	(0.84)	(0.84)
ln(p)	-0.09	-0.02	0.02
	(0.07)	(0.07)	(0.08)
Number of observations	3,868	3,607	3,607
Number of episodes	158	146	146
Number of failures	74	66	66
p value, Wald χ^2	0.0000	0.0000	0.0000

***p value < .01; **p value < .05; *p value < .10.

Notes: Dependent variable: Time to death (by any cause).

Negative coefficients indicate that increasing the variable in question decreases the risk of death.

t_0 indicates the year in which the democratic episode began. The variables measured at t_0 are time-invariant. The only time-varying variable is the economic growth rate.

I cannot measure military legacies over the time period I study, and thus cannot confidently disentangle legacy effects from EFR effects. However, EFRs should entail other effects, such as lower tax receipts and more rent extraction by the executive, not typically associated with military legacies per se. That EFRs indeed correlate with lower tax receipts has already been shown. They also correlate with higher perceived corruption.[27] Thus, we can parsimoniously explain a range of observed maladies afflicting presidential democracies by focusing on the budgetary process.

[27] For example, if one regresses Transparency International's corruption perception index on an indicator for a shutdown reversion, including all democracies as of 2000 in the analysis, one finds that democracies with shutdown reversions are perceived as significantly less corrupt than those with EFRs.

Quality of Democracy?

Another possibility is that the "quality" of a democracy at its birth, rather than whether it is presidential or parliamentary, determines its longevity. To explore this possibility, Table 11.3 controlled for each democracy's initial Polity 2 Score.

The initial Polity 2 Score is a significant predictor of democratic duration, when the indicator for a shutdown reversion is omitted from the model. However, when the budgetary reversion is controlled, the Polity 2 Score no longer systematically predicts democratic duration. Similarly, greater executive constraint (as measured by Polity) predicts democratic survival when the model excludes the budgetary reversion but not when the reversion is included.

Selection Bias?

Are the results in Table 11.3 generated by selection bias? To address this possibility, let's consider *why* countries chose the particular reversions they did at the onset of their respective democratic episodes.

One possibility is that countries copied their former colonial rulers' reversions. Consistent with this idea, most former French colonies began life with EFRs (similar to France V's), while most former British colonies began life with shutdown reversions. To the extent that initial reversions are exogenous inheritances, one can view them as if they were randomly assigned by the vagaries of European conquest in previous centuries. Such as-if random assignment makes it more plausible that democracies with EFRs died sooner because of some causal effects of EFRs.[28]

A second possibility is that each democracy's initial reversion was chosen in light of recent events. For example, perhaps founders favored EFRs in countries with more tumultuous politics, and democracy died more quickly in those places. Under this account, even if EFRs were strong medicine that helped preserve democracy, they might be associated with early democratic death – because the medicine was administered to the sickest patients.

One response to this concern is that more tumultuous democracies – as measured by Banks and Wilson's (2013) well-known index of riots, strikes, and protests – were no more likely to adopt EFRs than less

---

[28] Random assignment is not as helpful as it might be, because other features of French (British, etc.) constitutions may also affect the duration of democracies. In other words, the exclusion restriction may not be met.

tumultuous countries. So, the initial premise of the critique just offered is not met. Another response is that the effect of EFRs remains much the same, if one adds the Banks-Wilson index to the specification in Model 1.[29]

A third possibility is that more fragmented societies tend both to opt for EFRs and to have difficulty raising revenues for public goods. Such a supposition would gibe with work finding more powerful executives in countries with more fragmented party systems (Shugart 1998) and more fragmented ethnic compositions (Aghion, Alesina, and Trebbi 2004). To explore this possibility, I use Roeder's (2001) ethno-linguistic fragmentation (ELF) scores.[30] When I include initial fragmentation as an additional control in the duration analysis, it has no significant effect. Meanwhile, shutdown reversions have just as strong an effect as in Model 1.

Within-Country Comparisons

While budgetary reversions rarely change within a given democratic episode, thirteen countries have experienced some democratic episodes under shutdown reversions, and other episodes under EFRs. Focusing just on these countries, one finds that democratic episodes last on average eleven years longer, when the budgetary reversion is a government shutdown rather than an EFR. This effect is statistically and substantively significant.

EFRs, Coups, and Auto-coups

Table 11.1 has already shown that democracies die more quickly if they have EFRs. Table 11.1 does not tell us, however, the cause of death. Do democracies die due to the accumulation of power by an incumbent leader (auto-coup) or due to an extra-constitutional seizure of power by a new leader (coup)?

I classify the reason for a democracy's death as a "coup" if there was a constitutionally irregular entry into power in the year of the democracy's death.[31] Otherwise, I classify the cause of death as an "auto-coup," since

---

[29] The coefficient on the shutdown variable becomes -0.82, with a standard error of 0.38, very close to the corresponding estimates in Table 1, Model 1.

[30] These scores are available in only two years; I use the average of the available scores for each country.

[31] The Archigos data set is a widely used data set that codes all entries into power by national leaders over the period 1875–2004 as either constitutional or extra-constitutional. It can be found at http://www.rochester.edu/college/faculty/hgoemans/data.htm. Cf. Goemans, Gleditsch and Chiozza (2009). In principle, a democracy might die by auto-coup in year t and then suffer a coup later in the same year. In practice, that does not happen in my sample.

TABLE 11.5. *Auto-Coups, Coups, and Budgetary Reversions*

Independent Variables	Model 1: Auto-Coups (1875–2004)	Model 2: Auto-Coups (post-1914)	Model 3: Coups (1875–2004)	Model 4: Coups (post-1914)
Budgetary reversion is a government shutdown at t_0	-1.16** (0.55)	-1.61* (0.83)	-0.60 (0.64)	-0.11 (0.75)
GDP per capita at t_0	-0.10 (0.07)	0.03 (0.18)	-0.68*** (0.19)	-0.91** (0.44)
Growth rate at t	-1.68 (5.02)	1.51 (6.48)	-7.44** (3.38)	-8.22* (4.24)
Non-presidential regime at t_0	-0.28 (0.55)	-0.75 (0.86)	0.07 (0.52)	-0.13 (0.77)
Number of previous democratic breakdowns at t_0	-0.86 (0.54)	-0.82 (1.02)	0.67** (0.28)	0.92 (0.58)
Polity 2 Score at t_0	-0.14** (0.07)	-0.33** (0.15)	-0.04 (0.05)	-0.04 (0.11)
Decade dummies?	Yes	Yes	Yes	Yes
ln(p)	0.26** (0.12)	0.67*** (0.22)	0.002 (0.09)	0.07 (0.21)
Number of obs	3,607	1,063	3,607	1,063
Number of episodes	146	72	146	72
Number of failures	27	14	38	17
p value, Wald χ^2	0.0000	0.0000	0.0000	0.0001

***p value < 0.01; **p value < 0.05; *p value < 0.10.
Dependent variable in Models 1–2: Time to death by auto-coup.
Dependent variable in Models 3–4: Time to death by coup.

democracy ended, not due to a seizure of power, but rather due to some actions taken by the incumbent leader or regime.[32]

To explore how EFRs affect the incidence of auto-coups and coups, I use parametric survival models of the "cause-specific hazards" (Pintilie

[32] In principle, a democratic episode can also end due to the dissolution of a state (whether by conquest or agreement). In practice, I count one case that might be construed as a conquest (Vichy France) as a coup. There is also one case in my sample in which democracy ends due to state dissolution: Czechoslovakia began a democratic episode in 1990, which ended with the creation of two new states (the Czech Republic and Slovakia) in 1993. I get similar results either including this case in a residual category of "non-coups" or excluding it.

2007). That is, I conduct separate analyses of (a) the time a democracy lasts until it suffers an auto-coup; and (b) the time it lasts until it suffers a coup.[33] The control variables are the same as those used in Table 11.3. The results are presented in Table 11.5.

As Maeda (2010) has already pointed out in an important paper, the control variables should in theory relate differently to coups and auto-coups. To see why, consider each in turn.

First, higher rates of economic growth should deter coups, because good economic times bolster the position of the incumbent. For the same reason, however, higher growth rates should *not* deter auto-coups. Consistent with these expectations, poorer economic conditions strongly predict coups (Models 3–4) but not auto-coups (Models 1–2).

Second, higher levels of per capita income should deter coups, if the fighting that might then ensue would destroy larger stocks of capital assets (cf. Hirschman 1977). In contrast, auto-coups can be executed with or without violence, by biasing the electoral process in the executive's favor. Consistent with these observations, higher levels of GDP per capita strongly deter coups (Models 3–4) but not auto-coups (Models 1–2).

Third, note that countries with more previous democratic breakdowns are (insignificantly) *less* prone to auto-coups but (significantly) *more* prone to coups. One interpretation of this pattern is that coups are positively auto-correlated (cf. Londregan and Poole 1990), because their underlying structural causes persist. For example, some countries have powerful militaries with the constitutional standing to intervene in politics (Loveman 1993). Such countries are prone to cycling between civilian governments during democratic spells and military juntas during authoritarian spells. In contrast, auto-coups may be negatively auto-correlated due to political learning. For example, if a country begins another democratic episode after having experienced a prior auto-coup, politicians may seek to prevent the next incumbent from pursuing the same strategy.

Turning to the variable of primary interest, note that EFRs significantly boost the hazard of auto-coups, in both the full sample (Model 1) and the post-1914 sample (Model 2). Thus, we have evidence suggesting

---

[33] My analytical approach is essentially the same as Maeda's (2010). As Pintilie (2007) explains, the analyst has a choice between considering the "cause-specific hazard" and the "hazard of the subdistribution." Roughly speaking, in the present analysis, this choice depends on whether one is more interested in the marginal probability of an auto-coup occurring before time t or the probability of an auto-coup occurring before time t, conditional on an auto-coup occurring before a coup.

that the postulated causal path (EFRs → rents → auto-coups) has been well traveled.

In contrast, while EFRs boost the hazard of coups, the effect is statistically insignificant in both samples (Models 3–4). This is consistent with the idea that EFRs may help a leader defend against coups in ordinary times, while worsening his/her ability to bargain away from coups during crises.

A Word on the Tactics of Auto-coups

In a typical auto-coup, the executive shuts down the assembly after a long and acrimonious inter-branch conflict. How is this scenario consistent with my argument? In particular, why is there any conflict, if the executive wields an EFR?

The answer to this question is that all democracies endow their legislatures with the right to approve or reject new taxes. Thus, if the constitution also creates an EFR, it sets up what I called a *Rechtsstaat* budgetary process in Chapter 10. Such a system invites fiscal conflict, with MPs denying funds to an executive whose expenditure behavior they cannot control, and the latter trying to use budgetary power to undermine the assembly's independence and/or prerogatives. Thus, the typical auto-coup scenario fits my story well.

That said, a leader bent on establishing authoritarian rule need not suspend the legislature. He can also simply "buy" its members.

Conclusion

Most constitutions since the nineteenth century have required annual statutory budgets unlike those instituted in England after the Glorious Revolution. English MPs took care to ensure that their mere inaction would force key parts of the government to shut down. This was their method of ensuring that the Crown would in fact call Parliament, and that they would then have a strong bargaining position.

The bulk of the world's written constitutions, in contrast, have not mandated shutdown reversions. In that very fundamental sense they can be said not to have taken the first and most important step toward limited government.

In this chapter, I have shown that democracies lacking shutdown reversions share two problems common to the absolutist, Machiavellian and *Rechtsstaat* regimes examined earlier in the book. First, they collect fewer tax revenues as a percent of GDP. This may be because their MPs are less willing to support tax hikes, because they cannot control the resulting expenditures. Or, it may be because Parliament has lost control even over setting tax rates, resulting in tax evasion in the general populace. Second, they are more prone to tyranny. I show that democracies with EFRs lapse more quickly back into autocracy than do democracies operating under shutdown reversions. This seems due mainly to their executives gradually assembling enough power to permanently ensconce themselves in power.

12

Good Political Institutions

Are political institutions fundamental causes of economic growth, as a number of political economists have prominently argued (e.g., North, Wallis, and Weingast 2009; Acemoglu and Robinson 2012)? Are they fundamental causes of military prowess, as in the "strong democrats" thesis (Lake 1992)? Are they fundamental causes of financial credibility, so that democracies have a "borrowing advantage" (Schultz and Weingast 2003; Beaulieu, Cox, and Saiegh 2012)?

These general propositions derive, in good part, from particular understandings of England's Glorious Revolution. Indeed, one can rephrase each question in terms of that case. Did the Glorious spark the Industrial Revolution? Did the Revolution lead to England's many battlefield successes? Did the Revolution underpin England's financial revolution?

I have addressed the England-specific questions in Part I. In this conclusion, I focus on three broader questions. First, what are good political institutions? Second, in what sense are good political institutions fundamental causes of a state's ability to raise revenues or the health of its economy? Third, if good political institutions increase state revenue and economic performance, why haven't they been more widely imitated?

What Are Good Political Institutions?

In the view of Enlightenment theorists, good political institutions imposed "checks and balances." As James Madison wrote in Federalist #51, the trick was to "so [contrive] the interior structure of the government as that its several constituent parts may, by their mutual relations, be the means of keeping each other in their proper places." A bit more precisely, one must give "to those who administer each department [of government] the necessary *constitutional means* and *personal motives* to resist encroachments of the others" (italics added).

The "constitutional means" to which Madison referred have typically been construed as vetoes. Thus, we arrive at a classic formula for constraining the executive – namely, requiring that other constitutional veto players approve its decisions. I would, however, highlight three points that complicate the project of checking the executive by creating veto players.

First, as many have pointed out, if the executive appoints the other veto players, then it is unlikely they will use their powers to prevent tyrannical acts by the executive. Thus, formal veto powers must always be combined with sturdy reasons to expect that legislators and judges will be independent of the executive.[1]

Second, per Chapter 9, constraining the executive logically requires blocking all legal avenues – decrees, statutes, court decisions – by which s/he might seek to wriggle out of commitments. In other words, one needs a chain of independent veto players and executive constraint will be determined by the weakest link in that chain.

Third, if a polity successfully creates a chain of independent veto players to trammel the executive, then state capacity will be affected in two countervailing ways. Preventing unilateral executive action will *increase* state credibility and revenues but *reduce* the state's capacity to react quickly to events. The net effect on state capacity depends on how much revenues increase, how much decision-making slows down, and how one weighs money against speed of decision.

What Are Good Budgetary Institutions?

Among the most important of all state decisions are those concerning the expenditure of public revenues. In allocating decision-making authority between the executive and legislative branches, a polity faces risks from both actors. On one hand, there is the "executive commitment problem": if given legal discretion, the executive cannot commit to using it in the public interest (rather than for personal or factional gain). The main way to reduce executive discretion is to empower the

---

[1] Madison was aware of this issue (hence his reference to both "constitutional means" and "personal motives"). General discussions of veto player theory, such as Cox and McCubbins (2001) and Tsebelis (2002), also stress the importance of combining separations of power with separations of purpose.

legislature. But empowering legislators may create a "legislative commitment problem," since they can commit neither to refrain from championing special-interest spending nor to internalize the tax costs of public expenditure.

I define good budgetary institutions as those that (a) reduce the executive commitment problem by combining rule-of-law budgets with votes of no confidence; and (b) reduce the legislative commitment problem by giving the executive a monopoly on proposing expenditures. Such systems, Great Britain being the original example, have three main beneficial effects. First, they minimize the incidence of fiscal stalemate. Second, they make sovereign expenditure promises more credible, thereby increasing state revenues. Third, they improve fiscal discipline.

To clarify the logic behind my definition of good budgetary institutions, it helps to consider how each of the four budgetary processes (introduced in Chapter 10) manages the competing risks of executive and legislative misbehavior. This is illustrated in Figure 12.1, whose vertical and horizontal axes respectively measure how severe the executive and legislative commitment problems are.[2]

In constructing Figure 12.1, I assume an inevitable trade-off. Strengthening the legislature can reduce exposure to executive misbehavior but only at the cost of increasing exposure to legislative misbehavior. Thus, the ideal budgetary institution, which would be located at the origin in Figure 12.1, is not attainable.

At the top left of Figure 12.1 lie absolutist budgets, in which the executive can dictate both taxes and expenditures. Fiscal absolutism minimizes the danger from legislators by rendering them powerless, but maximizes taxpayers' exposure to executive misbehavior.

Machiavellian budgets give the legislature the right to set taxes, while retaining absolute executive control over expenditures. Such systems reduce the executive commitment problem because legislators can punish misbehavior by denying taxes at the next opportunity. At the same time, they potentially worsen the fiscal common pool problem – because legislators may clamor for local or special-interest expenditures as the price for their support of higher revenues. Thus, Machiavellian budgets are positioned below but to the right of absolutist budgets in Figure 12.1.

---

[2] I do not stipulate units of measurement. Thus, the locations of the various budgetary systems in Figure 12.1 have ordinal but not cardinal meaning. That is, whether one system is positioned above or to the right of another is meaningful but how far above or to the right is a matter of artistic license.

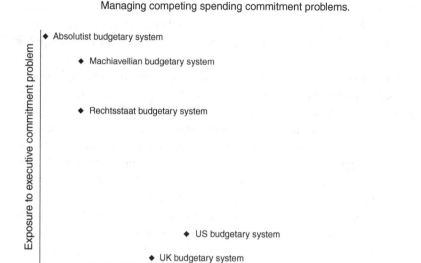

FIGURE 12.1. Managing competing spending commitment problems.

Rechtsstaat budgets are like Machiavellian ones, with one difference: the executive can no longer legally revise the expenditure plan on the fly, in response to events. Thus, although the executive still effectively dictates the annual expenditure plan, after that s/he must stick to it. *Rechtsstaat* budgets, as opposed to Machiavellian ones, lessen the executive commitment problem without worsening the fiscal common pool problem. Thus, in Figure 12.1, they are located directly below Machiavellian budgets.

Each of the first three budgetary processes preserves the executive's aboriginal ability to craft and sell platforms. Rule-of-law budgetary processes – those combining annual statutory budgets with shutdown reversions – create a parliamentary monopoly on platforms. This substantially reduces the risk of executive misbehavior, while simultaneously increasing the risk of legislative misbehavior. To illustrate how different rule-of-law countries address the remaining trade-off, consider the United Kingdom and the United States.

The United Kingdom further mitigates the executive commitment problem by allowing the House of Commons to remove ministers via a vote of no confidence. In contrast, the U.S. constitution specifically prevents Congress from removing the president from office (and empowers the latter to remove or retain ministers). Thus, U.S. legislators cannot trust executive officials as much as can their UK counterparts. To put it another way, *the executive commitment problem is larger in the United States.*

The United Kingdom reduces the legislative commitment problem by (1) giving ministers an exclusive right to propose expenditures; and (2) limiting backbenchers – whether in committee or on the floor – to granting, reducing, or denying such requests. In the United States, legislators are unwilling to give monopoly proposal power to the executive, because they cannot remove the executive. They do centralize the budgetary process in several important ways, seeking to force decision-makers to take a synoptic view of all costs and benefits.[3] However, whereas only one actor can propose expenditures in the United Kingdom, at least three can do so in the United States – the president, the House Appropriations Committee, and the Senate Appropriations Committee. Because the right to propose expenditures is more fragmented, *the United States' fiscal common pool is more exposed to overfishing than is the United Kingdom's.*

The United States' budgetary institutions, then, lie to the northeast of the United Kingdom's. American presidents are less able to commit to expenditure plans than are British premiers, and American legislators are more active in securing pork barrel expenditures for their districts and delivering favors to special interests than are British MPs. I consider some of the broader consequences of these differences later.

Do Good Budgetary Institutions Reduce the Incidence of Fiscal Stalemate?

Fiscal stalemate exists when: (1) the legislature refuses the taxes the executive requests; and (2) if the executive could credibly commit to spend revenues in particular ways, then a mutually acceptable deal would exist under which the legislature would grant higher taxes. In other words, fiscal stalemates are inefficient: the executive and legislature fail to reach available and mutually beneficial agreements due to the executive's lack of credibility.

As noted in previous chapters, fiscal stalemates sometimes precede civil wars, as in early Stuart England (before the Civil War), late Stuart England (before the Glorious Revolution), and late nineteenth-century Chile (before the Revolution of 1891). Even lesser stand-offs, such as the government shutdowns and debt ceiling crises marring American

---

[3] On the importance of centralizing the budgetary process, see Hallerberg, Strauch, and von Hagen 2010.

politics in the period 1995–2015, produce widespread popular anger and demands for political reform.

In this section, I consider how polities experiencing fiscal stalemate have reacted under the pressure of war. Warfare forces hard choices about cost-bearing and, at the same time, renders delay in making such choices dangerous. Polities can lower their structural risk of wartime fiscal stalemate either by reducing the executive's power over spending (ultimately creating a parliamentary monopoly) or reducing Parliament's power over taxation (ultimately creating absolutism). To illustrate the tendency for stalemate-prone budgetary systems to be driven either toward a more parliamentary or a more absolutist mold, I consider the first wave of European parliamentarism (1200–1700) and the second wave (1790–1900).

The First Wave

It is well known that parliaments, which had spread widely by the fourteenth century, were subsequently suppressed in most of the larger territorial states over the fifteenth and sixteenth centuries (Stasavage 2011, pp. 47–51; van Zanden, Luiten, Buringh, and Bosker 2012). From my perspective, these early parliamentary extinctions were natural consequences of endemic war and fiscal division. Because monarchs in the territorial states had complete legal authority to spend, parliaments granted revenues only when a Machiavellian promise looked credible. Unwilling to live with the meager resources that parliaments would voluntarily grant, and unwilling to cede control over spending, crowns sought to levy taxes by prerogative. In the larger states, they succeeded well enough that they could dispense more or less permanently with the parliaments.

Could these medieval European states have resolved their fiscal divisions by taking the other logically possible route away from stalemate – viz., establishing rule-of-law budgets? To do so would have required parliaments to meet frequently, to audit the state's revenues and expenditures, and to have some constitutional means to punish misappropriation. But could local notables trust their MPs? The more geographically extensive the polity, the weaker would be local elites' control over their own representatives, and thus the less attractive representative institutions vis-à-vis monarchism. Indeed, Stasavage (2011) finds a strong correlation in medieval and early modern Europe: parliaments in geographically extensive polities rarely exerted any influence over spending; and eventually lost their power to grant taxes. Thus, the only viable way to escape fiscal stalemate for most of the growing territorial states of early modern Europe was fiscal absolutism.

The main polities in which parliamentary prerogatives survived were the city-states, the Netherlands, and England – where smaller geographic scales (relative to the means of transportation) meant representatives could be better policed. Thus, by the dawn of the eighteenth century, endemic warfare had forced most of Europe's states to adopt budgetary systems less prone to fiscal stalemate – either absolutist or rule-of-law. The absolutist polities were larger but fiscally weaker. The rule-of-law regimes were smaller but fiscally stronger. The exceptions – states such as Poland that maintained Machiavellian budgeting regimes – suffered conquest and extinction.

The Second Wave

In the century after the onset of the Napoleonic Wars, most of Europe's absolutist polities revived their long-suppressed parliaments, endowed them with the right to control taxes, and instituted annual statutory budgets. In this second wave of European parliamentarism, one sees a repeat of the bifurcation process characterizing the first (medieval) wave. That is, states troubled by fiscal stalemates tended either to strengthen the executive's hand (e.g., Denmark 1885–1895) or to strengthen the parliament's (e.g., Denmark 1901).[4]

One again sees a similar bifurcation process when European parliamentarism spread to the various states emerging from colonial status. For example, under the pressure of war, Pakistan immediately opted for fiscal absolutism, while India opted for parliamentary monopoly.[5]

Beyond Stalemate

Avoiding fiscal stalemate is an important goal. If it were the only criterion for judging "good" institutions, then both absolutist and parliamentary rule-of-law systems would qualify. However, a broader criterion of a state's performance is its ability to extract revenues from its population.

---

[4] Due to the Transportation Revolution, the difficulties that geographic scale posed for the representational process diminished. Thus, the sorting out of fiscal processes into those dominated by Parliament and those dominated by the executive was less strongly tied to the size of the states.

[5] The mechanism of sorting was the governor-generalship. In Pakistan, Jinnah had himself appointed governor-general, thereby assuming the vast powers of that position of colonial control. In India, Nehru effectively put those powers in abeyance by retaining Lord Mountbatten as governor-general until a new constitution could be drafted to replace the Government of India Act.

And what the state then does with those revenues matters, too. In the next section, I take up these issues.

Do Good Budgetary Institutions Cause State Growth?

Evidence that budgetary institutions affect state revenue extraction comes in four main types. First, at any given point in time, states with "better" budgetary institutions have been able to extract more revenues per capita.

Consider, for example, the mean revenue extraction achieved by twelve pre-unification German states (including Austria) in the 1860s. The lone absolutist, Saxony, extracted less than one pound sterling per capita. The seven states with *Rechtsstaat* budgets (Austria, Baden, Bavaria, Brunswick, Hanover, Oldenburg, and Prussia) extracted an average of 1.26 pounds sterling per capita. Finally, the four states with rule-of-law budgets (Bremen, Hamburg, Lubeck, and Wurtemberg) collected 2.33 pounds sterling per capita.[6]

Much the same picture emerges if one expands the sample geographically. Table 12.1 shows the mean revenue per capita in twenty-eight European states circa 1850.[7] As can be seen, average *Rechtsstaat* revenues doubled absolutist receipts, while rule-of-law revenues were 40 percent larger than the *Rechtsstaat* average.

Finally, a similar snapshot correlation is evident 150 years later. As Chapter 11's study of sixty-seven democracies circa 2000 showed, revenues per capita are higher in democracies with shutdown reversions than in those without.

A second kind of evidence examines tax receipts before and after fiscal reforms in particular countries. Chapters 2 and 3 documented a sharp increase in British tax extraction after the introduction of annual statutory budgets in 1689. Chapter 11 showed that Brazil and Venezuela experienced the expected changes in their revenue collections, after they changed their budgetary reversions circa 2000.

A third and higher-octane form of evidence was presented in Chapter 10. Examining a panel data set documenting European states'

---

[6] The notes to Table 12.1 list the British Parliamentary Papers from which the tax data were extracted. I coded the budgetary institutions directly from each state's constitution.

[7] The sample consists of the twelve Germanic states mentioned in the text, plus six other central-west states (Belgium, Britain, Denmark, France, Netherlands, Sweden), plus seven states from southern Europe (Greece, the Papal States, Portugal, Sardinia, Spain, Tuscany, Two Sicilies), plus three states from eastern Europe (Hungary, Russia, and Turkey). Observations on revenues per capita are all within twenty years of 1850.

TABLE 12.1. *Revenue Per Capita in Europe Circa 1850*

Type of Budget	Mean Revenue (in Pounds Sterling) Per Capita	Polities with this Type of Budget
Absolutist or Machiavellian	0.66	7: Papal States, Russia, Sardinia, Saxony, Turkey, Tuscany, Two Sicilies
Rechtsstaat	1.37	11: Austria, Baden, Bavaria, Brunswick, Denmark, France, Hanover, Oldenburg, Portugal, Prussia, Spain
Rule-of-law	1.92	10: Belgium, Bremen, Britain, Greece, Hamburg, Holland, Hungary, Lubeck, Sweden, Wurtemburg

Sources: Revenue and population data are from the following British Parliamentary Papers: 1849 [1053], supplement to Part XIV; 1854–1855 [1985], XVIII; 1857 Session 1 [2149], XVIII; 1857–1858 [2447], XVIII; 1861 [2850], VII; 1862 [3067], VIII; 1864 [3397], IX; 1866, X; 1874 [1054]. Budget type was coded directly from the constitutions of the various polities (with the absence of a constitution coded as absolutism).

revenue extraction, a difference-in-differences approach found substantial revenue responses after fiscal reforms.

Finally, in the case of England, we can find evidence that is both within-country and within-year. As shown in Chapter 3, Parliament steadily expanded its purchase of the parliamentary platforms that fed the fiscal-military state but restrained its purchases of the royal platforms feeding the civilian government.

Are good budgetary institutions then causes of state revenue growth? I certainly think so. Theoretically, good institutions make executive platforms much more credible. With a better product to sell, more sales are made – and taxes go up. Empirically, no state with absolutist or Machiavellian budgetary institutions has ever reached the levels of revenue extraction observed in contemporary democracies; and only a few states with *Rechtsstaat* budgets have attained that level.[8]

The larger revenues that good budgetary institutions generate, moreover, are potentially compatible with economic growth – because they are only granted when the executive offers a package of goods and services sufficient to earn a majority in Parliament. If the goods offered foster

---

[8] I do not count mineral rents, since these are not voluntarily granted. Some states employ absolutist budgeting during military juntas or periods of emergency rule. But even these states did not grow their revenues during the juntas, although they may have been able to hold them stable.

economic growth and would not otherwise be supplied, the net effect of higher taxes on growth may be positive.

Do Good Budgetary Institutions Cause Economic Growth?

In this section, I suggest four ways good budgetary institutions might enhance economic performance. These suggestions overlap with Chapter 8's discussion of how England's Glorious Revolution might have led to its Industrial Revolution.

First, private actors supplying the government cannot make long-term plans as confidently when platforms are royal as when they are parliamentary. In this sense, *Rechtsstaat* and rule-of-law budgets are a fundamental cause of investment in those parts of the economy most directly tied to the government. As these government-tied parts of the economy are vast and include the military-industrial complex, the credibility of state budgets has a substantial effect on the overall performance of the economy.

Second, absent a ministerial monopoly on expenditures – for example, England's "rule of 1706," Germany's constructive vote of no confidence, France V's package vote – MPs may exploit their blocking power to extract budgetary concessions, producing budgetary and ministerial instability. By reducing such mischief, monopoly brokerage promotes fiscal discipline. As any fiscal indiscipline ramifies throughout the economy – in the form of debased currency, inflation, unsustainable debt burdens, and the like – this again is a big effect.

Third, good budgetary institutions increase the contestability of rents. Sneak attacks, whereby one interest group secures rents that burden another before the latter can organize to resist them, are less likely under monopoly brokerage than under any of the alternatives.

Fourth, good budgetary institutions, by facilitating bargaining over how to spend public revenues, help avoid inefficient fiscal stalemates. This helps explain why Britain progressed gradually toward political democracy, with violent intra-elite conflict never toppling an incumbent government and rarely threatening to do so. As challenge after challenge faced Britain's political class, it consistently found itself better able to craft credible deals – to avoid both inefficient fiscal conflict and large-scale political violence – than their contemporaries.[9]

---

[9] Of course, the British elite's ability to bargain with the disenfranchised was sometimes no better than in other states. Even here, however, suffrage rights were more valuable

An Aside on the United States, the United Kingdom, and Economic Growth

Is the executive commitment problem posed by rule-of-law presidential-ism a good thing for economic growth, allowing the United States to outperform the United Kingdom? Theoretically, the United States enjoys two substantial benefits – lower taxes and lower rents for the government and its legislative allies (Persson, Roland, and Tabellini 1997).

Against these advantages of presidentialism, however, must be weighed some disadvantages. First, as Persson and colleagues (1997) point out, parliamentary systems should typically provide more public goods than presidential ones. Second, as noted earlier, Congress's mistrust of the executive leads it to implement a less thoroughgoing solution to the fiscal common pool problem. Thus, presidentialism reduces public goods expenditure in favor of distributive expenditure. Third, Congress's mistrust of the executive leads it not only to keep taxes low but also, on occasion, to shut down the government and imperil the nation's credit. In addition to these obviously inefficient but rare tactics, Congress also resorts to less extreme but more common stratagems, such as refusing to confirm presidential nominees, underfunding departments, and the like (McCarty and Razaghian 1999; McCarty 2004). In other words, presidentialism does not just produce a smaller government, it also produces a systematically less efficient government (Moe and Caldwell 1994). This loss of efficiency must be counted as a cost.

It is not obvious whether lower taxes and lower rents trump a lower provision of public goods, greater distributive spending, and greater inefficiency. So, it is not obvious which country should have a better growth record. Empirically, there is little to choose between the two over the period 1875–2005.[10]

Why Are Good Budgetary Institutions Hard to Imitate?

Good budgetary processes – annual statutory budgets, shutdown reversions, ministerial monopolies, and responsibility – are hard to imitate for

in Britain than in polities without rule-of-law budgets (because the British parliament controlled the fisc whereas parliaments elsewhere had a more tenuous influence). Thus, when crises arose, Britain's political class could offer more valuable suffrage rights than could most of its competitors.

[10] The median difference between U.S. and UK annual growth rates over the period is –0.002, a slight UK advantage. The mean difference is a statistically insignificant 0.005, a slight U.S. advantage. Meanwhile, the U.S. growth rate exhibits significantly more variation from year to year than the United Kingdom's.

two main reasons. First, instituting reforms requires good aim. One can easily undershoot the mark by introducing insufficient constraints on the executive. This creates a fiscally divided state that will, when faced with fiscal stalemate, run a lottery in which some tickets lead to rule-of-law budgeting and others to fiscal absolutism. One can also overshoot the mark by failing to address the fiscal common-pool problem that necessarily attends legislative dominance. This leads to chronic instability and fiscal imprudence.

Second, while steering the ship of state between the Scylla of a too-powerful executive and the Charybdis of a too-powerful assembly, one must simultaneously compensate the incumbent rights holders. The right to spend other people's money is extremely attractive. Any political actor that currently enjoys a de jure advantage in controlling the expenditure of public revenues will never voluntarily surrender that advantage without compensation. While it is sometimes possible to arrange sufficient and credible compensation, at other times that proves insuperably difficult. Thus, moving toward good budgetary institutions may require a constitutional break. In England, for example, it took a Revolution to install a monarch willing to trade control rights for money.

References

Acemoglu, Daron, and James Robinson. 2005. *Economic origins of dictatorship and democracy*. Cambridge: Cambridge University Press.

2012. *Why nations fail*. New York: Crown.

Aghion, Philippe, Alberto Alesina, and Francesco Trebbi. 2004. "Endogenous Political Institutions." *Quarterly Journal of Economics* 119(2): 565–611.

Albert, W. 1972. *The turnpike road system in England, 1663–1840*. Cambridge: Cambridge University Press.

Allen, Robert. 2009. *The British Industrial Revolution in Global Perspective*. Cambridge: Cambridge University Press.

"An essay on the sinking fund; wherein the nature thereof is fully explained; and the right of the publick to that fund asserted and maintained. The second edition, corrected and much enlarged." 1737. Printed for J Peele, at Locke's Head, in Amen-Corner.

Anderson, Clifford B. 1962. "Ministerial Responsibility in the 1620s." *The Journal of Modern History* 34(4): 381–389.

Ansell, Benjamin, and David Samuels. 2014. *Inequality and democratization*. New York: Cambridge University Press.

Aylmer, G. E. 1957. "The Last Years of Purveyance, 1610–1660." *Economic History Review* 10(1): 81–93.

Azariadis, Costas, and John Stachurski. 2005. "Poverty traps." *Handbook of economic growth*, Volume 1A. Edited by Philippe Aghion and Steven N. Durlauf. London: Elsevier.

Baldez, Lisa, and John Carey. 1999. "Presidential Agenda Control and Spending Policy: Lessons from General Pinochet's Constitution." *American Journal of Political Science* 43(1): 29–55.

Banks, Arthur S., and Kenneth A. Wilson. 2013. *Cross-National Time-Series Data Archive. Databanks International*. Jerusalem, Israel.

Baron, David, and John Ferejohn. 1989. "Bargaining in Legislatures." *American Political Science Review* 83(4): 1181–1206.

Barzel, Yoram, and Edgar Kiser. 2002. "Taxation and Voting Rights in Medieval England and France." *Rationality and Society* 14(4): 473–507.

Bates, Robert H., and Da-Hsiang Donald Lien. 1985. "A Note on Taxation, Development, and Representative Government." *Politics & Society* 14(1): 53–70.

Bawn, Kathy, and Frances Rosenbluth. 2006. "Short versus Long Coalitions: Electoral Accountability and the Size of the Public Sector." *American Journal of Political Science* 50(2): 251–265.

Baxter, Stephen. 1957. *The development of the Treasury, 1660–1702*. Cambridge, MA: Harvard University Press.

Beaulieu, Emily, Gary W. Cox, and Sebastian Saiegh. 2012. "Sovereign Debt and Regime Type: Re-considering the Democratic Advantage." *International Organization* 66(4): 709–738.

Beck, Neal, and Jonathan Katz. 1995. "What to Do (and Not to Do) with Time-Series Cross-Section Data." *American Political Science Review* 89(3): 634–647.

Becker, Gary. 1983. "A Theory of Competition among Pressure Groups for Political Influence." *Quarterly Journal of Economics* 98: 371–400.

Beckett, John. 2014. "The Glorious Revolution, Parliament, and the Making of the First Industrial Nation." *Parliamentary History* 33(1): 36–53.

Berman, Sheri. 2001. "Modernization in Historical Perspective: The Case of Imperial Germany." *World Politics* 53(3): 431–462.

Besley, Timothy. 2005. "Political Selection." *Journal of Economic Perspectives* 19(3): 43–60.

2006. *Principled agents? The political economy of good government*. Oxford: Oxford University Press.

Binney, J. E. D. 1958. *Public finance and administration, 1774–92*. Oxford: Oxford University Press.

Bismarck, Prince Otto von. 1899. *Bismarck: The man and the statesman*. Trans. A. J. Butler. New York: Harper and Bros.

Blackstone, William. 1979. *Commentaries on the laws of England: A facsimile of the first edition of 1765–1769*. Chicago: University of Chicago Press.

Blossfeld, Hans-Peter, Katrin Golsch, and Götz Rohwer. 2007. *Techniques of event history modeling using Stata*. Mahwah, NJ: Erlbaum.

Bogart, Dan. 2005. "Did Turnpike Trusts Increase Transport Investment in Eighteenth Century England?" *Journal of Economic History* 65 (June): 439–468.

2011a. "Did the Glorious Revolution Contribute to the Transport Revolution?" *Economic History Review* 64(4): 1073–1112.

2011b. "British legal institutions and transaction costs in the early Transport Revolution." In *Law and long-term economic change*. Edited by Debin Ma and Jan Luiten van Zanden. Stanford, CA: Stanford University Press.

Bogart, D., M. Drelichman, O. Gelderblom, and J. L. Rosenthal. 2010. "State and private institutions." In *The Cambridge economic history of modern Europe, Volume 1: 1700–1870*. Edited by S. Broadberry and K. O'Rourke. New York: Cambridge University Press.

Bogart, D., and Richardson, G. 2011. "Property Rights and Parliament in Industrializing Britain." *Journal of Law and Economics* 54(2): 241–274.

Boix, Carles, Michael Miller, and Sebastian Rosato. 2012. "A Complete Data Set of Political Regimes, 1800–2007." *Comparative Political Studies* 46(12): 1523–1554.

Bolton, Patrick, and Mathias Dewatripont. 2005. *Contract theory.* Cambridge, MA: MIT Press.

Borchard, Edwin, and George Stumberg. 1931. *Guide to the law and legal literature of France.* Washington, DC: Government Printing Office.

Bowen, H. V. 1995. "The Bank of England during the long eighteenth century, 1694–1820." In *The Bank of England: Money, power and influence 1694–1994.* Edited by Richard Roberts and David Kynaston. Oxford: Clarendon Press.

Braddick, M. J. 1996. *The nerves of state: Taxation and the financing of the English state, 1558–1714.* Manchester: Manchester University Press.

Brewer, John. 1988. *The sinews of power: War, money, and the English state, 1688–1783.* Cambridge, MA: Harvard University Press.

Broz, J. L. 1998. The Origins of Central Banking: Solutions to the Free-Rider Problem. *International Organization* 52(2): 231–268.

Broz, J. L., and R. Grossman. 2004. "Paying for Privilege: The Political Economy of Bank of England Charters, 1694–1844." *Explorations in Economic History* 41: 48–72.

Bueno de Mesquita, Bruce, et al. 2003. *The logic of political survival.* MIT Press.

Burg, David. 2004. *A world history of tax rebellions.* New York: Routledge.

Carlos, Ann, et al. 2013. "Financing and refinancing the War of the Spanish Succession, and then refinancing the South Sea Company." In *Questioning credible commitment.* Edited by D'Maris Coffman, Adrian Leonard, and Larry Neal. Cambridge: Cambridge University Press.

Carruthers, Bruce. 1996. *City of capital: Politics and markets in the English financial revolution.* Princeton, NJ: Princeton University Press.

Chandaman, C. D. 1975. *The English public revenue 1660–1688.* Oxford: Oxford University Press.

Chapham, Sir John. 1945. *The Bank of England: A history.* Cambridge: Cambridge University Press.

Cheibub, Jose Antonio. 2007. *Presidentialism, parliamentarism and democracy.* Cambridge: Cambridge University Press.

Cheyney, E. P. 1897. *Translations and reprints from the original sources of European history,* Vol. 1, No. 6. Philadelphia: University of Pennsylvania Press.

Clark, Gregory. 1996. "The Political Foundations of Modern Economic Growth: England, 1540–1800." *Journal of Interdisciplinary History* 26: 563–588.

——— 2007. *A farewell to alms.* Princeton, NJ: Princeton University Press.

——— 2009. "The macroeconomic aggregates for England, 1209–2008." Working Papers, University of California, Department of Economics, No. 09,19.

Coase, Ronald. 1960. "The Problem of Social Cost." *Journal of Law and Economics* 3(1): 1–44.

Coffman, D'Maris. 2013. "Credibility, transparency, accountability, and the public credit under the Long Parliament and Commonwealth, 1643–1653." In *Questioning credible commitment: Perspectives on the rise of financial capitalism.* Edited by D'Maris Coffman, Adrian Leonard, and Larry Neal. Cambridge: Cambridge University Press.

Cole, Daniel H. 2007. "Political Institutions, Judicial Review, and Private Property: A Comparative Institutional Analysis." *Supreme Court Economic Review* 15(1): 141–182.

Comín, Francisco. 2010. "Public finance and the rise of the liberal state in Spain, 1808–1914." In *Paying for the liberal state.* Edited by José Luís Cardoso and Pedro Lains. Cambridge: Cambridge University Press.

Commons, John R. 1968. *Legal foundations of capitalism.* Madison: University of Wisconsin Press.

Congleton, Roger. 2011. *Perfecting parliament.* New York: Cambridge University Press.

Cox, Gary W. 1987. *The efficient secret.* Cambridge: Cambridge University Press.

2011. "War, Moral Hazard and Ministerial Responsibility: England after the Glorious Revolution." *Journal of Economic History* 71(1): 120–148.

2012. "Was the Glorious Revolution a Constitutional Watershed?" *Journal of Economic History* 72(3): 567–600.

Cox, Gary W., and Mathew D. McCubbins. 2001. "The institutional determinants of economic policy outcomes." In *Presidents, parliaments and policy.* Edited by Mathew D. McCubbins and Stephan Haggard. New York: Cambridge University Press, pp. 21–63.

Crawford, Vincent. 1987. "International lending, long-term credit relationships and dynamic contract theory." *Princeton Studies in International Finance* No. 59. Princeton, NJ: Department of Economics, Princeton University.

Cusack, Tom, Torben Iversen, and David Soskice. 2007. "Economic Interests and the Origins of Political Systems." *American Political Science Review* 101: 372–391.

De Krey, Gary. 2007. *Restoration and revolution in Britain.* New York: Palgrave Macmillan.

Debré, Michel. 1957. *Ces Princes qui nous gouvernent.* Paris: Librairie Plon.

1959. "La Nouvelle Constitution." *Revue Française de science politique* 9: 7–29.

Defoe, Daniel. 1710. "An essay upon publick credit, & c." Printed and sold by the book-sellers.

Desan, Christine. 1998. "Remaking Constitutional Tradition at the Margin of the Empire: The Creation of Legislative Adjudication in Colonial New York." *Law and History Review* 16(2): 257–317.

Devine, Tom. 2005. *The transformation of Scotland: The economy since 1700.* Edinburgh: Edinburgh University Press.

Dickson, P. G. M. 1967. *The financial revolution in England.* London: Macmillan.

Diermeier, Daniel, and Timothy Feddersen. 1998. "Cohesion in Legislatures and the Vote of Confidence Procedure." *American Political Science Review* 92(3): 611–621.

Dincecco, Mark. 2009. "Fiscal Centralization, Limited Government, and Public Revenues in Europe, 1650–1913." *Journal of Economic History* 69: 48–103.

2011. *Political transformations and public finances: Europe, 1650–1913*. Cambridge: Cambridge University Press.

Dincecco, Mark, Giovanni Federico, and Andrea Vindigni. 2011. "Warfare, Taxation, and Political Change: Evidence from the Italian Risorgimento." *Journal of Economic History* 71(4): 887–914.

Dixit, Avinash. 2009. "Governance institutions and economic activity." Delivered as the presidential address at the American Economic Association meetings on January 4, 2009.

Dixit, Avinash, and John Londregan. 2000. "Political Power and the Credibility of Government Debt." *Journal of Economic Theory* 94: 80–105.

Drelichman, Mauricio, and Hans-Joachim Voth. 2011. "Lending to the Borrower from Hell: Debt and Default in the Age of Philip II." *The Economic Journal* 121(557): 1205–1227.

Eaton, Jonathan, and Mark Gersovitz. 1981. "Debt with Potential Repudiation: Theoretical and Empirical Analysis." *Review of Economic Studies* 48(2): 289–309.

Eggers, Andrew, and Jens Hainmueller. 2009. "MPs for Sale: Estimating Returns to Office in Post-War British Politics." *American Political Science Review* 103(4): 513–533.

Einzig, Paul. 1959. *The control of the purse*. London: Secker & Warburg.

Epstein, Stephan. 2000. *Freedom and growth: The rise of states and markets in Europe, 1300–1750*. London: Routledge.

Epstein, S. R. 2005. "The rise of the West." In *An anatomy of power: The social theory of Michael Mann*. Edited by J. Hall and R. Schroeder. Cambridge: Cambridge University Press.

Fearon, James. 1995a. "Rationalist Explanations for War." *International Organization* 49(Summer): 379–414.

1995b. "Bargaining over Objects that Influence Future Bargaining Power." Chicago Center on Democracy. Working Paper, University of Chicago.

Ferejohn, John. 1999. "Accountability and authority: Towards a model of political accountability." In *Democracy, accountability, and representation*. Edited by Adam Przeworski, Bernard Manin, and Susan C. Stokes. New York: Cambridge University Press.

Ferejohn, John, and Frances Rosenbluth. 2008. "Warlike Democracies." *Journal of Conflict Resolution* 52(1): 3–38.

Findlay, Ronald, and Kevin O'Rourke. 2007. *Power and plenty: Trade, war and the world economy in the second millennium*. Princeton, NJ: Princeton University Press.

Finer, S. E. 1999. *The history of government from the earliest times*, vol. III. Oxford: Oxford University Press.

Fish, M. Steven, and Matthew Kroenig. 2011. *The handbook of national legislatures: A global survey*. New York: Cambridge University Press.

Flynn, John. 1988. "At the Threshold of Dissolution: The National Liberals and Bismarck 1877/1878." *Historical Journal* 31(2): 319–340.

Foord, A. S. 1947. "The Waning of 'The Influence of the Crown.'" *English Historical Review* 62: 484–507.

George, Robert H. 1940. "The Charters Granted to English Parliamentary Corporations in 1688." *English Historical Review* 55(217): 15–46.

Getzler, Joshua. 1996. "Theories of Property and Economic Development." *Journal of Interdisciplinary History* 26: 639–669.

Goemans, Henk, Kristian Gleditsch, and Giacomo Chiozza. 2009. "Introducing Archigos: A Dataset of Political Leaders." *Journal of Peace Research* 46(2): 269–283.

Gregg, Pauline. 1984. *King Charles I.* Berkeley: University of California Press.

Greif, Avner. 2007. "Toward political economy of implementation: The impact of administrative power on institutional and economic development." Unpublished typescript, Stanford University.

Groseclose, Timothy, and James Snyder. 1996. "Buying Supermajorities." *American Political Science Review* 90(2): 303–315.

Grotius, Hugo. 1949[1625]. *The law of war and peace.* New York: W J Black.

Guembel, Alexander, and Oren Sussman. 2009. "Sovereign Debt without Default Penalties." *Review of Economic Studies* 76: 1297–1320.

Guerra, José Guillermo. 1929. *La Constitución de 1925.* Santiago: Balcells & Co.

Guicciardini, Nicoló. 2005. "Isaac Newton, *Philosophiae Naturalis Principia Mathematica,* First Edition (1687)." In *Landmark Writings in Western Mathematics 1640–1940.* Edited by Ivor Grattan-Guiness. London: Elsevier.

Haber, Stephen, Noel Maurer, and Armando Razo. 2003. *The politics of property rights: Political instability, credible commitments, and economic growth in Mexico, 1876–1929.* New York: Cambridge University Press.

Hahn, Erich. 1977. "Ministerial Responsibility and Impeachment in Prussia 1848–63." *Central European History* 10(1): 3–27.

Hallerberg, Mark, Rolf Strauch, and Jürgen von Hagen. 2010. *Fiscal governance in Europe.* Cambridge: Cambridge University Press.

Harling, Philip. 1996. *The waning of "old corruption": The politics of economical reform in Britain, 1779–1846.* Oxford: Clarendon Press.

2001. *The modern British state: An historical introduction.* Cambridge: Polity Press.

Harris, Ron. 2000. *Industrializing English law.* Cambridge: Cambridge University Press.

2004. "Government and the economy." In *The Cambridge economic history of modern Britain,* vol. 1. Edited by Roderick Floud and Paul Johnson. Cambridge: Cambridge University Press.

2013. "Could the crown credibly commit to respect its charters? England 1558–1640." In *Questioning credible commitment: Perspectives on the rise of financial capitalism.* Edited by D'Maris Coffman, Adrian Leonard, and Larry Neal. Cambridge: Cambridge University Press.

Hayton, D. W. 2002. *The House of Commons 1690–1715.* Cambridge: Cambridge University Press.

Hayton, David. 1995. "Constitutional experiments and political expediency, 1689–1725." In *Conquest and Union.* Edited by Steven Ellis and Sarah Barber. London: Longman.

Hill, B. W. 1971. "The Change of Government and the 'Loss of the City', 1710–1711." *Economic History Review* 24(3): 395–413.

Hill, Brian W. 1976. *The growth of parliamentary parties 1689–1742*. London: George Allen and Unwin.

Hirschman, Albert. 1977. *The Passions and the Interests*. Princeton: Princeton University Press.

Hirst, Derek. 1986. *Authority and conflict: England 1603–1658*. London: Edward Arnold.

Hoffman, Philip T. 2009. "Why was it that Europeans conquered the world?" Unpublished typescript, California Institute of Technology.

2015. *Why did Europe conquer the world?* Princeton, NJ: Princeton University Press.

Hoffman, Philip T., and Kathryn Norberg, eds. 1994. *Fiscal crises, liberty and representative government, 1450–1789*. Stanford, CA: Stanford University Press.

Hoffman, Philip T., Gilles Postel-Vinay, and Jean-Laurent Rosenthal. 2000. *Priceless markets: The political economy of credit in Paris, 1660–1870*. Chicago: University of Chicago Press.

Hoffman, Philip T., and Jean-Laurent Rosenthal. 1997. "The political economy of warfare and taxation in early modern Europe: Historical lessons for economic development." In *The frontiers of the new institutional economics*. Edited by John N. Drobak and John Nye. New York: Academic Press, 31–35.

Homer, Sidney. 1963. *A History of Interest Rates*. New Brunswick: Rutgers University Press.

Hoppit, Julian. 1997. *Failed Legislation 1660–1800*. London: Hambledon Press.

2000. *A land of liberty? England 1689–1727*. Oxford: Oxford University Press.

2002. "Checking the Leviathan, 1688–1832." In *The political economy of British historical experience, 1688–1914*. Edited by Donald Winch and Patrick K. O'Brien. Oxford: Oxford University Press.

2011. "Compulsion, Compensation and Property Rights in Britain, 1688–1833." *Past and Present* 210: 93–128.

Horsefield, J. Keith. 1982. "The 'Stop of the Exchequer' Revisited." *Economic History Review* 35(4): 511–528.

Horwitz, Henry. 1977. *Parliament, policy and politics in the reign of William III*. Manchester: Manchester University Press.

Huber, John. 1996. *Rationalizing parliament: Legislative institutions and party politics in France*. New York: Cambridge University Press.

Jackson, Matthew, and Massimo Morelli. 2011. "The reasons for wars – an updated survey." In *The handbook on the political economy of war*. Edited by Christopher Coyne and Rachel Mathers. Cheltenham: Edward Elgar.

James, Herman. 1913. *Principles of Prussian administration*. New York: Macmillan.

Jha, Saumitra. 2008. "Shares, coalition formation and political development: Evidence from seventeenth century England." Stanford Graduate School of Business, Research Paper No. 2005.

2012. "Financial innovations and political development: Evidence from Revolutionary England." Unpublished typescript, Stanford University.

John, A. H. 1955. "War and the English Economy, 1700–1763." *Economic History Review* 7(3): 329–344.

Johnson, Noel, and Mark Koyama. 2014. "Tax Farming and the Origins of State Capacity in England and France." *Explorations in Economic History* 51: 1–20.

Jones, Eric. 2013. "Economics without History: Objections to the Rights Hypothesis." *Continuity and Change* 28(3): 323–346.

Jones, J. R. 1994. "Fiscal policies, liberties and representative government during the reigns of the last Stuarts." In *Fiscal crises, liberty, and representative government 1450–1789*. Edited by Philip T. Hoffman and Kathryn Norberg. Stanford, CA: Stanford University Press.

    1996. *The Anglo-Dutch wars of the seventeenth century*. London: Longman.

Jones, W. R. 1975. "Purveyance for War and the Community of the Realm in Late Medieval England." *Albion* 7(4): 300–316.

Katzenstein, Peter. 1985. *Small states in world markets*. Ithaca, NY: Cornell University Press.

Kelly, Morgan, Joel Mokyr, and Cormac Ó Gráda. 2014. "Precocious Albion: A New Interpretation of the British Industrial Revolution." *Annual Review of Economics* 6: 363–389.

Kemp, Betty. 1957. *King and Commons, 1660–1832*. London: Macmillan.

Kiser, Edgar, and April Linton. 2001. "Determinants of the Growth of the State: War and Taxation in Early Modern France and England." *Social Forces* 80(2): 411–448.

    2002. "The Hinges of History: State-making and Revolt in Early Modern France." *American Sociological Review* 67(6): 889–910.

Klerman, Daniel, and Paul Mahoney. 2005. "The Value of Judicial Independence: Evidence from Eighteenth Century England." *American Law and Economics Review* 7: 1–27.

Kletzer, Kenneth M., and Brian D. Wright. 2000. "Sovereign Debt as Intertemporal Barter." *American Economic Review* 90(3): 621–639.

Kuran, Timur. 2011. *The long divergence: How Islamic law held back the Middle East*. Princeton, NJ: Princeton University Press.

Lake, David. 1992. "Powerful Pacifists: Democratic States and War." *American Political Science Review* 86(1): 24–37.

Lamoreaux, Naomi. 2009. "Scylla or Charybdis? Historical Reflections on Two Basic Problems of Corporate Governance." *Business History Review* 83(Spring): 9–34.

    2011. "The Mystery of Property Rights: A U.S. Perspective." *Journal of Economic History* 71(2): 275–306.

Landes, David S. 1983. *Revolution in time: Clocks and the making of the modern world*. Cambridge, MA: Harvard University Press.

Lavaux, Phillippe. 1988. *Parliamentarisme rationalize et stabilité du pouvoir executif*. Bruxelles: Bruylant.

Lemire, Beverly. 1997. *Dress, culture and commerce: The English clothing trade before the factory, 1660–1800*. New York: St Martin's Press.

Levi, Margaret. 1988. *Of rule and revenue*. Berkeley: University of California Press.

Linz, Juan. 1990. "The Perils of Presidentialism." *Journal of Democracy* 1(1): 51–69.

Little, David. 1969. *Religion, order and law: A study in pre-Revolutionary England.* Chicago: University of Chicago Press.

Londregan, John, and Keith Poole. 1990. "Poverty, the Coup Trap, and the Seizure of Executive Power." *World Politics* 42(2): 151–183.

Loveman, Brian. 1993. *The constitution of tyranny.* Pittsburgh: University of Pittsburgh Press.

Macaulay, Thomas. 1848. *The history of England from the accession of James II.* Philadelphia, PA: Porter and Coates.

MacDonald, James. 2013. "The importance of not defaulting: The significance of the election of 1710." In *Questioning credible commitment: Perspectives on the rise of financial capitalism.* Edited by D'Maris Coffman, Adrian Leonard, and Larry Neal. Cambridge: Cambridge University Press.

Machiavelli, Niccolò. 1979[1513]. *The prince.* In *The portable Machiavelli.* Edited by Peter Bondanella and Mark Musa. New York: Penguin.

Madison, James. 2009[1788]. *The Federalist papers.* New Haven, CT: Yale University Press.

Maeda, Ko. 2010. "Two Modes of Democratic Breakdown: A Competing Risks Analysis of Democratic Durability." *Journal of Politics* 72(4): 1129–1143.

Maitland, F. W. 1908. *The constitutional history of England.* Cambridge: Cambridge University Press.

Major, J. Russell. 1960. *Representative institutions in Renaissance France, 1421–1559.* Madison: University of Wisconsin Press.

Marongiu, Antonio. 1968. *Medieval parliaments: A comparative study.* London: Eyre and Spottiswoode.

Marshall, Monty, Ted Robert Gurr, and Keith Jaggers. 2014. "Political regime characteristics and transitions, 1800–2013: Dataset users' manual." Center for Systemic Peace.

McCarty, Nolan. 2004. "The Appointments Dilemma." *American Journal of Political Science* 48(3): 413–428.

McCarty, Nolan, and Rose Razaghian. 1999. "Advice and Consent: Senate Responses to Executive Branch Nominations 1885–1999." *American Journal of Political Science* 43(4): 1122–1143.

McGuire, Martin, and Mancur Olson. 1996. "The Economics of Autocracy and Majority Rule: The Invisible Hand and the Use of Force." *Journal of Economic Literature* 34(1): 72–96.

McNeill, William H. 1982. *The pursuit of power.* Chicago: University of Chicago Press.

McNulty, William. 1912. "Eminent Domain in Continental Europe." *Yale Law Journal* 21(7): 555–570.

Meltzer, Alan, and Scott Richard. 1981. "A Rational Theory of the Size of Government." *Journal of Political Economy* 89(5): 914–927.

Milgrom, Paul, Douglass North, and Barry Weingast. 1990. "The Role of Institutions in the Revival of Trade: The Law Merchant, Private Judges and the Champagne Fairs." *Economics and Politics* 2(1): 1–23.

Mitchell, B. R. 1962. *Abstract of British historical statistics.* Cambridge: Cambridge University Press.

1988. *British historical statistics.* Cambridge: Cambridge University Press.

Moe, Terry, and Michael Caldwell. 1994. "The Institutional Foundations of Democratic Government: A Comparison of Presidential and Parliamentary Systems." *Journal of Institutional and Theoretical Economics* 150(1): 171–195.

Mokyr, Joel. 2002. *The gifts of Athena.* Princeton, NJ: Princeton University Press.

2008. "The institutional origins of the Industrial Revolution." In *Institutions and economic performance.* Edited by Elhanan Helpman. Cambridge, MA: Harvard University Press.

2009. *The enlightened economy: An economic history of Britain 1700–1850.* New Haven, CT: Yale University Press.

Mokyr, Joel, and John Nye. 2007. "Distributional Coalitions, the Industrial Revolution, and the Origins of Economic Growth in Britain." *Southern Economic Journal* 74(1): 50–70.

Montesquieu, Charles de Secondat. 1989[1748]. *Spirit of the laws.* Cambridge: Cambridge University Press.

Mork, Gordon R. 1971. "Bismarck and the Capitulation of German Liberalism." *Journal of Modern History* 43(1): 59–75.

Morrill, John Stephen. 1974. *Cheshire 1630–1660: County government and society during the English revolution.* Oxford: Oxford University Press.

Mundill, Robin R. 2010. *The king's Jews: Money, massacre, and exodus in medieval England.* New York: Continuum.

Murphy, Anne L. 2012. *The origins of English financial markets: Investment and speculation before the South Sea Bubble.* Cambridge: Cambridge University Press.

2013. "Demanding 'Credible Commitment': Public Reactions to the Failures of the Early Financial Revolution." *Economic History Review* 66(1): 178–197.

Murrell, Peter. 2009. "Design and evolution in institutional development: The insignificance of the English Bill of Rights." Unpublished Typescript, University of Maryland.

Muthoo, Abhinay. 1999. *Bargaining theory with applications.* New York: Cambridge University Press.

Myerson, Roger. 2008. "The Autocrat's Credibility Problem and Foundations of the Constitutional State." *American Political Science Review* 102(1): 125–140.

Neal, Larry. 1990. *The rise of financial capitalism: International capital markets in the age of reason.* Cambridge: Cambridge University Press.

North, Douglass C. 1981. *Growth and structural change.* New York: Norton.

North, Douglass, John Joseph Wallis, and Barry R. Weingast. 2009. *Violence and Social Orders.* Cambridge: Cambridge University Press.

North, Douglass, and Barry Weingast. 1989. "Constitutions and Commitment: The Evolution of Institutions Governing Public Choice in Seventeenth-Century Britain." *Journal of Economic History* 49(4): 803–832.

Nye, John. 2007. *War, wine, and taxes: The political economy of Anglo-French trade 1689–1900.* Princeton, NJ: Princeton University Press.

O'Brien, Patrick. 1988. "The Political Economy of British Taxation, 1660–1815." *Economic History Review* 2d series 41(1): 1–32.

2002. "Fiscal exceptionalism: Great Britain and its European rivals from civil war to triumph at Trafalgar and Waterloo." In *The political economy of British historical experience, 1688–1914*. Edited by Donald Winch and Patrick K. O'Brien. Oxford: Oxford University Press.

2005. "Fiscal and financial preconditions for the rise of British naval hegemony 1485–1815." Working Paper No. 91/05. Department of Economic History, London School of Economics.

O'Donnell, Guillermo. 1994. "Delegative Democracy." *Journal of Democracy* 5(1): 55–69.

Olson, Mancur. 1993. "Dictatorship, Democracy and Development." *American Political Science Review* 87(3): 567–576.

Parthasarathi, Prasannan. 2011. *Why Europe grew rich and Asia did not.* Cambridge: Cambridge University Press.

Payling, Simon. 2009. "The House of Commons, 1307–1529." In *A short history of Parliament.* Edited by Clyve Jones. Woodbridge: The Boydell Press.

Peck, Linda Levy. 1990. *Court patronage and corruption in early Stuart England.* Boston, MA: Unwin Hyman.

Pelizzo, Riccardo, and Rick Stapenhurst, eds. 2004. *Legislatures and oversight.* Washington, DC: IBRD/World Bank.

Perotti, R. and Y. Kontopoulos. 2002. "Fragmented Fiscal Policy." *Journal of Public Economics* 86(2): 191–222.

Persson, Torsten, Gerard Roland, and Guido Tabellini. 1997. "Separation of Powers and Political Accountability." *Quarterly Journal of Economics* 112 (4): 1163–1202.

2000. "Comparative Politics and Public Finance." *Journal of Political Economy* 108(6): 1121–1161.

Pincus, Steve. 2009. *1688: The first modern revolution.* New Haven, CT: Yale University Press.

Pincus, Steve, and James Robinson. 2011a. "What really happened during the Glorious Revolution?" NBER Working Paper 17206.

2011b. "What really happened during the Glorious Revolution – and why it matters for current fiscal crises." Posted on www.voxeu.org August 7, 2011.

2014. "Wars and state-making reconsidered: The rise of the interventionist state." Unpublished typescript, Yale University.

Pintilie, Melania. 2007. "Analysing and Interpreting Competing Risk Data." *Statistics in Medicine* 26: 1360–1367.

Pool, Bernard. 1966. *Navy Board contracts 1660–1832.* Hamden, CT: Archon Books.

Poole, Keith B., and John Londregan. 1990. "Poverty, the Coup Trap, and the Seizure of Executive Power." *World Politics* 42(2): 151–183.

Powell, Robert. 1999. *In the shadow of power.* Princeton, NJ: Princeton University Press.

Power, Eileen. 1942. *The wool trade in English medieval history, being the Ford Lectures.* London: Oxford University Press.

Przeworski, Adam, and Michael Wallerstein. 1982. "The Structure of Class Conflict in Democratic Capitalist Societies." *American Political Science Review* 75: 215–238.

Przeworski, Adam et al. 2000. *Democracy and development*. Cambridge: Cambridge University Press.

2013. Political Institutions and Political Events (PIPE) Dataset. Department of Politics, New York University.

Quinn, Stephen. 2001. "The Glorious Revolution's Effect on English Private Finance: A Microhistory, 1680–1705." *Journal of Economic History* 61(3): 593–615.

2004. "Questioning a stylized fact: When did the Bank of England become a delegated bureaucrat?" Unpublished typescript, Texas Christian University.

2008. "Securitization of sovereign debt: Corporations as a sovereign debt restructuring mechanism in Britain, 1694 to 1750." Unpublished typescript, Texas Christian University.

Ramey, Garey, and Joel Watson. 2002. "Contractual Intermediaries." *Journal of Law, Economics and Organization* 18(2): 362–384.

Redlich, Josef. 1908. *The procedure of the House of Commons: A study of its history and present form*. Translated by A. E. Steinthal. London: Archibald Constable & Co.

Reenock, Christopher, Jeffrey Staton, and Marius Radean. 2013. "Legal Institutions and Democratic Survival." *Journal of Politics* 75(2): 491–505.

Reitan, E. A. 1970. "From Revenue to Civil List, 1689–1702: The Revolution Settlement and the 'Mixed and Balanced' Constitution." *Historical Journal* 13(4): 571–588.

Reiter, Dan, and Allan Stam. 1998. "Democracy, War Initiation, and Victory." *American Political Science Review* 92(2): 377–389.

Reynolds, Susan. 2010. *Before eminent domain*. Chapel Hill: University of North Carolina Press.

Roberts, Clayton. 1956. "The Growth of Ministerial Responsibility to Parliament in Later Stuart England." *Journal of Modern History* 28(3): 215–233.

1959. "Privy Council Schemes and Ministerial Responsibility in Later Stuart England." *American Historical Review* 64(3): 564–582.

1966. *The growth of responsible government in Stuart England*. Cambridge: Cambridge University Press.

1977. "The Constitutional Significance of the Financial Settlement of 1690." *Historical Journal* 20(1): 59–76.

Robinson, James. 2006. "Debt repudiation and risk premia: The North-Weingast thesis revisited." Unpublished typescript, Harvard University.

Rodger, N. A. M. 2004. *The command of the ocean: A naval history of Britain, 1649–1815*. New York: W. W. Norton.

2010. "War as an Economic Activity in the 'Long' Eighteenth Century." *International Journal of Maritime History* 22(2): 1–18.

Roeder, Philip G. 2001. "Ethnolinguistic Fractionalization (ELF) Indices, 1961 and 1985." http://weber.ucsd.edu\~proeder\elf.htm.

Romer, Thomas, and Howard Rosenthal. 1978. "Political Resource Allocation, Controlled Agendas and the Status Quo." *Public Choice* 33(4): 27–43.

Root, H. L. 1989. "Tying the King's Hands: Credible Commitment and Royal Fiscal Policy During the Old Regime." *Rationality and Society* 1(2):240–58.

1994. *The fountain of privilege: Political foundations of markets in Old Regime France and England*. Berkeley: University of California Press.

Rosenthal, Jean-Laurent. 1990. "The Development of Irrigation in Provence, 1700–1860: The French Revolution and Economic Growth." *Journal of Economic History* 50(3): 615–638.

1992. *The fruits of revolution: Property rights, litigation, and French agriculture, 1700–1860*. Cambridge: Cambridge University Press.

1998. "The political economy of absolutism reconsidered." In *Analytic narratives*. Edited by Robert Bates et al. Princeton, NJ: Princeton University Press, 64–108.

Roseveare, Henry. 1973. *The Treasury, 1660–1870*. London: George Allen and Unwin.

Rydz, D. L. 1979. *The parliamentary agents*. London: Royal Historical Society.

Sacks, David Harris. 1994. "The paradox of taxation: Fiscal crises, parliament, and liberty in England, 1450–1640." In *Fiscal crises, liberty, and representative covernment 1450–1789*. Edited by Philip T. Hoffman and Kathryn Norberg. Stanford, CA: Stanford University Press.

Saiegh, Sebastián. 2011. *Ruling by statute*. New York: Cambridge University Press.

2012. "Political institutions and sovereign borrowing: Evidence from nineteenth-century Argentina." *Public Choice*.

Santiso, Carlos. 2004. "Legislatures and Budget Oversight in Latin America." *OECD Journal on Budgeting* 4(2): 47–76.

Schedler, Andreas. 2002. "The Menu of Manipulation." *Journal of Democracy* 13(2): 36–50.

2006. *Electoral authoritarianism*. New York: Lynne Rienner.

Schultz, Kenneth, and Barry R. Weingast. 2003. "The Democratic Advantage: The Institutional Sources of State Power in International Competition." *International Organization* 57: 3–42.

Schumpeter, Joseph A. 1918[1954]. "The crisis of the tax state." In *International economic papers: Translations prepared for the International Economic Association*. Edited by Allan Peacock et al. New York: MacMillan.

Scott, William Robert. 1912. *The constitution and finance of English, Scottish and Irish joint-stock companies to 1720: Companies for foreign trade, colonization, fishing and mining*, Vol. 2. Cambridge: Cambridge University Press.

Shaw, William A., ed. 1931. *Calendar of Treasury books*, Volume 9. London: Printed for Her Majesty's Stationery Office.

ed. 1952. *Calendar of Treasury books*, Volume 21. London: Printed for Her Majesty's Stationery Office.

Shugart, Matthew. 1998. "The Inverse Relationship between Party Strength and Executive Strength: A Theory of Politicians' Constitutional Choices." *British Journal of Political Science* 28(1): 1–29.

Siavelis, Peter. 2002. "Exaggerated presidentialism and moderate presidents: Executive-legislative relations in Chile." In *Legislative politics in Latin America*. Edited by Scott Morgenstern and Benito Nacif. New York: Cambridge University Press.

Stasavage, David. 2003. *Public debt and the birth of the democratic state.* Cambridge: Cambridge University Press.

2007. "Partisan Politics and Public Debt: The Importance of the 'Whig Supremacy' for Britain's Financial Revolution." *European Review of Economic History* 11: 123–153.

2011. *States of credit: Size, power and the development of European politics.* Princeton, NJ: Princeton University Press.

Stith, Kate 1988. "Congress' Power of the Purse." *Yale Law Journal* 97: 1343–1396.

Stoebuck, W. B. 1972. "A General Theory of Eminent Domain." *Washington Law Review* 47: 553–608.

Stourm, Rene. 1917. *The budget.* New York: D. Appleton and Company.

Sussman, Nathan, and Yishay Yafeh. 2006. "Institutional Reforms, Financial Developments and Sovereign Debt: Britain 1690–1790." *Journal of Economic History* 66(3): 906–935.

Sussman, Nathan, and Yishay Yafeh. 2013. "Institutions, deficits, and wars: The determinants of British government borrowing costs from the end of the seventeenth century to 1850." In *Questioning credible commitment: Perspectives on the rise of financial capitalism.* Edited by D'Maris Coffman, Adrian Leonard, and Larry Neal. Cambridge: Cambridge University Press.

Sutherland, Donald. 1973. *The Assize of Novel Disseisin.* Oxford: Clarendon Press.

Svolik, Milan. 2008. "Authoritarian Reversals and Democratic Consolidation." *American Political Science Review* 102: 153–168.

Szostak, Rick. 1991. *The role of transportation in the Industrial Revolution.* Montreal: McGill-Queens University Press.

Tilly, Charles. 1966. "The Political Economy of Public Finance and the Industrialization of Prussia, 1815–1866." *Journal of Economic History* 26(4): 484–497.

1990. *Coercion, capital and European states, AD 990–1990.* Cambridge, MA: Blackwell.

1995. *Popular Contention in Great Britain, 1758–1834.* Cambridge, MA: Harvard University Press.

Todd, Alpheus. 1867. *On parliamentary government in England.* London: Longmans, Green and Co.

Tomz, Michael. 2007. *Reputation and international cooperation: Sovereign debt across three centuries.* Princeton, NJ: Princeton University Press.

Tsebelis, George. 2002. *Veto players: How political institutions work.* Princeton, NJ: Princeton University Press.

van Caenegem, R. C. 1973. *The birth of the English common law.* Cambridge: Cambridge University Press.

van Zanden, Jan Luiten, Eltjo Buringh, and Maarten Bosker. 2012. "The Rise and Decline of European Parliaments, 1188–1789." *Economic History Review* 65(3): 835–861.

Waugh, Scott L. 1991. *England in the reign of Edward III.* Cambridge: Cambridge University Press.

Wehner, Joachim. 2010. "Cabinet Structure and Fiscal Policy Outcomes." *European Journal of Political Research* 49(5): 631–653.

Weingast, Barry R. 1997. "The political foundations of limited government: Parliament and sovereign debt in seventeenth- and eighteenth-century England." In *The frontiers of the new institutional economics*. Edited by J. N. Brobak and J. V. C. Nye. San Diego, CA: Academic Press.

Weiser, Brian. 2003. *Charles II and the politics of access*. Woodbridge and Suffolk: Boydell Press.

Wells, John, and Douglas Wills. 2000. "Revolution, Restoration, and Debt Repudiation: The Jacobite Threat to Britain's Institutions and Economic Growth." *Journal of Economic History* 60(2) (2000): 418–441.

Wheeler, J. S. 1996. "Navy Finance, 1649–1660." *Historical Journal* 39(2): 457–466.

Whipple, Edwin P. 1879. *The great speeches and orations of Daniel Webster*. Boston, MA: Little and Brown.

Wiener, Frederick. 1972. "The Register of Writs: Seed-Bed of the Common Law." *American Bar Association Journal* 58: 498–504.

Williamson, Oliver. 1983. "Credible Commitments: Using Hostages to Support Exchange." *American Economic Review* 73(4): 519–540.

Wilmerding, Lucius. 1943. *The spending power*. New Haven, CT: Yale University Press.

Woodhouse, Caleb. 1974. "The Defense Question and Danish Politics, 1864–1914." *Scandinavian Studies* 46(3): 201–228.

Zahedieh, Nuala. 2010. "Regulation, Rent-Seeking, and the Glorious Revolution in the English Atlantic Economy." *Economic History Review* 63(4): 865–890.

Ziblatt, Daniel. 2006. *Structuring the state: The formation of Italy and Germany and the puzzle of federalism*. Princeton, NJ: Princeton University Press.

Index

in Spain, 142
tax revenue, 160–163
trends from 1875–2005 in, 158–160
within-country comparisons, 172
Bulgaria, budgetary reversion in, 160n.11
business syndicates, medieval sale of
monopolies to, 22–23

Calico Act, 108–109, 129
capital expenditure
British military intervention and
expansion of, 111–115
Transportation Revolution and mobility
of, 102–107
Carruthers, Bruce, 73
centralized government, revenue growth in
Europe and, 146–148
Chancellor of the Exchequer, monopoly
proposal power and, 46–48
charitable assets, property rates of return
and, 85–86
Charles I (King of England), 22–23, 95
Charles II (King of England), 22,
25, 59, 78
Cheibub, Jose Antonio, 169
Chile
budgetary process in, 155–156
EFR and democracy in, 165–172
fiscal stalemates in, 181–184
City of London, King's Bench judgment
against, 25–26
civil expenditures
parliamentary appropriations for, 43
royal appropriations for, 28–32
Civil List
parliamentary appropriations and
revenues of, 41–43, 49
royal appropriations for, 28–32
Clark, Gregory, 4, 84–86, 92–93
class structure
suffrage rights and, 186n.9
technological innovation and, 114
coal industry, British military intervention
and growth of, 111–115
Coffman, D'Maris, 79n.10
colonial regimes, budgetary reversions in,
171–172
Commission on the Budget (France), 45–46
Committee of Supply, stopped orders
and, 78–79
Committee on Public Accounts, 47

"common fame" evidence, 30n.8
common law
English property rights and, 90–91
executive discretion limits and, 91–92
judiciary as veto player and, 105
Commonwealth, establishment of, 4
communication networks, lobbying of MPs
and, 109
competition, lobbying tactics and, 109
compulsory purchase of property,
86, 88–89
Comtat Venaissan Estates, 103–104
conciliar courts, 23
property rights and, 84
conciliar responsibility, parliamentary push
for, 29–32
Congress (U.S.)
budgetary controls in, 134n.2, 157n.5
mistrust of executive in, 187
separation of powers and, 180–181
Congressional Budget and Impoundment
Control Act of 1974, 138n.5
Consolidated Fund
creation of, 66–67
parliamentary charges on, 28
constitutional reforms
charter revocation and, 94–95
consequences and causes of, 128–129
debt seniority and funding and, 50–51
to eminent domain, 105–107
European adoption of, 138–145
European debt credibility and, 73n.3
executive-favoring budgetary reversions
and, 158–160, 163–165
executive powers in, 154–155
government shutdowns and budgetary
reversions and, 154–155, 158–160
history of, 67–68
Industrial Revolution and, 100–101,
118–130
interest rates and, 75–77
political institutions and, 177–178
in Prussia, 142–145
senior and well-funded debt, 53
sovereign debt credibility and, 50–56, 75
in Spain, 142
weakest-link theory of executive
constraint and, 119–122
constitutional school of sovereign
credibility, 2
Glorious Revolution and, 4–6

Other Books in the Series (continued)